Quality Enhancement of University Teaching and Learning

Quality Enhancement of University Teaching and Learning

Claus Nygaard
Nigel Courtney
Paul Bartholomew

Foreword by Professor John Biggs

THE LEARNING IN HIGHER EDUCATION SERIES

LIBRI
PUBLISHING

First published in 2013 by Libri Publishing

Copyright © Libri Publishing

Authors retain copyright of individual chapters.

The right of Claus Nygaard, Nigel Courtney and Paul Bartholomew to be identified as the editors of this work has been asserted in accordance with the Copyright, Designs and Patents Act, 1988.

ISBN 978-1-909818-12-5

A CIP catalogue record for this book is available from The British Library

Cover design by Helen Taylor

Design by Carnegie Publishing

Printed in the UK by Short Run Press

Libri Publishing
Brunel House
Volunteer Way
Faringdon
Oxfordshire
SN7 7YR

Tel: +44 (0)845 873 3837

www.libripublishing.co.uk

Contents

Foreword

Universities have, in the past ten years or so, dramatically increased participation rates and at the same time have shifted from being publicly funded institutions to becoming businesses, run on corporate lines. Funding is provided in large part from student fees, with students justifiably demanding value for money. Universities, like other corporate institutions, thus rely heavily on quality assurance procedures which, in part, involve key performance indicators for assessing the performance of staff. Quality assurance procedures may be appropriate in the business context but in the academic context they can actually interfere with teaching effectiveness, undermine staff morale and compromise the conduct and reporting of research (Hil, 2012; Meyers, 2012).

Furthermore, there is a logical problem. The quality assurance of teaching and learning attempts to ensure that the standards at present reached in degree programmes meet external criteria. If they do not, the best that can evidently be done is to blame those involved and order them to do better next time. But the horse has already bolted.

As this book makes clear, and as I have long maintained, universities should be concerned not with quality assurance, which is summative and operates retrospectively, but with quality *enhancement* of teaching. Quality enhancement is formative and proactive in that it monitors ongoing teaching and learning, takes steps to prevent problems and attempts to solve those that do arise. Quality enhancement ensures that whatever the standard of teaching is currently, it will be better in future. Therefore quality enhancement to a large extent subsumes quality assurance. All that time spent in form-filling and other busywork associated with quality assurance procedures can be better spent in paying attention to the improvement of teaching through staff development and by putting in place quality enhancement procedures.

As outlined in the first chapter, quality enhancement involves taking intentional steps at the level of the institution to enhance the quality of learning prospects; it is about improving quality, not controlling quality. There is a huge cultural difference here. Controlling quality operates within a culture of compliance - which McGregor (1960) calls a 'Theory X' institutional climate - that, as Hil and others point out all too clearly, radiates a demoralising lack of trust in teachers. On the other hand, improving quality involves a culture of innovation; a 'Theory Y' climate that is not about supporting the status quo but about making room for new ideas, for collegiality and for participation in a positive working system.

Three agents are involved in quality enhancement: the teacher, the student and the institution. Recognising this leaves room for institutions to follow their individual approaches to quality enhancement in line with their theories of teaching and their available resources. So quality enhancement is not just about an individual teacher practising action research – although that is important – but teachers, students and institution working together as an interactive system. The contributions to this volume variously address these foci: six chapters address quality enhancement in relation to students, two chapters in relation to teachers and four chapters in relation to the institution, providing a thoughtful range of quality enhancement strategies. Although these contributions are presented as "perspectives" from nine countries, the aim is not to compare approaches from different countries but rather to demonstrate the universality of the issues (that said, it is a pity that Asia and North America aren't represented). The overall message, and it is an important one, is to seek the active engagement of all participants to instil a culture for enhancing the quality of student learning through reflective practice, initiative, creativity, collaboration and shared experiences among stakeholders.

I say 'Amen' to all that. But it seems to me, speaking now largely from an Australian perspective, that a major problem is that management all too frequently operates in a self-created Theory X climate in which key performance indicators, which claim to assure quality but rarely do, are a demoralising part. The business model applied to academe is counter-productive because it subjects academics to devices for exerting control. The way to go in the academic context is not by applying business models that operate within a culture that is alien to academe. A truly academic culture, and one that is essential for quality enhancement, operates in a trustful and supportive Theory Y climate within which academics have freedom to teach, to innovate, to conduct untrammelled research and to publish without fear or favour.

Underlying quality enhancement, then, is the unspoken but necessary assumption that the university is an academic, not a business, enterprise. Those who are truly concerned with quality teaching and learning will benefit enormously from this comprehensive book, which has been carefully designed to address the interacting levels of student, teacher and institution in enhancing teaching and learning at university.

John Biggs
February, 2013

About the Author

John Biggs is Honorary Professor of Psychology at the University of Hong Kong. His influential work on quality enhancement in higher education is captured in 'Teaching for Quality Learning in University', co-authored with Catherine Tang (Biggs & Tang, 2007). He can be contacted at this email: jbiggs@bigpond.com

Chapter One

Theoretical and Empirical Perspectives on Quality Enhancement in Higher Education

Claus Nygaard, Nigel Courtney and Paul Bartholomew

Quality Enhancement in Higher Education

This book is written by a group of international scholars and academic practitioners who have in common an ambition to enhance the quality of university teaching and learning. After a year of writing, the group of authors met on Iceland under the visionary guidance of quality director Sigrún Magnúsdóttir from University of Akureyri, to collaborate on finalising the manuscript for publication. Ultimately, our aim with this book is to improve the learning outcomes of students, the graduateness of students, the employability of students, the professional identity of students and, overall, the quality of students' future work and social life balance. In short: *to generate a culture of quality in Higher Education.*

Doing so means concurring on a general definition of quality enhancement. Although all 13 chapters of the book make a concerted attempt to get to terms with the various understandings and practices relating to quality enhancement of teaching and learning at universities around the world, the definitions of quality enhancement vary slightly from chapter to chapter. Such definitions depend on the focus of the quality work referred to, and in this book authors have chosen to write from three different viewpoints: 1) the student, 2) the teacher, 3) the institution.

Speaking of definitions, it has been argued that the notion of 'quality' itself lacks a solid theoretical foundation (Harvey & Newton, 2004). As a concept it is not fixed; its perceived meaning is relative to the mechanisms and local contexts presented in terms of desired results. Some Higher Education Institutions (HEIs) link their quality work to the improvement of students' learning outcomes, others to improvements in curriculum design, and yet others to the improvement of teaching practices. And these are just a few examples of the kind of ambitions and aims that may drive quality work at HEIs. In this book, those different approaches to quality enhancement of teaching and learning can be seen in the way our authors present cases from Australia, Belgium, Denmark, England, Finland, Iceland, Portugal, Scotland, and United Arab Emirates. Although the cases are different and may rest on differing understandings of quality enhancement, a consensus emerges based on the authors' shared aspiration to search for improvement in teaching and learning practices. Furthermore, independently of the mechanism and focus of action, they place centrally the improvement of students' learning experiences as the primary purpose of undertaking their quality enhancement work.

Therefore, in this introductory chapter, we discuss the importance for universities of establishing a framework for quality enhancement which explicitly focuses on the relationship between the activities of learning and teaching and students' learning outcomes. In our experience the efficacy of the framework that is chosen will be strongly affected by institutional context and culture; a QE initiative may tend to focus on development of the student or the teacher or the institution although, clearly, the three approaches are not mutually exclusive. We will review the analytical and empirical dimensions which characterise each chapter and briefly present its core arguments to show how the different approaches can be interrelated.

To start with we will outline similarities and differences between quality assurance and quality enhancement in order to locate quality enhancement as a concept within the wider, 'quality' context of HE.

Is Quality Assurance the same as Quality Enhancement?

This anthology is concerned with quality enhancement of university teaching and learning. As a concept, quality enhancement (QE) should not be mistaken for quality assurance (QA); and, perhaps just as importantly, QE and QA should not be seen as entirely opposing ideas. As we will show in this section, they are distinctly different, particularly in relation to aspirations for change, but they are also interrelated.

The Ideals of Quality Assurance

In recent years the literature on Higher Education has increasingly focused on QA as a result of growing political and institutional pressures to document and control quality. Today, HEIs need to meet national and international requirements for QA which include national institutional accreditations, national programme evaluations, and international requirements for harmonisation (Biggs, 2001; Jeliazkova & Westerheijden, 2002; Hodson & Harold, 2003; Billing, 2004; Perellon, 2005). In their own countries, HEIs operate within politicised and public contexts. HE and how it is managed and funded are hot political and social topics – particularly in these times of global economic slowdown, austerity measures, debates around the need for national competitiveness, and concerns about 'value for money' for HE provision. These newly framed pressures have changed national conceptions of the purpose of HE, what 'successful' provision might look like, and (crucially in relation to quality assurance) how such 'success' might be measured.

Of course, success encompasses more than just that which relates to 'fitness for purpose' in the service of broad socio-economic goals; QA also encompasses those mechanisms that allow for the oversight and management of academic standards. In Europe, the ten action lines of the Bologna Accord have also increased the focus on QA. QA is described by the Quality Assurance Agency (QAA, cited in Oliver, 2009) as the means by which an institution guarantees and validates that the circumstances are in position for students to attain the standards set by the institution or set for them by an external body. According to Filippakou & Tapper

(2008), QA can be regarded as a substitute for state intervention; it is among the policy avenues that enable the State to achieve closer control in developing the system of higher education. This sometimes instrumental focus on QA – as an exercise in quantitative data collection to document student grades, student satisfaction, student/staff ratios, contact hours, student retention, average salary of graduates, and the like – appears to stem from an ever increasing political focus on obtaining value for money for the taxpayer. The political institutions governing the HE sector seem to be driven by a belief that transparency in certain key performance indicators across institutions will increase quality. Sadly this instrumental approach runs the risk of ignoring, and so devaluing, the richness and diversity of the myriad of innovative and non-standardised approaches available for enhancing the quality of learning and teaching.

QA frameworks are chiefly based on student consultation activity in which frameworks are based on analyses of student responses to management-led prompts rather than meaningful student engagement. This consultation-based mechanism ignores the scope of student engagement into learning. Bramming (2007) likewise questions the approaches in quality assurance that are based on surveys of student satisfaction that merely attribute a numerical value to the data. The surveys do not always reveal higher academic attainment and they tend to disregard transformation by learning. The implementation of surveys of student satisfaction in QA produces few direct measurements of the learning experience but, instead, tends to offer meandering measures of academic content and narrow interpretations of student achievement.

There is no proof that quality monitoring, whether internal or external, has a significant effect on the processes of learning and teaching (Gvaramadze, 2011). QA procedures rarely deal with the micro-level human interactions that impact upon learning, but are more concerned with compliance with assessment regulations, with reporting, and performance indicators. The processes totally negate research into solutions and innovations in learning. Where student involvement in QA processes does occur, it seldom (if ever) captures or adequately represents the true and full nature of the learning experience. A QA framework that considers performance and achievement but negates student experience necessitates continuous compliance and alterations of quality markers (Coates, 2005). It would be more appropriate to address the extent of student engagement in learning through qualitative means and discuss pertinent institutional capabilities that improve the quality of learning experiences.

The Ideals of Quality Enhancement

Quality Enhancement (QE) on the other hand is the course of taking intentional steps at the level of the institution to enhance the quality of learning prospects. Therefore, quality enhancement is the element of institutional quality management designed to safeguard the quality of learning prospects in the context of the limitations within which an institution operates. The definition of enhancement leaves room for institutions to follow their individual definitions of enhancement. This opens the door for approaches that seek out and value novel and effective practices and disseminate these where appropriate. QE often uses formative evaluations and qualitative indicators to understand the everyday practices of HEIs. QE is about ongoing engagement of stakeholders and alignment of structures; it focuses on the internal processes of improvement through relational management of stakeholders and institutional operational structures. QE can be said to be about developing and sustaining mechanisms through which usable and negotiated parameters of quality can be understood and acted upon.

Crystallising the Differences between QA and QE

The key characteristics of QA and QE are summarised below in Table 1.

	Quality Assurance (QA)	Quality Enhancement (QE)
Definition	A process by which HEIs account for the quality of their services.	A process by which HEIs enhance the quality of their services.
Key purpose	Controlling quality.	Improving quality.
Key driver	External: National QA-agencies (accreditation, evaluation, assessment, audits).	Internal: Management group / project groups of the HEI.
Type of pressure	A political pressure on HEIs for external adaptation to rules and regulations in relation to academic services.	A collegial or managerial pressure on HEIs for internal integration of actors, processes and structures in relation to academic services.
Key methods	External evaluation, internal self-evaluation, peer reviews, site visits, audits.	Staff competency development, creation of a learning organisation, relational management, work with values, creation of a quality culture.

Table 1: Comparison of the main characteristics of QA and QE.

Table 2 presents an overview of the role of internal and external factors in improving and controlling quality achieved through QA and QE-practices.

	Internally driven	Externally driven
Quality enhancement (improving quality)	Competence development of staff. Relational management. Quality seminars. Research and publication on quality-related issues such as teaching, learning and assessment practices and students' learning outcomes.	Benchmarking. Accreditation.
Quality assurance (controlling quality)	Self-assessment. Benchmarking.	Assessment. External review. Externally formulated standards and criterias. Accreditation. Certification. On-site visits by external reviewers / agency staff. Review panels.

Table 2: QA and QE as internally and externally driven processes of either control or improvement.

Drawing on Oliver (2009), we can sum up some of the prominent perspectives on QA and QE:

- QA and QE are dissimilar. The former deals with establishing that aims and objectives are achieved, while the latter deals with making improvements. QE is part of a broader framework wherein quality assurance, quality control, transformation, and quality enhancement are phases in quality management. The common understanding that QA naturally leads to QE is wrong, as most QA efforts are focused on accountability which is not necessarily connected to enhancement and may even oppose it;

- QA may either be retrospective or prospective depending on the kind of quality it intends to assure. Retrospective assurance reviews the past to create a judgment with emphasis on accountability, while prospective quality deals with the present and future, emphasising quality as standards to be met. QE may also be retrospective or prospective; retrospective activity is related to reflections on practice and formative learning while prospective activity is related to systemically acting on findings and ensuring that the data collected is really used for development.

Culture of Compliance or Culture of Innovation?

Applying Coppieters' (2005) research, HEIs need to focus on the dynamic and complex processes and relations that create their learning environments in order to move from a 'culture of compliance' to a 'culture of enhancement'. This can be done by systematically working to analyse and understand the role of the everyday practices of stakeholders (students, teachers, researchers, administrators, managers) and the administration of academic structures (curricula, resources, organisation, rules, norms, etc.). The outcome should be a culture (with the necessary accompanying supportive academic infrastructure) where ownership of the institutional quality enhancement agenda extends down to the point of delivery. A culture where academics, either as individuals or in their programme teams together with students (and other stakeholders including employers), research the effectiveness of their provision and collaborate on the development of interventions to enhance the learning experience of students.

McCulloch (2009) suggested a co-production model where students and other stakeholders are jointly involved in a collaborative enterprise emphasising generation, distribution, and (crucially) use of knowledge. This relationship decreases the distance between the students and their universities, supports profound learning, and enhances collaborative and collegiate learning approaches. This process engages innovation to transform knowledge, academics, and students. Gvaramadze (2011) argues that how the co-production based model of student and university through student engagement directly leads to QE processes in higher education. Such student engagement results in transformations in overall decision-making processes include that which impact on learning and teaching. This reflects the transformation of processes at the institutional level, including establishing and implementing quality mechanisms. This also suggests transformations at the level of the course and programme, expected activity of the student, strategies in teaching and learning, and student-instructor relationships. Delivering student engagement necessitates not only establishing sufficient student representative organisations but also additional important opportunities for empowering students.

By collaborating with students in QE activity, not only are interventions likely to be better informed and targeted, and thus more effective, but the engagement with students, in and of itself, leads to the development of a culture that promotes student empowerment and a sense of 'belonging'. Interestingly, this sense of belonging can be related directly to student retention and progression (Thomas, 2012) – factors which are among the primary markers for success as valued by those who favour QA approaches to quality management.

The Structure of this Anthology

The chapters in this book focus on QE rather than QA and our aim has been to provide a 'road map' of the chapters so that it is easier for you, the reader, to navigate directly to information that addresses QE issues that are currently of particular relevance to you.

During an intensive, 4-day symposium facilitated by the editors the chapter authors reviewed and debated distinctions between chapters. A consensus emerged: a successful QE initiative must always involve jointly the student, the teacher and the institution. However, it was agreed that some chapters deal with QE from a student-centric viewpoint, some champion a teacher-centric view of QE and some examine QE from an institution-centric perspective. The authors then decided that each chapter could be characterised as taking a macro-level or a micro-level approach to development of the three constituencies.

These views precipitated the model depicted in Figure 1.

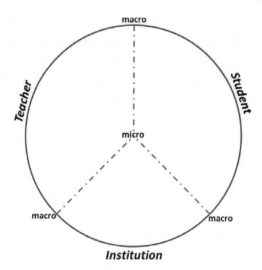

Figure 1: A model for a QE initiative in Higher Education that distinguishes the three constituencies to be developed.

Authors then found they could position precisely the 'centre of gravity' of their chapter on the mapping space offered by this model. See Figure 2.

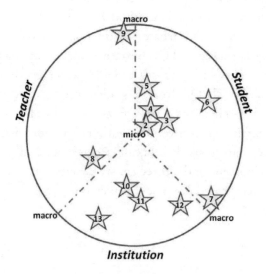

Figure 2: The model as a mapping space to locate the chapters in this anthology.

We have used this mapping to sequence the chapters in three parts: student-centric QE initiatives, teacher centric initiatives and institution-centric initiatives. In each part we start with a chapter addressing a micro-level approach to quality enhancement in HE and progress to those offering a macro-level perspective.

Part One: Practising QE in Relation to Students

The relatively recent student engagement movement has shifted the traditional equilibrium of qualitative and quantitative information towards more innovative quality enhancement mechanisms (Gvaramadze, 2011:32). It has led institutions and academic staff in HE to embark on novel strategies and tactics for learning and teaching. One example is seen in Scottish universities. The Enhancement Led Institutional Review (ELIR) reports for HEIs in Scotland show that the new strategies were designed to improve the learning experience of the students and mould them to be autonomous learners (Gvaramadze, 2011). These strategies included the strengthening of curriculum design, new learning and teaching approaches, tutorials, supervising student research, and providing distance-learning opportunities that reflect how HEIs have redefined their theoretical conceptions of learning. Activities to develop learning opportunities within a QE paradigm inevitably embrace innovation and foster a migration away from an often stale *status quo*. Learning environments informed by QE approaches are characterised by innovative practice, higher uses of technology, a greater volume of dialogue with stakeholders and a general willingness to advance pedagogy.

In their novel QE strategies, institutions often pay better attention to putting in place virtual learning settings and strengthening student engagement. The virtual setting in institutions becomes a vital source of training resources and information for students, but where exploited to the full the technology broadens the interface between academics and students (and between students and their peers). As newly formed student forums form, they become a supplemental space for engagement and communication. The learning experience is also enhanced through academic staff support of students by giving advice, feedback, and guidance. Together, these generate opportunities for additional enhancement of the learning experience.

Six chapters are featured in Part One. By way of introduction, each author(s) has succinctly summarised their key message as follows.

Chapter	The key message of the author(s)
2	Marja Mäensivu, Tiina Nikkola and Pentti Moilanen offer a Finnish perspective.
	"In supervisory situations where students have a more equal role with educators, students can see themselves as an active agent and controller of their own learning and that enables them to take more responsibility for their studying."
3	Swapna Koshy offers a UAE perspective.
	"My chapter evaluates the benefits of using differentiated assessments to enhance the learning experience of tertiary students. Multiple modes of assessments in the form of role plays, videos, letters to the editor, production of a career guide, blogs, posters, and games are demonstrated in order to cater to the varied skills and tastes of the students."
4	Andrew Green offers an English perspective.
	"Students commence their courses with established personal expectations about independent studies. Lecturers in higher education need to use these subjective expectations to build and challenge students' abilities and repertoire as independent learners to enhance the quality of teaching & learning."
5	Jennifer Rowley and Peter Dunbar-Hall offer an Australian perspective.
	"We explore music students' learning through the lens of a different culture's learning and teaching practice. The two main quality enhancement mechanisms that allow this to happen are experiential learning and immersion in diverse learning environments."
6	Isabel Huet, Ana Vitória Baptista and Carla Ferreira offer a Portugese perspective.
	"Undergraduate students' learning is enhanced by engaging them in research activities. These enable them to develop generic competencies which impact on and enhance their learning."
7	Andrea Raiker offers an English perspective.
	"My chapter explores using blended physical/virtual communities of enquirers as a methodology for teachers to organise and generate their own enlightenment to develop and focus their professional identities and their power to influence high level educational change."

Part Two: Practising QE in Relation to Teachers

Peer review of teaching increasingly focuses on the essentiality of university teaching and is seen to enhance teaching quality by sharing good practices among staff. Peer review of teaching is the deliberate method of observation in which a lecturer attends a colleague's teaching session with the purpose of providing feedback (Lomas & Kinchin, 2006). Peer review is regarded more as a QE tool than a QA tool because its primary purpose is to help academics study their teaching to self-improve and establish good practices for enhancing student learning (Lomas & Nicholls, 2005). Academics are starting to realise that focusing on facts and mastering data *"must give way to more active forms of learning; those that bring students to a deeper understanding"* (Lomas & Nicholls, 2005:139). Such approaches to teaching need to be comprehended and distributed department-wide by managers and academics. The three major arguments for the peer review are to:

1. strengthen cooperation among academics to share concepts and good practice;

2. ascertain that teaching enhancement is mainly the professionals' remit rather than of outside agencies;

3. supplement student assessment of teaching and offer several sources of information (Lomas & Nicholls, 2005).

These elements necessitate that academics are actively involved in the quality of teaching, directly engaged in gathering proof to demonstrate what they actually do, and show the knowledge behind the taken actions. This resonates with the argument made above where we advocate institutional QE mechanisms which extend right through to the point of delivery. In implementing peer review, the organisational culture and subcultures have to be understood. The fundamental values and beliefs of the academic staff should be discussed in order to generate an awareness of the significance of continuous enhancement and the worth of peer review as a practice to further that aim.

Managing change can be a difficult and intricate task, with academic staff frequently failing to react to what is forwarded by innovators. Innovators need to 'persuade and cajole' if success is to be guaranteed in peer review of teaching (Lomas & Nicholls 2005:140). High degrees of commitment, leadership skills, and perseverance are needed to successfully remove the constraints. By way of meeting this challenge, Bartholomew and Bartholomew (2011) demonstrate that it is possible to teach academics to be more innovative, to negotiate institutional cultures more successfully in the pursuit of successful innovation, to draw from the effective practice of others, and to generate evaluation evidence that is crucial in persuading peers to change their practice.

The development of learning-centred HE builds upon contextual learning theories (Bandura, 1975; Kolb, 1984; Vygotski, 1987; Lave & Wenger, 1991; Wenger, 1998). Contextual learning allows for linking the thoughts, feelings and actions of the learner to the contextual aspects of the curriculum. Learning is seen as an embedded process, affected by the learner's identity (Wenger, 1998; Greenwood, 1994) and social position (Lawson, 1997) in ongoing systems of social relations (Granovetter, 1992). Curriculum developers can use this knowledge to facilitate learning activities which build purposefully upon knowledge of the ways in which students constitute their identity when engaged in education (Nygaard & Serrano, 2010). The learning context constantly changes, and unique, ongoing systems of social relations are created each time students and teachers (and other key actors) take part in a learning activity (Nygaard & Andersen, 2005). We follow the definition of competence put forward by Nygaard *et al.* (2008:34-35), where competence is *"the ability to apply one's qualifications (knowledge and skills) in such a way that the task at hand is carried out to the standards of performance required in a particular context so the person is seen as competent by relevant peers."*

Part Two features two chapters:

Chapter	The key message of the author(s)
8	Christopher Klopper and Steve Drew offer an Australian perspective.
	"Quality enhancement through the peer review of teaching for learning and learning for teaching - a process and an outcome."
9	Sigridur Halldorsdottir offers an Icelandic perspective.
	"The quality attributes of the transformative teacher are presented and discussed in the form of a synthesised theory. The theory can be used in teacher education and training, in teachers' self-assessment, and in dialogues between teachers (e.g. as part of teachers' enhancement)."

Part three: Practising QE in Relation to Institutions

On the institutional level, the challenge is to develop an internal quality system which takes into consideration the above important aspects regarding students and teachers. As mentioned earlier in this introductory chapter, recent socio-political rhetoric has brought pressure to bear on HE, with an expectation that it rejuvenates its contribution to the economy in order to prepare better graduates for the 'market place' and to do so in a way that acknowledges and responds to the needs of employers. Although we have made some play of the necessity to develop QE approaches that embrace innovation and the 'discovery' of more effective pedagogies, we have not forgotten that such enhancements are never just in their own service. We see them as a valid response to aims that are common to those who subscribe to QA and QE paradigms; those of preparing more effectively graduates who can confidently and competently contribute to the wider world.

In order to accommodate the broad diversity of cultures and traditions in HE and surmount the fear of standardisation, QE paradigms offer flexibility to meet the students' specific needs and provide 'vibrancy, vitality, and variety' in a student and learner centred culture (Gvaramadze, 2008). In a mature QE framework, the student is placed at the centre of the education system; their capability to learn and their learning experience, as well as their engagement and participation, are requirements for high quality. Focusing on the learning experience leads to better transparency in devising specific objectives for study programmes while considering the wider societal context that remains a socio-political reality (Gvaramadze, 2008).

Because the student is placed at the core of internal quality system, a quality culture generates new roles for students; it sustains individual learners in their learning processes and enables them to become autonomous learners. The process encourages critical thinking, reflexivity, and self-reflection; it develops the student's awareness of the learning-teaching process and culture of the institution, it fosters community membership, and develops self-identity (Gvaramadze, 2008). All these have a positive impact for producing a learning context oriented towards continuous quality enhancement.

Curriculum development is, in many ways, an acute manifestation of institutional quality management. For most academics, designing new (or re-designing existing) study programmes brings them into an unfamiliar level of contact with academic regulations, occupational standards, stakeholder expectations and pedagogic planning. Those engaged in this work will experience the institutional quality management paradigm in a concentrated form; accordingly the institution, through the proxy of its policy and management practices, can have profound influence on the learning opportunities that emerge from this process. It is during these times that the principles guiding curriculum development should be reinforced to address important priorities and values that relate to learning and teaching. Teaching has to relate to current practice and to reflect evidence-based ideals.

Curriculum development should take into account the learning processes of students. It is our argument that universities can best fulfil their role and meet these requirements within the frame of contextual learning. Moreover, curriculum development needs to be rooted in an organisational culture in which there is a will (and the way) to experiment and to challenge existing world views, including allowing for non-conformist ideas that are different from the ideas of academic peer groups. Otherwise it will be extremely difficult to move away from the traditional syllabus-driven paradigms. Learning is about challenging current conceptions and breaking through boundaries. It is easy to understand why many HE institutions reproduce the old practice of simply lecturing what has been said in the text book. Such institutions generally focus on teaching or imparting knowledge rather than learning or learning to learn. Typically, they will lack a coherent set of principles to guide their curriculum development, and they may treat academic professionalism as synonymous with the achievement of high levels of academic knowledge and skills.

We believe that institutional cultures which place a QE paradigm at their centre are better able to support innovation and to reap the rewards that cascade from such activity. Furthermore, we believe that learning-centred education is more likely to emerge from such institutional contexts. Learning-centred education is the best way to secure competency development. In learning-centred education, the curriculum becomes a learning-centred action plan that unfolds while students are learning and thus becomes both responsive and agile to the dynamic worlds of education and wider society.

Part Three is informed by four chapters which address institution-centric QE:

Chapter	The key message of the author(s)
10	Lesley Lawrence and Helen Corkill offer an English perspective.
	"Our chapter shows how the introduction of action research into a postgraduate certificate in academic practice helps to develop a quality culture. This is achieved by supporting and empowering inexperienced teaching staff to change practice using evidence-informed approaches, thus enhancing the enhancers."
11	Jesper Piihl and Jens Smed Rasmussen offer a Danish perspective.
	"Course evaluation systems (CSE) can serve not only the purpose of quality control but also enhancement. We discuss a case on how design and style of use of a CSE can create multiple arenas for discussions on quality enhancement making stakeholders able to take responsibility."
12	Paul Bartholomew, Stuart Brand and Luke Millard offer an English perspective.
	"Three discrete projects are used to illustrate an institutional response to quality enhancement. A partnership with students delivers a sense of belonging and enhances student success. This is compatible with the enhancement of the student engagement dimension of the process variable of academic quality."
13	Lorenzo Vigentini and Laurent Ledouc offer a Belgian and a Scottish perspective.
	"Quality enhancement is considered as part of the strategic activities of two European learning and teaching centres. Despite significant differences in their context and strategic approach, there are similarities which reveal the effectiveness of such centres in affecting teaching and learning, ultimately enhancing students' learning experience."

Conclusion

In this introductory chapter we have argued that innovative quality enhancement initiatives provide a better way to handle intricate learning processes of students. The practice of quality enhancement has called into question the capability of those HE institutions that are centred upon a QA paradigm to generate systemic transformation and embed an effective quality culture. This shift is leading away from forms of quality assurance that create a culture of compliance to one that innovates and calls forth the active engagement of students, academic staff, and the institution. It requires partnership and collaboration among the stakeholders and a sharing of experiences. A quality enhancement paradigm delivers collaborative frameworks for change in institutions through joint endeavour. By allowing academic staff to take risks, and to own up to and learn from mistakes, the institution is able to embrace innovation and to become more effective.

While this creates some uncertainties and perceived risks, the uncertainty can be viewed as desirable in the sense that it guarantees change. This is exemplified by the political and social changes brought on by the global financial crisis. Even stalwarts of QA paradigms have come to understand that the *status quo* is no longer a viable option if we are to safeguard the role of Higher Education as a fundamental part of the knowledge (and wider) economy.

About the Authors

Claus Nygaard is Professor in Management Education at Copenhagen Business School, Denmark, and Director of LiHE. He can be contacted at this email: lihesupport@gmail.com

Nigel Courtney is Honorary Senior Visiting Fellow at Cass Business School, City University London, UK and Visiting Fellow at the University of Technology, Sydney. He can be contacted at this email: nigel@courtneynet.com

Paul Bartholomew is Director of Learning Innovation and Professional Practice at Aston University. He can be contacted at this email: p.bartholomew@aston.ac.uk

Chapter Two

Students Constructing the Curriculum – An Experiment to Increase Responsibility

Marja Mäensivu, Tiina Nikkola & Pentti Moilanen

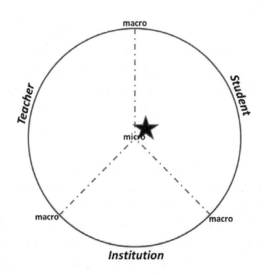

Introduction

At university, students' responsibility is considered automatic but, in reality, power relationships, for example, affect how students interpret their position of responsibility. This chapter presents a case of quality enhancement through action research that focuses on increasing students' responsibility for engagement in study.

An action research approach is well suited to enhancing the quality of teaching and learning (Biggs & Tang, 2007; Kember, 2000; Lawrence & Corkill, this volume). Firstly, action research enables practitioners to be active agents in developing their own work. Secondly, enhancement of one's own work is a continuous process where the cyclical nature of action research can be beneficially useful (Kember, 2000). Thirdly, action research can be used to clarify those perceived problems or weaknesses which need to be addressed in the future, and which are the starting point for the quality enhancement of teaching and studying (see D'Andrea & Gosling, 2005; van Vught, 1994).

In the Critical Integrative Teacher Education (CITE) programme, an alternative pathway for master's level university students studying to become primary school teachers, quality enhancement is based on precisely this kind of research-based evaluation of one's own activity. CITE endeavours to find an alternative to the routines of school and education and use research -to continuously assess the operating practices of the training programme, to identify factors hindering and promoting learning and to develop alternative modes of implementation. One of the challenges discovered through CITE research is that the constraints of studying still include various features which prevent student autonomy and responsibility (Mäensivu, 2012). Although students in CITE have more opportunity to influence and more freedom of action than regular teacher education students, they nevertheless seem to have adapted to the dominant position of the supervisor and perceive that the supervisor has the responsibility for teaching situations and sometimes even for students' working and learning.

Since our research indicates that accepting responsibility is challenging, we tried to tackle this problem in the CITE programme and improve our own teaching so that it would enable students to take responsibility for engagement in study. Our position is that supervision and responsibility can be constructed in an interactive teaching intervention. We have used several micro-pedagogical interventions to support the increase of student responsibility. In our latest intervention students were allowed to design a new curriculum for their training programme.

In this chapter we describe our own attempt to enhance the quality of teaching and studying by means of the curriculum planning process (Figure 1). We begin by describing one of the obstacles to the goal of increasing student responsibility: the hierarchical relationship existing between supervisor and student. We then describe the intervention and the teaching and studying methods employed in the attempt to improve students' responsibility in both supervisory situations and work processes. We then go on to present some of the features we discovered in supervisor-student interaction which helped students to assume responsibility, but also some which unintentionally impeded it. We describe these features in more detail using two supervision episodes.

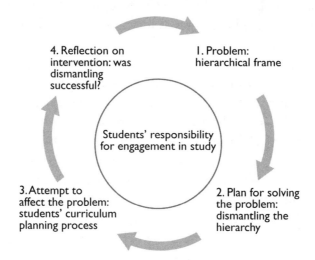

Figure 1: Our action research cycle for quality enhancement, adapted from Kember (2000:26).

The Hierarchical Frame – the Challenge of Fostering Student Responsibility

Quality enhancement offers an opportunity for teachers themselves to define what is meant by good teaching, studying and learning (Bamber & Anderson, 2012; Little & Williams, 2010). In CITE we consider one of the goals of a good studying process to be that students feel that they are not just receivers of information but active and independent agents (Dobozy, 2011) who take responsibility for their own studies and learning. This kind of student engagement is an important indicator of educational quality (Gibbs, 2010), yet this is far from being self-evident even for university students.

The construction of student responsibility and autonomy in a study context can be examined using Goffman's (1986) concept of frame. According to Goffman, the individual does not him/herself define a social situation but the definition already exists – as some kind of 'frame'. The student endeavours, often unconsciously, to find appropriate definitions for study situations by answering the question. *"What is it that's going on here?"* (Goffman, 1986:8). In the study situation, students are easily directed by an understanding that the supervisor and student are not equal, meaning that one of the frames related to the study situation is constructed on the hierarchy existing between student and supervisor (Mäensivu, 2012).

According to Mäensivu (2012) the students' responsibility for engagement in their own learning and studying decreases, and sometimes even disappears, when they interpret the study situation as hierarchical with controlling authority in the hands of the supervisor. The frame determines what appropriate behaviour in the study situation is so that when students interpret a study situation according to a hierarchical frame, they regress into subordinates who do not fully accept or understand their responsibility. As subordinates, they devote considerable energy to pleasing their supervisor and, not assuming an active role; they only do as they are told.

According to our observations, the hierarchical frame is particularly strong, for example, in teacher education. We asked educators if they could do something to break the frame and increase students' responsibility. If the hierarchical frame can be broken, the student's resources might be more effectively directed towards studying. If the student does not need to try to interpret and guess what the supervisor wants studying is structured through the student's own active decision-making. According to Shor (1996), by distributing authority and by questioning the teacher's traditional role, the students could assume greater responsibility for their training and become more active agents.

Dismantling the hierarchy, however, does not mean completely removing it from the supervisory relationship. Professional relationships always involve tensions and asymmetries which are not possible or even appropriate to discard (e.g., Gerlander & Isotalus, 2010). By denying their own authority status, educators may give an impression of being incompetent teachers and indicate that 'anything goes'. That is why, for example, Shor (1996) thinks that in order to organise changes in power relations educators must use their authority status. Dismantling the hierarchy then is more a question of recognising the consequence of hierarchy – responsibility-free subservience – and of questioning and invalidating the associated traditional modes of activity (Mäensivu, 2012). This chapter deals with our attempts to break that hierarchical frame in a teaching intervention where students were given the task of drawing up a curriculum for their training programme.

The Students' Curriculum Planning Process – a Place for Taking Responsibility

Designing the curriculum was devised as a continuation of the two-year CITE programme for primary school student teachers developed at the University of Jyväskylä's Department of Teacher Education (Nikkola et al., 2008). At the beginning of their studies one group of thirteen students has the opportunity to join this self-selected non-traditional programme and then, during their first two years, most of their studies take place in CITE. Even though CITE has a clear theoretical basis and its operational methods differ from other Teacher Education Department teaching, the programme has not had its own formal curriculum and its activities have to be adapted to fit in with the official general class teacher education curriculum. For example, in contrast to traditional separate teaching units, CITE studies have been arranged in the form of an extensive totality but, because CITE students and students taking the conventional route are all working towards the same teacher qualification on parallel pathways, CITE students have to obtain credits from the same official units as the other students. As it has developed, however, CITE has increasingly distanced itself from the general curriculum and consequently there has been a need for CITE to have its own curriculum.

On completion of their CITE studies and after merging with the general study pathway in their third year, one group of students in the CITE programme was offered the opportunity to participate in designing the CITE curriculum, as an additional unit (3 credits) of their CITE studies. The idea was that by creating the curriculum, students could contribute to CITE developmental work and it would also clarify the 'big picture' of CITE studies, not only for the students themselves but also for educators and future CITE students. Designing the curriculum was part of a wider project on action research quality enhancement (for more, see Critical Integrative Teacher Education, 2012).

The Means for Dismantling Hierarchy in the Curriculum Planning Process

Since the quality of learning outcomes is one of the consequences of the study methods employed in the learning process (Marton & Säljö, 1984; Ramsden, 1992), we tried to construct the curriculum design task in such a way that it would help to break down the hierarchical frame and increase students' responsibility. In the curriculum planning process, the idea was that demolishing the hierarchical frame would enable students to assume increased responsibility for engagement in study because they would no longer construe responsibility as belonging solely to the supervisor but rather see it as being more mutual (see Bartholomew *et al.*, this volume).

The curriculum planning process had some similarities to experience-based learning approaches, which often assume a relatively equal relationship between teacher and student (Andresen *et al.*, 2000). In the intervention, as in problem-based or project-based learning, the roles of the supervisor and student were transformed and control was transferred to the hands of a learner (Helle *et al.*, 2006; Hmelo-Silver, 2004). Questioning and invalidating the associated traditional models of activity happened in the following ways:

- the experiment was a voluntary part of their studies so students took part out of their own interest;

- students were working with a real curriculum and not completing a task for their educators;

- the students were given the chance to create something new where there was no one correct solution; it was emphasised that the educators themselves did not have a ready-made answer or solution as to what the curriculum should be like;

- the students could organise their work themselves and decide on how the process advanced;

- the educators acted as mirrors for the students' processes and not as process leaders or transmitters of information.

Additionally, in the curriculum process, the students were able to make use of information that the educators did not have: the students' own 'lived experience' of the programme (see Bartholomew *et al.*, this volume). In the intervention, students also had an opportunity to develop the future work of the educators by curriculum planning and this factor helped to transform the traditional relationship between educators and students.

Implementing the curriculum planning process

In autumn 2011, the student group (n=12) began working on their task of drawing up a proposal for the form and content of the CITE curriculum. The students already had two years' experience of working together as a group and the bases for the work were the students' own experiences of the programme and the material collected during it. The autumn term and half the spring term were set aside for the process. The students mostly worked together and decided themselves on their own working methods, progress and organisation.

The students also had access to two educators for consultation. Joint meetings between educators and students dealt with progress (Table 1). The educators tried to structure the students' work by discussing their observations of the group's work, asking questions and keeping the group on task. The joint meetings also involved setting timetables and resolving practical issues. In addition to meetings, the educators also monitored the group's work with minutes and other email messages sent to a joint mailing list.

spring 2011	Students made aware of opportunity to be involved in designing CITE curriculum.
13.9.2011	Agreement with students on the curriculum task and the preliminary course timetable.
4.10.2011	Process guidance on the basis of students' questions: students present curriculum content they themselves consider important. Students also raise issues related to their internal organisation.
8.11.2011	Process guidance on the basis of students' questions: discussion on the structure of the curriculum, etc.

13.12.2011	Process guidance on the basis of students' questions: students present their ideas on alternative forms of the curriculum. One of the educators promises to send out material (e.g., on various curricula) for the next meeting.
10.1.2012	Dealing with material sent out in advance by the educator.
21.2.2012	Dealing with curricula sent in by students. Curriculum process educators and two external CITE instructors give comments.
16.3.2012	Discussion and evaluation of the curriculum process and experiment as a whole.

Table 1: Supervisory meetings related to the students' process.

After the last supervisory meeting students sent in the final version of the curriculum via email (22.5.2012).

Data from the Curriculum Design Process

The process described above generated considerable data that we have used in analysing the teaching experiment (Kember, 2000). We have the notes and the reflective diaries kept by two of the teaching intervention educators during the seven process meetings, each lasting from two to four hours. In addition, we have used memoranda made by the student group and the email exchanges that took place through a shared list. We have also recorded and videoed the four-hour reflective discussion carried out at the end of the process (16.3.2012) with the aim of analysing the students' process.

We analysed the data to find features that were somehow significant from the viewpoint of the hierarchical frame. We reflected especially on the influence that supervision had on dismantling the hierarchy and increasing students' responsibility. For example, we analysed the joint meetings by looking for the different roles of the educators and students and the degree to which students assumed or shirked responsibility. Our analysis was directed by the following questions: How successfully had we accomplished our aim of dismantling the hierarchical structure and increasing students' responsibility? Where did we succeed well? Where, on the other hand, did we have less success and why?

Did we Succeed in Dismantling the Hierarchical Frame?

We examine hierarchy dismantlement by means of two significant episodes present in the supervisory process. Those episodes were the most critical moments concerning the role transformation and role constancy of educators and students. In one, the emphasis is on allocating responsibility in supervisory situations and in the other, on taking responsibility for one's own work.

Supervision may Involuntarily Exempt the Student from Responsibility

The joint meetings between the student group and two educators began promisingly from the viewpoint of dismantling the hierarchy since the students did not feel that their role in the supervisory situations was that of responsibility-free subordinates but rather of active agents. At the start of the process, the student group did not assume that educators would take charge but they themselves had prepared for the meetings with educators and assumed responsibility for the progress of such meetings. The students had decided what kind of issues they wanted to discuss and, in addition, for the first time in the CITE programme, they had chosen a chairperson and secretary from among themselves for a meeting also attended by educators. Generally, the chairperson and secretary had only functioned in meetings among students, with educators expected to run other meetings. Because students assumed more responsibility than earlier in supervisory situations, the planned means for dismantling the hierarchical frame worked.

Apparently, in supervisory situations where educators had the responsibility for planning and teaching, the students did not regard this as teaching but rather as helping their process forward. In these cases, the students themselves were best informed about the kinds of questions that needed discussing with the educators and they bore the responsibility for bringing them up. This required allowing the students to take the leading role in the situation while the educators acted as facilitators.

Although at the outset of the teaching intervention both educators and

27

students succeeded in breaking away from their traditional hierarchical roles and students were able to take responsibility for the contents and progress of the supervisory meetings, the students very quickly resumed the role of subordinates without responsibility. After the students' initial enthusiasm, when it came to deciding the direction in which to begin developing the curriculum, work came to a standstill. One of the educators tried to help the students' process by sending material in advance for the first scheduled meeting of the spring term (10.1.2012). The idea was that considering that material would open up a new perspective for the students on their own curriculum process, but this intervention by an educator seemed to mean a relinquishing of the role of 'responsibility bearer'. The educator's effort to help and the resulting responsibility-free subordination of students impacted that first spring meeting and the subsequent process at many levels.

First of all, students had not prepared themselves for the first meeting of the spring term in the same way as for previous occasions when they had assumed responsibility for the course of events:

> "I don't think we had either a chair or a secretary, and I wasn't at all clear myself about what we had agreed on before the vacation and whether we had fixed up some task for the group to think about. I at least hadn't written anything down and so I hadn't done anything." (Student's email message 23.1.2012)

Clearly, the students were interpreting the situation differently than earlier supervisory situations: the duty of the educator seemed to be to make sure the session ran smoothly and the students' task was merely to be present. It was never revealed in the session whether the material sent by the educator failed to interest or was not felt to be significant. Maybe because the default position of students is to be passive, it was left to the educator to try and involve the students in the discussion.

This change from earlier meetings may have been because the students interpreted the educator sending material as a sign that this particular meeting would be the supervisor's responsibility. On the other hand, the transfer of responsibility to the educator may have been because the student group had not had a collective meeting to decide on preparations and their roles.

In addition to leaving responsibility for the meeting to the educator, the students treated the task of considering the advance material like a school assignment. Because the supervisor had not specified a more precise task, many had just glanced through the material without thinking what it could contribute to their own process. They considered their part done when they had scanned the material. This is perhaps the reason why students did not seem to make any substantive comments during the ensuing discussion:

> "It feels like an uphill battle. Not one of them has any comments on anything, just a few keep up some kind of discussion. Could it be that this curriculum [that was sent to them] isn't interesting for the students after all? Should I have been able to ask about it in a more interesting way? Should they have been left alone to think about it before being asked? On the other hand, I assumed that they would have familiarised themselves with it so that they could say something about it." (Educator's diary 10.1.2012)

The students responded to the material sent by the educator as subordinates without responsibility: they did not question the necessity for material to be sent by an authority yet they did not feel any obligation to show interest in the material or try and further develop any ideas from it.

The educator's attempt to help not only affected the students' responsibility in that particular meeting but it also made the students reshape their own activities as the process advanced. Although the educator had meant the material as just one example of a curriculum and in no way whatsoever as a model, the students grasped it like a straw, forgot their own original ideas and began to work on their curriculum using the material as a model. The same kind of leader dependence has also been observed, for example, in problem-based learning: the students view the tutor's comments as the truth (Hammar Chiriac, 2008). Perhaps the students' interpretation was that the educators had initially given them the freedom to implement their own ideas but were using this intervention to rein in that freedom.

The educator's well-intentioned attempt to help the students in their process may have become an obstacle to the dismantling of the hierarchical frame. The students interpreted the educator's effort to help as an opportunity to deflect their responsibility and, furthermore, to redirect their work in order to please the educator. In this situation, fracturing the student's role of subordinate without responsibility would have required the educator to recognise the hierarchical frame and to react to it:

> "It is only now afterwards that I realise I should have interrupted the situation when I understood it wasn't working. The situation became more a matter of getting through it. Because the students hadn't prepared for this situation as a group and hadn't chosen a chairperson, I had responsibility for the situation and they didn't." (Educator's diary 10.1.2012)

Even though the educator realised that something was wrong, she lacked the necessary understanding to end the situation and to question her role as the person responsible because she went along with the students' interpretation of the situation as hierarchical (see about role confusion in problem-based learning Papinczak *et al.*, 2009; Bowman & Hughes, 2005). Consequently, in this meeting, dismantling the frame was unsuccessful. The students pushed responsibility onto the educator whereupon she attempted to carry it and was unable to reassign it to the students.

Shifting Responsibility Back to the Students Requires Tolerance of Uncertainty

The second example of a situation regarding the relation of supervision and student responsibility was the meeting planned to conclude the course (16.3.2012). The purpose of the last meeting was to discuss the working process and evaluate this pioneering intervention as a whole. The meaning of the meeting changed, however, since the students had in fact not put the finishing touches to their curriculum, although this action had been agreed on in the previous meeting where the students' draft curriculum had been reviewed through discussion. In that discussion, students talked about their intention to carry on developing the curriculum and it was agreed that students should make the decisions about necessary changes. Despite what had been agreed, the students had not met once as a group after the feedback meeting and, partly as a result of this, had not finished the curriculum.

At the meeting, the students were unable to explain why they had neglected to do the work and their understandings of the task were contradictory. At the start of the session one of the students spoke up in defence of not completing the work. According to her, the task of finishing off the assignment had been misunderstood and yet she felt it had indeed been completed. Another student offered an opposing view that the activity of the group had quietly subsided after their initial enthusiasm and in fact the group had abandoned work on the final version of the curriculum after the feedback session:

> "We just like left it, you know, unfinished, just like that. I feel that the last time we students met each other there was this idea right from the start that we'd done it." (Student's comment at the meeting on 16.3.2012)

Apart from one comment, the group did not seize on this viewpoint that emphasised their own responsibility. Rather, it leaned toward defensive explanations that underplayed its own responsibility and emphasised, for example, misunderstanding the educators' instructions, the negative impact on the group's creativity of the material sent out by the educator, and the difficulty of guessing what the instructors' wishes were. On the other hand, the view that the task had been completed was constantly present in the discussion along with the excuses. One explanation for these seemingly contradictory experiences may be that during the process the students learned much about the nature of curricular work but, in spite of this, they gave up when as a group they should have made challenging concrete decisions: applying what they had learned to their own activity.

The fact was, however, that the learning agreed upon in the course still required work, even though many of the constraints, such as timetables and the assumption that the course would end with this session, worked against this. For this reason, the student group was not allowed to escape the fact that work on the curriculum appeared incomplete. Consequently, the first stage of dismantling the hierarchical framework was to have the students recognise and acknowledge their responsibility as active agents.

The key to initiating discussion of the students' responsibility was when the educator related her own experiential interpretation of the confusion and frustration generated by their failure to complete the task. After this, many of the students started to talk about their responsibility and acknowledged their avoidance of cooperative work. Until the educator expressed her frustration, the students had concentrated on arguing that they had finished or misunderstood the requirements. The educator's human and sensitive comments seemed to open up to the students the opportunity to talk more honestly about their own activity and also about its less admirable aspects.

When the students admitted to neglecting their responsibility, they nevertheless began to expect the educators to 'forgive' them for it. Although students acknowledged their responsibility superficially, they did not want to 'own' it. The framework had not been completely dismantled, but in fact the strategy for maintaining the subordinate framework had altered. By granting forgiveness, the educators would have charged themselves with responsibility and so the hierarchical roles would not have changed at all.

Benevolent understanding or forgiveness was not the answer to moving on to the next stage of dismantling the framework. For that to happen, the educator had to hand questions of shirking responsibility back to the students for them to deal with. At the end of the session, an effort was made to agree on how the work could be concluded but, even though the educator repeatedly mentioned the incomplete work, the student group failed to pick up on it. They killed it with their silence. With the group expecting to give the assignment only the finishing touches, it was disagreeable to point out that they had failed to complete the agreed tasks. However, the educator's task was to remind them categorically what was required of them to complete the course and to stick to this requirement while leaving them to bear the responsibility. In our experiment this meant, for example, insisting that the group completed the task, and acknowledged the unpleasant issues and re-assessing the timetable.

Because the educators did not allow the students to neglect their responsibility and handed the task back to them, the students recommenced their work on the curriculum after the meeting, although it was originally planned to conclude the course. The students themselves were keen to move their work forward and they also felt responsibility for its completion. If the students had felt they were responsible to their educators, according to the hierarchical frame, they would have carried out their educators' suggestions. The reallocation of responsibility seemed to have succeeded because the attitude of the students to the task was not that of subordinates who were working under orders from above or gratifying their supervisors. This was seen in the final meeting when the students discussed the educators' wishes and suggestions for the curriculum. Their attitude was critical, with some suggestions being accepted but the majority rejected.

Based on the episode described above, we can conclude that dismantling the hierarchical framework in the supervisory process requires the educator to tolerate uncertainty in his or her own work. In this case, uncertainty was caused, for example, by the unpredictability of the consequences of one's own interventions and the breakdown of the agreed timetable. It is characteristic of situations of uncertainty that they arise unpredictably and it is often challenging to tackle them. Such situations require the educator to have the skill to continuously analyse study situations and react to each of them appropriately (Nikkola, 2011). This viewpoint on the uncontrollability of reality is not necessarily taken into account enough in teaching quality enhancement.

In Conclusion

This case is part of the ongoing action research quality enhancement process in our CITE training programme. Our idea was to increase students' responsibility for engagement in study by demolishing the hierarchy. In a short intervention of this kind, breaking the hierarchical frame meant a novel way of interpreting situations where educators and students meet and not the total removal of the hierarchy. By investigating our own activity we discovered factors in the supervisory process that influenced the construction of responsibility amongst students.

At the first stage of quality enhancement, the course must be planned in such a way that the study structures themselves make it possible to create opportunities for the student to move from the frame of responsibility-free subordinate towards a more active and accountable role. It must be taken into account that the state of responsibility-free subordination is not a characteristic of students but rather a deeply entrenched model for functioning in training situations; the purpose is not to use planning in an attempt to 'fix' the students but to improve the university teaching culture. The structure of the course we planned gave the students increased decision-making power and a more equal role with the educators and made the students act accountably in supervisory situations. We were thus partly successful in enhancing study quality during the experiment by transforming the roles of teacher and student.

In our intervention we discovered that even good planning is not sufficient. The other factor that influenced the construction of responsibility among students was the supervisor's sensitivity in unpredictable situations. The reality of teaching can never be exhaustively planned because it is always full of surprises and more multidimensional than we assume (Britzman, 2009). The educator can plan an environment where the hierarchy could crumble but, in addition to planning, it also requires sensitivity in supervision (see Papinczak *et al.*, 2009). This kind of sensitivity is part of an educator's existential competence (Halldórsdóttir, this volume)

Breaking the student's role of responsibility-free subordination requires the educator to abandon 'benevolently responsible' supervision of the situation as well as those measures that would undoubtedly simplify the practicalities. It is a matter of clarifying questions of responsibility and reassigning to students the responsibility that is theirs. For the individual, this uncompromising approach may be irksome and may complicate the running and planning of one's own work smoothly. In the hectic work of a university the breakdown of timetables is annoying for all parties. Some might find it easier to turn a blind eye to students' shortcomings on the task, award the marks for the course and consider the matter settled.

Furthermore, the educator cannot forcibly dismantle the framework for the student or assume that once the hierarchy has been successfully broken, the students will automatically begin to act more responsibly in all situations. Even a small hint from the educator may derail a well-planned course, meaning that quality enhancement from the viewpoint of dismantling the hierarchical framework requires constant work. In this experiment, we did succeed in returning responsibility on certain points, though far from all.

The results of our research will benefit others who see students' responsibility for their own learning as a precondition of a good studying process. Because the quality enhancement process does not only concern predictable situations, time and resources must be set aside for supervision and its constant evaluation and modification according to the situation. The educator must evaluate the effects of his/her own action and what is required of him/her in the supervisory situation in order to facilitate student accountability. Follow-up discussion with a colleague not participating in the supervisory situations benefits this evaluation (Biggs & Tang, 2007; see also Klopper & Drew, this volume, on peer review of teaching) and it would be of special benefit to have collegial support in place during the supervisory interaction. For university teaching, this means moving from the tradition of individual teaching towards joint planning, supervision and evaluation, thus allowing more flexible reaction to unpredictable situations.

About the Authors

Marja Mäensivu is a Doctoral Student at the Department of Teacher Education at the University of Jyväskylä, Finland. She can be contacted at this email: marja.f.maensivu@jyu.fi

Tiina Nikkola is a Postdoctoral Researcher at the Department of Teacher Education at the University of Jyväskylä, Finland. She can be contacted at this email: tiina.nikkola@jyu.fi

Pentti Moilanen is a Professor at the Department of Teacher Education at the University of Jyväskylä, Finland. He can be contacted at this email: pentti.moilanen@jyu.fi

Chapter Three

Differentiated Assessment Activities: Customising to Support Learning

Swapna Koshy

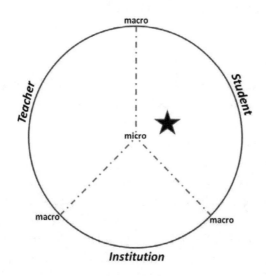

Quality Enhancement to Benefit Students

Quality Enhancement in simple terms *"is about getting teachers to teach better"* (Biggs, 2001:227). Educational institutions have always been engaged in enhancing quality to satisfy various stakeholders including governments, accreditation bodies and patrons. The enhancement of the quality of every/any stage of the complicated process of delivering education benefits all stakeholders. This chapter focuses on quality enhancement through improving assessment practices that positively and immediately impact student learning. These 'micro-quality enhancements' initiated by reflective practitioners and applied in the 'microcosm' of the classroom are critical to overall quality enhancement. When they attain critical mass, 'macro-quality enhancement' measures such as policy changes will have to be put in place. 'Individual learning' is as much a component of a learning organisation as is 'organisational learning' (Hodgkinson & Brown, 2003:340). Periodic review and improvement of current pedagogic practices is essential for quality enhancement in a dynamic environment where *"new content knowledge, educational innovations, a changing student population, and changing conditions in the institution and society, all make such a review necessary"* (Biggs, 2001:223). As learning/knowledge organisations, universities should encourage and accept the productive innovative practices initiated by pedagogy-focused teachers who can best assess students' needs.

The Context

This chapter evaluates the benefits of using differentiated assessments – offering varied assessment formats – to enhance the learning experience of tertiary students in a private Western University in the Emirate of Dubai in the United Arab Emirates (UAE). Differentiated teaching and assessments are used by educators whose goal is to be inclusive. Today's classroom, with its eclectic mix of students, warrants a customised approach. This is especially true in the UAE which is a veritable salad bowl of cultures. The population of the UAE consists overwhelmingly of expatriates; they account for 88% of the population (Emirates24/7, 2012). The majority of these expatriates come from the Indian Sub-continent, Iran and neighbouring Arab countries. Schools offer national curricula as well as western curricula including American, British, Australian and International Baccalaureate®. Most Emiratis pursue tertiary education in government colleges and are fully funded by the government. Expatriates have to choose from the various private universities offering western or other degrees accredited internationally and in India and Iran.

The course reviewed in this chapter is a Business Communication course for first year undergraduate business students. This course is also subscribed to by a number of final year students because the topics it covers include preparing for job interviews and writing curriculum vitae. The learning outcomes expected were:

1. comprehend the foundations of communication, its contexts, processes and the skills required to be an effective, culturally sensitive and humane communicator;

2. analyse communication barriers and difficulties with a view to developing solutions to overcome them;

3. demonstrate skills in finding, organising and presenting ideas orally and in writing;

4. propose methods to manage mediate and resolve conflicts in communication.

The cosmopolitan student population at the university embraces close to 130 nationalities, mirroring the population make-up of the UAE. Some 30 to 40 nationalities are represented in a typical lecture cohort. Students' different learning experiences and learning styles add to the cultural variety. Students who graduate from schools following western curricula are trained in communication from their formative years; this is not the case with some other curricula. This creates perceivable differences in communication skill levels. Oral and written skills in the English language also vary considerably.

As instructor, I was responsible for successfully delivering the course, managing tutors and tutorials, preparing subject content and assessments. I decided that the eclectic mix of students warranted the use of differentiated assessments. Instead of the earlier practice of offering a single assessment format like reports, oral presentations or posters for the whole cohort, I changed to multiple modes of assessment. These include role playing, presenting self-produced videos on communication topics, writing letters to the editors of local dailies on socially relevant topics, collating relevant local information for a career guide, presenting students' own social interest websites and blogs, poster presentations, educative games and so on.

Students were given a choice of themes as cues to work on. Alternatively they could choose any topic related to Business Communication.

The Need for Differentiated Assessment

Differentiated instruction is gaining wider acceptance the world over, especially in primary and secondary schools which cater to special needs students and those from impoverished and otherwise diverse backgrounds. These students have explicitly different learning needs which have to be addressed. The benefits of differentiated instruction have been documented by several educators including Tieso (2001) and Tomlinson (2000). The role of differentiated assessments in facilitating differentiated instruction has also been confirmed. Rock *et al.*'s (2008) extensive survey of literature on differentiated instruction identified *"five quality indicators that reflect major factors(variables) associated with differentiated instruction: (a) teacher, (b) content, (c) learner, (d) instruction, and (e) assessment."*

Assessment synthesises the other four indicators of quality. Tomlinson and Kalbfleisch (1998) attempted to identify elements that make a differentiated classroom successful and found that a key factor was the need for *"varied assessment options"*.

More recent developments in pedagogy that facilitate customisation include Personalised Learning strategies (Leadbeater, 2004; Miliband, 2004). To me, a Personalised Learning strategy recognises aspects like the needs of the individual student, the students' individual learning styles, and the students' motivation for studying and learning. It also recognises the role of teaching and learning methods in relation to the individual student's learning process. Personalisation is achieved mainly through technology, close interaction with the teacher in small classrooms, and partnering with parents beyond the classroom. Differentiated learning and assignments are definitely easier to implement and require fewer resources. In the four practical cases that follow in this chapter I show how to deal with Personalised Learning strategies in practice.

Chapman and King (2005:xix) offer a lucid definition of the concept of differentiated assessment: *"Differentiated assessment is an ongoing process through which teachers gather data before, during, and after instructing from multiple sources to identify learners' needs and strengths. Students are different in their knowledge and skills. They differ in the ways and speeds at which they process new learning and connect it to prior knowledge and understanding. They also differ in the ways they most effectively demonstrate their progress. This necessitates a strong and continued commitment from the lecturer."*

Another characteristic of differentiated assessments is that they are usually formative in nature. Wormeli (2006:4) observes that

> *"...summative assessments like unit tests and final projects are done post learning. The real powerhouse is formative assessment. This is made of smaller assessments and checkpoints done en route to mastery. Students get regular and frequent feedback in a timely manner that they can use. Teachers should spend at least as much energy designing their formative assessments as they do their summative assessments."* Wormelli (2006:4)

Therefore, summative assessments, such as final exams, do not lend themselves easily to differentiated assessment. The use of differentiated assessments in the Business Communication course mentioned was expected to:

- avoid transmitting information to students – what Biggs (2001:13) calls *"dubbing an audio tape"* – but to help them learn by *"interacting with the world"*. The world here is inclusive of the material, instructor, peers, media of presentation etc. Deep learning results from active engagement in a self-chosen activity';

- accommodate individual variations in student learning. Researchers have observed that each student's experience is unique as he/she interacts with the *"learning context"* (Prosser & Trigwell, 1999:16);

- help low achievers to improve performance. As Martin Richardson observes *"with differentiated assessment even low achievers can learn to high standards and succeed with higher order thinking skills"* (reported in Chapman & King, 2005:xvi).

The Practice: Choosing Assessment Activities

As the instructor, I was able to estimate the skill level and learning preferences of most of my students because they had completed a minimum of two courses with me. Individual consultations were offered to students in the second week of the 13-week course to review the topic chosen. Students were given five to seven minutes in class to discuss with the teacher, in addition to the announced out-of-class consultation hours. Giving students the chance to choose their preferred theme was intended to increase their engagement with the topic. Some students seemed to lack clarity on how to proceed and these were advised based on their past performance, social milieu and personality. A second session of individual consultations was offered two weeks before the assessment presentations were due to begin. This was to ensure that students were progressing well and were ready to present their work. As some of them had chosen formats they had never worked in before it was imperative for the teacher to offer help. This individual attention helped students air their doubts and concerns and receive practical guidance.

Students with a fear of public speaking were given individual coaching; students who could not locate information were directed to useful resources, and students with poor time management skills were helped to develop weekly schedules to complete their assessment effectively and on time.

Close monitoring by the instructor is necessary for differentiated assessments to succeed. As students are engaged in different activities they cannot always rely on their peers or prior experience as much as in standard assessments. McLoone (2007) used formative assessment to facilitate student learning and recommended that, when using differentiated assessment, they should be individualised and supervised properly.

Having discussed differentiated assessment from an academic point of view, let me turn to four different cases in which I have practiced differentiated assessment.

Learning by Interacting with the World: 4 Cases

The four cases presented below were chosen because they exemplify the role of differentiated assessment in improving student learning by increasing engagement with the task, gaining higher grades, and achieving holistic improvement. These cases offer a representative sample that highlights some of the benefits reaped by using differentiated assessments. The cases also represent four different assessment formats.

Case I: Active Learning

Students of all ages learn best when they are actively engaged in the learning process. To engage actively in a learning activity, it should be interesting and should also encourage learning. The instructor must therefore strive to create interesting learning environments which will motivate students to interact with the world. This will encourage both acquisition and application of information. As Biggs (2001:13) confirms, it is not the assimilation of information but its application that brings about a *"conceptual change"*.

One mode of assessment, for instance, encouraged students to produce videos on job searches and career guidance focusing on local requirements. These could be uploaded on the university website and were intended for current and future students of the university and the general public. Students were instructed not to duplicate information that is easily available in the mass media but to identify relevant and specific information on the topic which would be valuable and beneficial for the community. Many students chose this assessment activity and produced videos that incorporated local information of value to job seekers in the region.

A male Emirati student, whose family has multiple businesses, was encouraged to interview the human resource (HR) managers of four major local companies to find out what they expected to see on curriculum vitaes of prospective employees in their respective industries. Unlike expatriate students, this student had easy access to executives of large companies and was happy to engage in the task. The student was a consistently poor achiever and had failed several courses. However, he had his own web site and an active blog on arts and music which had attracted over 60,000 visitors in the span of a few months. The student had also uploaded several amateur videos and enthusiastically shared these with the instructor.

His familiarity with the media and his penchant for creative work made the video assessment an ideal choice for him. The HR managers interviewed by the student represented four diverse industries: aluminium production, healthcare, premium car franchise, and local banking.

Unlike assignments which involve only arm-chair research, in this case the student had to identify four different industries where graduates could find employment, get appointments with the HR managers of the companies, prepare a set of interview questions that would utilise the time allotted for the interview beneficially, prepare a video of the interview and present it to the class. This involved much more work and skill than would be required for a report or oral presentation. After his presentation the student confirmed that he enjoyed the work, was excited to do it and he commented that he found it easy. He had started work on the project the day after he chose the topic. Later, he shared the video and the *"best grades I ever got"* with his proud family.

The output was exceptional and he scored a high distinction for it. What the student learned from engaging in the learning activity was varied and valuable. In addition, the community benefit from the assessment was high. The full-fledged interaction with the learning activity at every stage led to deep learning. He proudly shared the high profile interviews with the class and declared *"this was such a fun assessment. I love this subject"*.

During an informal interview conducted to assess the merit of differentiated assessments, the student remarked that he was motivated by the uniqueness of the assignment and the fun in doing it and also because the outcome would be appreciated by an external audience (when displayed on the university career department web site). As Biggs (2001:13) says: *"Motivation is a product of good teaching not its prerequisite"*. The onus is on the instructor to create a learning environment which inspires students to learn effectively.

Case 2: An Holistic Change

In this example, the student was a particularly timid 24 year old non-local Arab male whose younger sister was also a student at the university. She had approached me several times for information about the course but the student himself was too nervous to approach me. The student was encouraged to meet me and, when information was not passed through his sister, he did. It took several sessions for him to decide on a topic and his extreme fear and nervousness was worrying. He was very quiet in class too and had few friends. However, he improved with continued support and he chose to present a poster on the topic 'active listening'.

For the poster presentation, students were expected to display information on B1 sized posters. They were encouraged to use bullet points and graphics and avoid copying and pasting text from internet sources. On the day of the presentation they were to display their poster on the classroom wall and answer queries from the instructor and fellow students in the class. These students needed a sound understanding of the topic; information learned by heart would not be sufficient to answer questions effectively.

The poster presentation involved interaction with peers individually and in groups, as well as with the instructor. This format was ideal for a student with fear of public speaking as he only needed to interact with individuals and small groups rather than addressing the whole class. The task was intended not merely to test content knowledge but also to allow practice in communication, meeting and greeting strangers, personal grooming and research skills.

On the day of the presentation the student chose the remotest corner of the classroom to display his poster. He started slowly, speaking to one visitor at a time. By the time I approached him to discuss his work a few students had gathered around and he spoke with confidence. I had expected him to be uneasy but was amazed at the transformation. During the informal interview after the presentation the student said that working on the poster helped as he could internalise the material; this familiarity with the material boosted his confidence and he felt well prepared to speak.

The fact that he was addressing small groups or individual students who came by to discuss the poster, rather than the whole class, minimised fear of public speaking. It also helped that he was not being graded by them. The pressure of memorising and remembering a scripted speech was absent as he only had to respond to queries raised by his audience, not present the whole topic. He would have found it difficult to address the whole class and engage in a question-answer session. Because I had spent several sessions explaining the task and reviewing the work he was familiar with the material. The poster format was the right choice for him. This student also commented that the course and his interactions with the instructor and students had changed his personality and boosted his confidence.

Case 3: Motivation through Challenging Work

The female student in this case chose to submit a well-researched 1000-word article which would be of use to job seekers; if shortlisted it was to be featured in a proposed career guide. During the first consultation, the student confirmed that she would conduct primary and secondary research to identify industries with the highest recruitment rates. This information was expected to assist job seekers including current students, alumni of the university and the general public. During the second consultation the student submitted a draft of her work; this was several weeks before it was due. She had put together a 20-page document that would serve as a comprehensive guide to job seekers in the region. The instructor inferred that the student had misunderstood the activity assigned to her. She had spent three weeks researching, interviewing potential employers and collating the information into a booklet format with attractive graphics and catchy headings. The topics covered included the UAE job market, information for local and expatriate applicants, interview tips, top recruiters and useful websites. All content was specific to the region and this could easily be the most comprehensive local career guide catering to fresh graduates.

During an informal interview after the submission the student clarified that she had not misunderstood the activity but was inspired to do extra work because it would be beneficial to her and fellow students. The fact that it would be made available on the university website and a hard copy would be released officially was added motivation. She enjoyed the activity and was happy to have done extra work for no extra marks. In my experience, encountering students who put in extra effort due to intrinsic motivation is both rare and rewarding.

Case 4: Seizing Opportunities

This is the case of two conservative female students and their choice of role-play for the assessment activity. As they were not outgoing and did not volunteer to participate in class activities I was apprehensive about their choice of assessment format. They chose to present a role play on interviewing to the whole lecture cohort of 150 students. During the second consultation they said they had scripted the play and it involved humour. They were advised that humour was difficult to pull off as it required theatrical skills and perfect timing. They reassured me that they had completed the script and that it was quite entertaining.

On the day of their presentation they surprised the whole class by acting naturally to a humorous script. They effectively conveyed to the students how important it is for both interviewee and interviewer to practise and prepare for interviews. During the debriefing after the presentation several students commented that because the role-play effectively highlighted the need for preparedness they would not go un-prepared for an interview. The assessment activity had achieved its purpose successfully.

The presentation was effective and members of the audience were asked to volunteer to participate. This added interest, engagement, and a better learning experience. During the debriefing, the students were asked if they were seasoned actors; one replied that "*this is a first in our life experience*" and both wished every subject had this option for assessment. They had enjoyed writing the script, incorporating the humour elements and rehearsing it. Shortly after the role play the students volunteered to participate in a poster display for academics as part of the activities of the professional development centre. They were nervous and met with me several times for reassurance that a poor performance in the voluntary academic activity would not harm them in relation to their studies. On the day of the poster display, they presented themselves well and confidently communicated to senior professors. They later thanked me for what they had found to be "*a great learning opportunity*" and they volunteered to work with the Students' Speaking Club.

Assessment for Learning

The four short cases described above throw light on the benefits of differentiated assessments and how this creates an inclusive classroom catering to different learning styles, skill levels, aptitudes and culture. As I have reported, the differentiated assessment activities I used offered experiences which were enjoyable and extremely beneficial for all the students in this cohort. The close involvement of the instructor with the students in order to facilitate differentiated assessments led to the creation of personalised learning environments which further benefited students. As a result, I can recommend that assessors should offer diverse platforms for students to work on.

Table 1 compares the performance of the students mentioned in the cases in a standardised assessment, differentiated assessment, and summative final exam in the same subject. The right-hand column compares their final grades in this subject with that of all subjects completed so far

– around 10-15 subjects for most students. All students have performed better in the differentiated assessment and this has helped them to score high grades.

	Standardised Assessment (Debate)	Differentiated Assessment	Summative Final Exam	Total score	Comparison to grades in other subjects
Case 1	57%	93%	45%	62%	Highest grade in qualitative subject
Case 2	71%	88%	61%	71%	Highest grade in qualitative subject
Case 3	95%	100%	90%	95%	Highest grade in qualitative subject
Case 4	71%	95%	68%	76%	Second highest grade in qualitative subject

Table 1: Comparison of grades for standardised and differentiated assessments.

In my observation, differentiated assessments tend to heighten engagement (for both instructor and students) even though the same mode of assessment was used throughout a 13-week semester. In general, students were more involved and interested in the activities when the activities were presented in an informal setting. The assessments also improved interaction between students. Students were free to walk around and learn things at their own pace. The most important outcome from my point of view was the improved performance of those students who had previously earned mediocre grades. Most students, including the high achievers, enjoyed and performed well in the differentiated assessment. Students confirmed during focus group interviews that they enjoyed the activities and the participation of the non-presenters proved that they wanted to be actively involved. Students could show their full potential because the activities catered to different learning styles – visual, auditory and kinaesthetic. They were motivated by the success they achieved and it is hoped that they would use the experience to improve performance in other subjects also. Stiggins (2002) believes that school children become more confident learners as they watch themselves succeed; and teachers, parents, school administrators all win in the process. The same seems to be true of tertiary education.

Reflection on the use of differentiated assessments also informed my teaching philosophy and the benefits can be transferred to other courses taught. Reflective teaching that improves practice is a characteristic of the 'Level 3' theory of teaching put forward by Biggs. The focus here is on *"What the student does"* and *"on teaching that leads to learning"* (Biggs, 2001:224).

Another important benefit of using differentiated assessment was that it aided modification of teaching to suit student learning needs better. The process of designing, monitoring and assessing differentially gave the instructor clear and in-depth understanding of students' diverse needs. Differentiated assessment differs from personalised learning in that instructors do not have to cater to every student but can create a portfolio of assessments that will suit a broad spectrum.

Further Applications

Different skills, learning styles and capacities require differentiated teaching and assessment methods. What excites one student may not motivate another. Motivation is a prerequisite of active learning if it is to promote engagement with the work and give a deep understanding that will aid future application of the concepts studied. Accordingly, the design of appropriate and varied assessment activities is imperative for good learning and teaching. The Business Communication course has been on offer for several years at the university and I had taught it to over 12 cohorts. However, this was the first time I used differentiated assessments. The usual practice was to assess students through written reports and group oral presentations. Since it was a communication course it was important to optimise communication time for students. To facilitate communication, I decided to use posters as an assessment format in 2010. The use of posters offers many advantages, including reducing plagiarism, engaging non-presenting students in the assessment process and facilitating quick feedback (Koshy, 2011:220). However, student feedback indicated that not all students were happy to work on a poster. This led me to experiment with differentiated assessments in Spring 2012.

Stiggins (2007:24) observes that the role of assessment is changing from: *"ranking students according to their achievement"* to *"helping all students succeed in meeting standards"* by using *"assessments that support learning – that is, assessments for learning".*

Differentiated assessments can be successfully used in several subjects, particularly as a formative assignment. However, its application in a practical, experience-based course like Business Communication was particularly relevant because of the flexibility it offered. The practice of using differentiated assessments warrants reflection, planning, preparation, consultation with students and, on the whole, much more dedication and time investment by the instructor. The benefits from investing time and effort are many and all stakeholders – primarily the students – stand to gain. Differentiated assessment has been successfully used to enhance quality in schools and I strongly recommend that instructors apply this assessment format at university level.

In short, assessment *for* learning should replace assessment *of* learning. The use of differentiated assessments was expected to help with this process.

About the Author

Swapna Koshy is an assistant professor at the University of Wollongong in Dubai. She can be contacted at this email: swapnakoshy@uowdubai.ac.ae

Independent Studies in Higher Education: Great Expectations or Hard Times?

Andrew Green

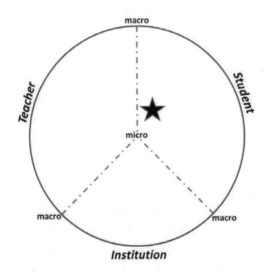

Introduction: Quality Enhancement and Independent Study

This chapter presents a case of quality enhancement (QE) focusing on the issue of the independent work students are expected to undertake during their studies in Higher Education. It draws on quantitative and qualitative data gathered as part of a large-scale research exercise involving

113 undergraduate and 128 sixth form students of English. It goes on to explore the changing nature and role of students' subjective expectations by presenting data gathered through individual student interviews in which students reflect upon the factors shaping their independent learning experiences. Following the trajectory of expectations illustrated in Figure 1, it sets out a range of pedagogic interventions in this process, assessing outcomes via individual student interviews.

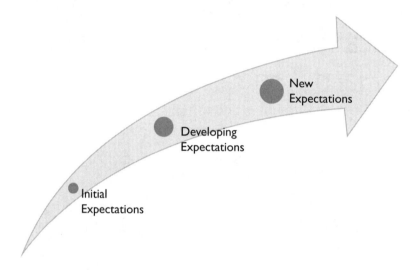

Figure 1: Trajectory of expectations.

Learning to manage independent studies effectively has a significant impact upon the quality of students' learning experiences (Snapper, 2009; Green, 2010). This to a large extent depends upon understanding and managing expectations. For Booth (1997) academic expectations represent a crystallisation of students' experiences of study to date and function as a powerful internalised force as they approach HE. The Higher Education Academy in the UK (HEA, 2008) identifies engaging with student expectations and using them as a means of developing appropriate and effective practices as a key factor in promoting QE.

The question of how QE relates to teaching and learning is not straight forward. In its most general sense, QE may be seen as *"deliberate steps"* (HEA, 2008:33) to improve students' learning opportunities. Gvaramadze (2008:450) takes this further, seeing QE as *"a constant effort to improve the quality of programme design, implementation and delivery".*

If we are to measure effectively the extent to which the quality of students' independent learning can be enhanced we need to look to process-based rather than content-based mechanisms which will help students develop strong transferrable processes as independent learners as they (re)define themselves in relation to knowledge and knowledge acquisition.

As the range and diversity of students proliferates, so HE needs to develop responsive practices to handle a widening corpus of needs. In the field of independent studies, this means enabling students to accept and cope with the significant challenges of managing academic uncertainty and risk in an autonomous environment. QE relating to independent studies moves away from the traditional focus of QE initiatives on developing contiguous (face-to-face) learning environments.

Constructing effective independent learning in non-contiguous space (Moore, 1973) poses particular challenges, as students and lecturers cannot engage in dialogue at the point of learning. In their independent studies, students encounter the provisional nature of knowledge and have to face this insecurity on their own. As Rogers observes (1969:104), *"no knowledge is secure, ... only the process of seeking knowledge gives a basis for security."* In so doing he identifies the epistemological/ontological conflict which lies at the heart of teaching and learning and which is heightened. It is the contention of this chapter, therefore, that in order to enhance the quality of independent learning, it is essential to discuss) the changing cognitive and metacognitive demands of subject (Atherton, 2006; Marland, 2003), teaching practices (Green, 2005a; Hodgson & Spours, 2003; Ballinger, 2003), and study patterns (Green, 2011; Bluett et al., 2004; Stewart & McCormack, 1997) explicitly. This creates shared understandings rather than allowing incorrect assumptions to breed, and maximises the conditions for effective independent learning. Wingate (2007) explores this specifically in relation to agendas of learning to learn, ways in which students perceive their 'knowing' and how knowledge is acquired.

Fallows and Steven (2000) indicate that, despite Rogers' conceptualisation of learning, academics are often unwilling to engage with pedagogy, preferring to focus on content rather than process. Faced with limited curriculum time, there is a clear QE case for explicitly developing students' awareness of epistemological dimensions of subject, as these enhance their abilities to understand the processes of their learning in both face-to-face and independent learning environments (Banks *et al.*, 1999; Grossman *et al.*, 1989).

Students' perceptions of learning in HE are coloured by assumptions based upon prior experience (Green, 2010; Smith, 2003, 2004). Students' personal responses to the demands of the HE environment need to be understood and addressed if QE is to be effectively managed (Booth, 1997; Clerehan, 2003; Cook & Leckey, 1999). Blackwell and Blackmore (2003) identify that, within the UK context, QE developments surrounding teaching and learning tend to be subject-based, but if interventions are effectively to drive change in students' understanding of their independent learning, explicit pedagogic focus is necessary (Green, 2010). This will encourage the quality transformation envisaged by Harvey (2002) as students develop an holistic vision of their studies, including critical independent study.

To address QE in independent studies, we must first consider how difficulties in this area can be conceptualised. Bourdieu's (1990:205) notion of the habitus, *"the site of the internalisation of externality and the externalisation of internality"*, is illuminating here. In this site, he contends, reside personal expectations, dispositions and schemas. The students best fitted to succeed in HE are those who have developed strong transferable processes as learners – those Baird (1988) decribes as effective independent learners. Where there is a hiatus between students' and lecturers' expectations, however, a potential conflict emerges (Bourdieu & Passeron, 1977). Vygotsky (1978) identifies the importance of socially constructed and culturally transmitted rules, which operate as internalised guiding systems. These individual systems naturally reside on a spectrum. Some will be largely enabling, whilst others may tend to create expectational barriers and misunderstandings.

Both of these philosophical stances reflect on independent study and provide useful starting points when considering how to enhance its quality. For Vygotsky, experimental play is central in learning. This play is not spontaneous but rigorously defined by internalised rules which provide cognitive and process touchstones against which new experiences can be measured. These *"socially formed and culturally transmitted"* rules (Vygotsky, 1978:126) come close to Bourdieu's habitus. In independent study, students employ rules internalised from previous learning as a benchmark. By engaging specifically with students' personal rules lecturers can develop appropriate interventions to enhance the quality of students' independent learning (Green, 2010). It is, therefore, important to consider how teaching processes can be used explicitly to address independent study practices.

Using the model set out in the introduction, we will explore how lecturers can work with students' subjective expectations, devising pedagogic interventions to challenge and adapt these to the new contexts of HE (see Figure 2).

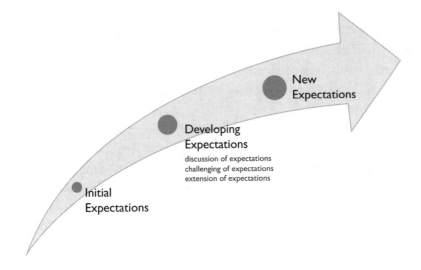

Figure 2: Developing student expectations.

Teaching for Quality Independent Learning

The changing nature and amount of contact time at university is a significant factor. Many students anticipate receiving greater input than they in fact do. In a survey of 128 sixth formers, 85% anticipated receiving six or more contact hours per week. Only 13% percent of 113 undergraduates surveyed, however, received more than six hours and none more than ten hours per week. This means that students face considerably more independent study than they typically expect. As Yorke (1994) observes, students increasingly perceive face-to-face teaching as a measure for quality learning. The role and management of independent studies is, therefore, a core issue for QE. It is important to ensure students perceive their independent studies as a necessary and logical 'emergent' from contiguous teaching; as a built-in rather than as a *post hoc* or additional component of learning (Yorke, 1994).

Lowe and Cook (2003:63) identify that *"about one-third of the cohort appear to expect teaching styles associated with school"*. This is only natural. However, in reality the pedagogic range of HE is typically narrower and less supportive than they expect (Green, 2005a). Lectures and seminars are unfamiliar formats to many new students (Snapper, 2009; Rosslyn, 2005), and using these as the basis for extensive independent study is very challenging. Much learning at post-16 level tends to be activity-based, focussing on short extracts of text and working over extended periods of time through set texts (Atherton, 2012; Snapper, 2011). Students are expected to work independently, but this is often highly structured, as is reading of primary and secondary sources (Smith, 2003, 2004; Green, 2005a; Atherton, 2012).

In HE, students concurrently follow multiple modules, each addressing at least one full text each week, each requiring the preparation of primary and secondary materials, often selected from a large reading list. This is clearly very different from their previous experiences, yet students are assumed to be autonomous and capable of handling and evaluating the quality of large quantities materials for themselves (Mishra, 2008). This requires a shift from content- to problem-centred conceptualisations of learning (Knowles, 1984, 1990). The quality of support for independent studies can be enhanced by involving students in developing materials (e.g. VLEs) and study processes. This promotes shared understanding of the function, process and content of independent studies (Adjieva & Wilson, 2002; Srikanathan & Dalrymple, 2002).

Levels of pressure to complete and support for work are very different as students progress from school into HE (Ellis, 2008; Hodgson, 2010). Interviews repeatedly revealed a lack of understanding and organisation in relation to independent studies. Students were often unable to conceive of and shape their response to literary study on a large scale – a legacy of their previous studies (Snapper, 2009; Green, 2010). Using process-based discussions, VLEs and course handbooks to model effective study practices and as platforms for dialogue about independent study is a central QE tool. It helps if students conceptualise their studies not as one large activity, but rather as a two related and iterative stages (see Figure 3). Understanding these interdependent phases of study enhances student engagement and with improved quality of participation come increased levels of student satisfaction. This is, thus, an essential component of QE.

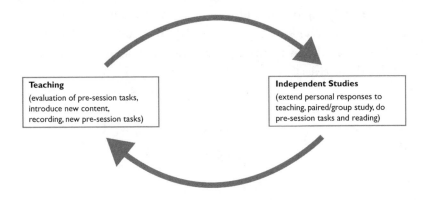

Figure 3: The study cycle (adapted from Green, 2009:46).

By exploring this learning cycle and related processes, students are empowered to deal with the contingent demands of their studies. By looking backwards and forwards through their learning, students establish how previous experiences inform or limit new learning. Figure 4 demonstrates how lectures, seminars and independent study relate to each other. Through discussing such structures, students can revise and challenge previous concepts or opinions; learning becomes a connected and dynamic process. For lecturers, such structured interventions provide insight into students' developing conceptualisations of subject and related processes, as envisaged by Rogers (1969). This enhances the quality of student experiences, of independent study and its outcomes and also specifically addresses student expectations, internalised rules and habitus. The challenges of overcoming such implicit expectations are also explored by Maensivu *et al.* (this volume).

Understanding Independent Study

School literature courses tend to focus on a narrow range of content. HE literary studies, by contrast, emphasise breadth of study, and this change in intellectual process poses a major challenge for students. This can be intimidating but also liberating, as students have more time and space to pursue a wider range of materials and ideas. Students need to be actively introduced to these possibilities, not simply left to discover them for themselves.

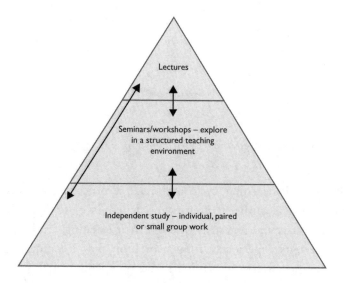

Figure 4: Teaching & learning in HE (Green, 2009:26).

The following case study explores a variety of possible forms for independent study, which need not always be synonymous with individual study, and which can utilise the kinds of social construction and intellectual play Vygotsky (1978) advocates. Working in a variety of organised group contexts, for example, can be fruitful and rewarding and prevents independent study becoming an isolating and unmediated experience.

First it is useful to consider students' perceptions of independent study at school and university. One comments in particular on *"the independence one receives"*, identifying the *"contrast to school"* where work is much more closely structured and monitored. Faced with this, undergraduates allocate inadequate time to independent study. Of 113 undergraduates surveyed, 70% spent ten hours or fewer per week on independent study. Only 11% reported spending 21 or more hours per week (Green, 2005b).

Interview data indicate that sometimes the cause is non-academic activities – sports, social engagements, employment, etc. – but often it is lack of understanding of independent study processes (as outlined by Rogers, 1969) or poor organisation and planning. Support and guidance in syntactic dimensions of subject (Grossman *et al.*, 1989) and the modelling of study practices assists students to function more effectively and leads to improved understanding (Green, 2010).

Independence in HE is often viewed in a negative light by in-coming students, used to the much greater levels of structured input schools tend to provide.

Student 2 observes the pressure she feels *"to take control of my own research and education, which could have a negative effect on my work."*

Student 3 also expresses fear of autonomy, which contrasts with the perceived security of learning in the school environment: *"The idea of independent study at university worr[ies] me, as I like the security of having teachers at hand. I worry that it would be entirely different."*

Similar views are expressed by undergraduates, who draw a clear distinction between their experiences at school and at university.

Student 4 felt under-prepared for the demands of HE, *"since at university most — nearly all — learning is done on your own. Whereas in college you are almost spoon-fed."*

Student 5 recognises the differing nature and function of independent studies in school and HE: *"Sixth-form education . . . was very different to the study of English at degree level. Individual thinking was not nearly as encouraged and the emphasis was on teacher-based learning rather than independent study."*

Student 6 reflects: *"University is about working and thinking on your own and for yourself."* Student 7 simply observes, *"The mode of study is completely different. I had no idea how independent I would have to be in study terms."*

Implicit in these interview data is a sense that students feel isolated and unsupported in their HE independent studies (Grebennikov & Shah, 2012). This is not to say, however, that they do not perceive and welcome the opportunities for personal development increased independence allows; it is simply that they require support in learning to function more autonomously. This is a significant issue in ensuring effective QE, as lack of appropriate support for independent learning can be a significant contributory factor to attrition rates (Ashby, 2004; Birch & Miller, 2006; Grebennikov & Skaines, 2008; Yorke & Longden, 2008).

Pace of Study

Pace of study is another important issue. The number of texts covered in HE and the rate at which they are covered comes as a surprise to many students and has a significant impact on their ability to manage their independent studies (see Figure 5).

A level	
The Tempest	*Regeneration*
Read Act 1 independently. Close reading: prepare in detail Act 1, Scene 2, ll. 1-180.	Read chapters 1 to 4. Prepare in detail chapters 1-2. Read extracts in class as basis for discussion.
Read opening section of Act 1, Scene 2 as a class. Read extract from critical introduction.	Read Rivers' paper "The Repression of War Experience".
University	
Poetry	*Middle English*
Read Seamus Heaney's collection *North* for lecture.	Read "The Wife of Bath's Prologue and Tale" for lecture.
Prepare in detail a selection of ten poems for detailed seminar discussion.	Prepare for group presentation on the view of medieval views of women, using historical sources.
Read background on The Troubles in Northern Ireland.	
Shakespeare	*The Rise of the Novel*
Reread *Othello* for this week's lecture.	Refamiliarise *The Italian*, Ann Radcliffe for lecture and seminar.
Read *King Lear* for next week's lecture.	
Read *Shame in Shakespeare*, Ewan Fernie, to compare presentation of shame in the two plays.	Read *The Monk*, Matthew Lewis for next week's lecture.
	Read Radcliffe's *On the Supernatural in Poetry* and Burke's *A Philosophical Enquiry into the Origin of Our Ideas of the Sublime and the Beautiful* as views of Gothic literature.

Figure 5: Weekly reading in school and HE (Green, 2010:146).

Not surprisingly, such a radical shift in gear causes many new undergraduates problems. Where students are not appropriately prepared, they encounter difficulties:

Student 2: *"I have gone from spending an entire term on* Hamlet *to four hours, which is understandable given that we cover far more texts here…"*

However, it emerges that not all students understand the nature of independent studies in HE.

Student 8 observes the pace of coverage and simplistically equates this with lack of depth: *"There isn't a lot of time spent on in-depth knowledge. It seems to be basic overviews and moving on to the next topic."*

The same is true of Student 9: *"I was expecting to look at literary pieces in more depth, but some of what is done feels quite basic. I hoped to be challenged more. Also we don't seem to be given the chance ourselves to analyse pieces of literature. More in-depth discussions would make me enjoy the course much more."*

Here again coverage is perceived as lacking in depth, and the role of independent studies in providing the desired 'in-depth discussion' and 'challenge' is overlooked. There is a fundamental misunderstanding of the function of independent studies, and this has significant QE implications. Such potential for misunderstanding illustrates that it is not productive to leave students to fend for themselves in the early stages of their HE. Support is needed initially in managing independent preparation for teaching.

Student 10: *"It would give … more structure, because it would allow the seminar to be more focused as well. If everyone focused on something or like five themes, everyone could go in with all their points and really go for it, because everyone's done it. I don't know how many people prepare — it can be really wishy-washy and you just touch one thing then move on to the next topic and it just doesn't work. It's really messy."*

Where preparatory tasks are made the subject of metacognitive and process-based discussion, students learn more effectively how to challenge existing learning paradigms (Bourdieu) and to play with learning (Vygotsky) as they engage in autonomous literary study. These tasks can (and should) steadily be withdrawn as time progresses.

Such practices enhance students' understanding that HE is less about narrow content focus and more about developing generic processes that can be brought to bear on a wide variety of material; that it is about using independent and wide reading to discover connections across their learning. It cannot simply be assumed that students will know how to plan for this kind of work.

Using Module Handbooks and VLEs

Module handbooks and Virtual Learning Environments (VLEs) are powerful vehicles to engage students specifically with processes of independent study, and can therefore be used to secure QE gains. Particular attention was paid through a sequence of structured interventions to:

- reading of primary and secondary texts;

- revisiting and completing notes after teaching;

- discussions with peers;

- preparation for assignments.

These provided a specific focus for quality input into independent studies (Green, 2009). The supporting resources for students to use in an unadministered environment needed to be unambiguous, responsive and anticipatory (Moore, 1973). Handbooks and VLEs were used to establish what would be covered in teaching (contexts, themes, theoretical perspectives, etc.) and to provide stimulating questions or activities. These structured intellectual 'play' with concepts and content both prior to and following teaching, thus tightening the relationship between taught and independent components of study. As Maslow (1968) identifies, the extent to which learners are required to display and/or cede their autonomy is situationally dependent, and the interventions described assist students in locating themselves.

Here is an example drawn from the handbook for a first-year Shakespeare course. The primary fields for inquiry are clearly stated at the beginning of the handbook:

- the plays as theatre and as text;

- the genres Shakespeare employs;

- use of language;

- historical-cultural context both at the time of the plays' composition and today.

This introduction provides significant insight into the approaches the course adopts. It is to introduce 'the close study of a wide range of Shakespeare's plays' and is not to be the full extent of students' engagement. Lectures and seminars modelled the kind of close readings (or textual 'play') that students are expected to develop through independent studies, and these relate specifically to interim peer-assessments and lecturer-moderated chat-room seminars. Lectures are thus the first, not the last word on Shakespeare and students are guided through session notes to forge independent and creative responses to the plays. Chat-rooms and other on-line materials are used post-teaching to stimulate further thought and development through subsequent studies. Teaching and learning is thus not an end-stopped activity, but becomes an iterative process.

The module handbook also provides teaching and learning outlines on a week-by-week basis. Broad aims and objectives presented in the introduction are used to provide more detailed guidance for study. Here are the outlines for two related teaching sessions on *The Merchant of Venice*.

Week One: *Introduction: The Merchant of Venice 1*
Why does Shakespeare matter? *The Merchant of Venice*. Is the play a comedy? How important are the issues of trade and finance to the play? What does the play value? What is its view of "aliens" and "outsiders"? What is its view of love or of revenge?

Figure 6: Week One: Introduction: The Merchant of Venice 1.

The provision of open questions to promote critical thinking prior to teaching, develops high quality problem-centred learning, as advocated by Knowles (1984). Some questions are broad in nature. They are intended to encourage reflection on personal, cultural, and literary values: for example, 'Why does Shakespeare matter?' Others lend themselves to exploratory reading. 'Is the play a comedy?', for example, prompts reading on genre and Shakespearean comedy in particular. The final four questions guide students' developing responses to certain issues in the play.

> Week Two: *The Merchant of Venice 2*
>
> This special lecture will introduce performance approaches to Shakespeare, focussing on post-Holocaust interpretations of *The Merchant*.

Figure 7: Week Two: The Merchant of Venice 2.

Here the guidance is very different. There are no detailed questions. Instead 'performance approaches' and 'post-Holocaust interpretations' are highlighted as two ways of reading the play. The emphasis upon the play as theatre and as cultural-historical phenomenon focuses students on theoretical issues of textual production and reception.

When students revisited and developed materials gathered during teaching, they were guided via questions and tasks in the VLE to reflect in more refined ways upon teaching (e.g. through developing personal critical responses to particular productions of the play, and considering how these reveal developing perceptions of anti-semitism). Suggestions were also provided about how to follow up learning through additional library work, discussions with peers, contact with lecturers, and how to generate further cycles of study within and across modules.

While much independent study inevitably takes place alone, studying in pairs and groups has great QE and learning benefits (Vygotsky, 1978). The opportunity to discuss learning with peers is very important for a number of reasons. Detailed suggestions about how to work in pairs and groups were discussed:

- sharing and evaluating opinions;
- working through personal difficulties;
- clarifying complex ideas and theoretical issues;
- developing confidence in discussing primary and secondary texts;
- discussing teaching.

Before paired study, students were encouraged to spend time preparing in order to maximise focus and direction. Issues for discussion were agreed in advance with input from lecturers. The conditions for independent learning were thus situationally mediated (Maslow, 1968) to reflect developing levels of student autonomy and encouraging new understandings of process (Rogers, 1969; Huet *et al.*, this volume). Primary and secondary reading was also established. These tasks could, of course, be undertaken individually, but are more dynamic and useful if undertaken in pairs.

Encouraging students to think clearly about the desired outcomes and processes of the shared study session also proved useful. Before teaching, students developed introductory notes and questions and frameworks for taking notes during seminars and lectures. In the early stages of preparation for an assignment, such sessions were directed towards establishing important areas for coverage.

Group study was also facilitated. The larger group format, however, brought certain difficulties:

- the logistics of finding a time mutually convenient for all group members;

- finding a space that is suitable for meeting (though virtual learning environments can help overcome this);

- agreeing on a shared focus for the group;

- agreeing the outcomes for sessions.

Meetings of the group may be formal or informal. Sometimes students met informally to chat about reading — related or unrelated to their modules. Where there were more formal agendas, students agreed upon a weekly schedule for contribution. Some groups met via the VLE, and lecturers suggested the means by which formal extended contributions could be made (e.g. pre-circulated individual papers, podcasts, visual stimulus, audio files, etc.). On a weekly basis, individuals or small groups took responsibility for organising session content and outcomes were monitored by lecturers. This ensured that responsibility for these sessions did not fall too heavily upon any one person and that all students benefited from their participation.

Students following this module were asked to reflect upon their experiences and to consider how it had enhanced their learning experience. The impact of the interventions described is effectively captured in some of their responses. It is clear that students appreciated the specific input into their studies, feeling that it had increased their confidence in lectures and seminars.

Student 4 observes: "*It has given me more confidence to sort of question what's being said and I feel more engaged with what's happening whereas the times that I haven't done it it's felt like I'm just sitting here taking notes and the thing gets passive rather than active.*"

Student 10 comments specifically on the value of directed preparation: "*We were given a worksheet ... with a list of bullet points saying while reading this text look for this, that or the other and just make brief notes and then maybe go into the lecture and they develop on them, so then you're not going into the lecture with nothing on your mind. You know what to expect.*"

The benefits of structured preparatory reading are the focus of Student 5's attention: "*It's not just reading the primary text, it's reading all the other things that are around it. You know, the critics to see what they say, and the different perspectives on it. And it really does widen your knowledge of that book by getting lots of other views as well.*"

All of these benefits can be summed up in the succinct response of Student 3, who observes that as a result of the structured interventions, "*you do not feel like you're reacting.*"

Conclusion

Independent studies, like any other area of teaching and learning, is an important focus for QE. The structured interventions to guide independent studies explored in this chapter served an important purpose in developing the quality of undergraduate students' understanding of the processes of literary study. By assisting students to engage with some ways they could play with learning (Vygotsky) and challenge their pre-established expectations, students developed in autonomy and confidence. The interventions described enabled them to find new ways to (de)construct their own learning and (re)define themselves as learners in HE. As a direct result of this the quality of their learning and their transferable abilities as students of literature were enhanced. Figure 8 illustrates the final outcomes of this dynamic process of pedagogic development, during which students were empowered to reshape their perceptions of subject and their expectations of themselves as independent learners.

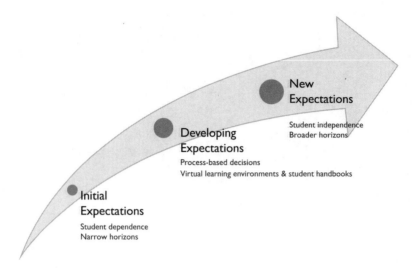

Figure 8: New expectations.

Whilst placing additional demands upon staff, whose input is essential to the development of the QE mechanisms outlined, the on-going student autonomy fostered by these mechanisms should amply repay the effort in terms both of student engagement and student satisfaction.

About the Author

Andrew Green is a Senior Lecturer in Education and English Literature at Brunel University, UK. He can be contacted at this email: andrew.green@brunel.ac.uk

Chapter Five

Enhancing Music Students' Learning and Pedagogic Understandings through Cultural Exchange

Jennifer Rowley and Peter Dunbar-Hall

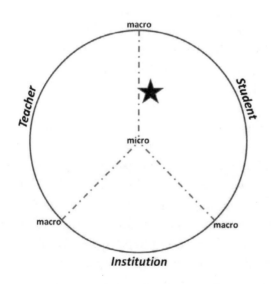

Introduction

In training to become music teachers, students from an Australian University have the opportunity to study, engage in, and learn through cultural exchange. Students can undertake part of their teacher training through a short period of international fieldwork where they learn music and dance in Bali (Indonesia), and analyse and adapt the pedagogic methods of Balinese musicians to develop their pedagogic practice. As an exercise in enhanced learning and teaching, this fieldwork experience raises students' awareness that different cultures have different learning and teaching practices. Students develop an understanding that both processes and outcomes of learning are essential for being a successful higher education learner and an effective music teacher. In these ways, cultural exchange is positioned as a means for quality enhancement in higher education.

In this chapter we discuss an initiative of quality enhancement of training music teachers, both in terms of teaching practices and of learning outcomes. The quality enhancement is measured by improving student learning outcomes and the mechanism by which it is done is immersion and experiential learning. In this curriculum initiative, students engage in learning music and dance through a period of international fieldwork in Bali *alongside* a group of Balinese musicians. The fieldwork experience discussed here investigates tertiary music students' learning and their development as future music teachers. This is one element of an ongoing, research-led teaching enhancement directed approach to the University's teacher training of these students and an example of quality engagement. Alongside other initiatives, it forms a significant approach to the transformational nature of the degree program, rather than the design of the subject, as part of the four-year undergraduate curriculum that students undertake.

Other curriculum initiatives in the degree program are: interactions with Indigenous Australian music and dance (Marsh, 2000); the internationalisation of Practice Teaching (Power & Dunbar-Hall, 2001); experimental immersion in music ensembles (Renwick & Webb, 2008); ethnomusicologically influenced music pedagogy (Dunbar-Hall, 2009); an understanding of emerging musician and teacher identities (Rowley, 2010); classroom uses of multimedia (Webb, 2010); and IT assisted learning (Dunbar-Hall *et al.*, 2010; Rowley, 2011). All of these curriculum interventions are to be seen as ways to engage students in learning contexts through which they can reflect on their own directions as they develop the pedagogical skills, knowledge, and practices required of music teachers. The case study presented in this chapter supports the theory of productive pedagogy and confirms the impact of research enhanced learning and teaching.

As literature on quality enhancement indicates (The Higher Education Academy, 2008), each quality enhancement project differs according to its context, purposes, expected outcomes, logistics and possibilities. It is through investigating these qualifying research parameters of fieldwork and its effect on students' development of pedagogical skills, knowledge, and practice that we demonstrate quality enhancement in our case study. Indeed, the idea of transformational curriculum change – which implies a process rather than an abrupt difference in education – is about enhancement and *"shows how contextually and culturally determined academic understandings, expectations, preferences, priorities and constraints are key influences in the process of educational change"* (Sin, 2012:1).

Students can be partners in the change process, assume responsibility, and develop a thorough understanding of their own learning and teaching practices. Through this change process the students can become more capable of controlling their own learning (Mäensivu *et al.*, this volume) to include a strong student voice as the researchers become co-learners with the students. The case study described in this chapter demonstrates the essence of research-led teaching and has the potential to be replicated in other disciplines, which is how we can position our discussion of a field-work trip as quality enhancement of student learning. The methodology of the fieldwork can be summarised, therefore, as follows:

1. preparation of students for fieldwork;

2. removal of students from their usual music learning contexts;

3. confrontation between students and new teaching and learning experiences;

4. reflection by students on their experiences and their reactions to these;

5. construction by students of pedagogic practice in relation to themselves as current music learners and future music teachers.

We validate the enhancement of learning by triangulating the data presented here which has come from students and researchers – both as observers and co-learners as researcher became co-learners with the students. The following discussion is based on analysis of filmed observations of the students in Bali, a fieldwork journal kept by one researcher and student reflections from focus group interviews held after their return to Australia.

Transformation of Student Learning

We perceive the experiences described in this chapter as ways of raising *"internal disciplinary tension"* (Filippakou & Tapper, 2008) in the area of music education, and in the training of future music teachers. In this way we draw attention to a range of educational philosophical positions, pedagogic practices, implicit and explicit learning styles, and ideologies of music education as an ethnomusicological undertaking. In line with the theorising of Harvey and Knight (1996) on quality enhancement, we see student fieldwork in Bali as an agent of transformation, and the students involved as stakeholders in their own learning, their own musical identity development, and their ideas of themselves as developing teachers. Drawing on Knight's (2006:29) analysis of quality enhancement, the experience of learning music and dance in Bali is positioned as 'extensive' and a form of 'practice-based learning' through which the professional development of trainee music teachers is achieved through 'the creation of working environments that favour certain kinds of professional formation'. The methods of teaching and learning music in Balinese culture differ greatly from those of students' Western music learning backgrounds, and music and dance are readily observable parts of Balinese people's daily lives. Quality enhancement of music students' learning, therefore, is a product of intersections between students' familiar concepts of learning music (and from that, their nascent views of teaching music), and their immersion in and participant observation roles in Balinese enacted and performative culture. These aspects of students' teacher training are influenced by the musical and non-musical elements of learning in a foreign setting.

This chapter focuses on how this fieldwork experience influences students as they develop as future music teachers — that is, as the processes of their own learning become influential in their understandings of the processes of teaching. Cultural exchange is seen therefore as more than a source of teaching content or teaching practices/strategies for valuable pedagogy. It is multi-layered in its applications of the ideology of teaching and learning music, positioning cultural difference as a site of personal development and self-realisation. It relies on students being removed from their musical, pedagogical, social, and cultural 'comfort zones.' Through this, cultural confrontation is read as a force in the processes and outcomes of music students' learning; thus our position as researchers that cultural confrontation can act as a pathway to quality enhancement of music students' learning experiences with graduate attributes are explicitly mapped into the curriculum. The aim of the study, therefore in relation to quality enhancement, is developing trainee teachers' pedagogic practice.

The methodology for our research involved three stages. First, the researchers worked with students involved before the fieldwork trip took place, making sure that students were musically and socially prepared for aspects of the experience. To ensure that their experiences of teaching and learning in Bali would not be prefigured, students were not explicitly told to expect a different type of pedagogy from that of their day-to-day learning experiences. In the second stage of the process, staff worked *with* students in Bali on a daily basis, observing lessons, filming activities, and discussing students' reflections on and reactions to fieldwork and its expectations of learning Balinese music and dance. Third, students were interviewed after the fieldwork trip, to gauge how they saw the experience as influential in realisations of their development as learners first as we were interested in them as learners. The students were asked also to project how this could influence their eventual directions as music teachers and professional practitioners. Through this multi-layered approach, students' occupied a number of contrasting and continually shifting identities: learners, nascent ethnomusicological researchers, pedagogy analysts, performers, curriculum conceptualisers, self-analysts, and potential teachers – although not all students took on all these identities. Through these identities, students' voices could be heard as they considered their teacher training as a period of learning enhancement and reported greater affinity with diverse music learning and teaching than previously understood. The filmed material, the observational data and the interviews provide insights into quality practices that assisted trainee music teachers' learning outcomes and pedagogic practice, and the project improved the quality of university teaching and learning.

Before discussing the outcomes of the project, it is necessary to explain its purposes and context, and the logistics of the fieldwork involved.

Curriculum Structured to Enhance Learning

Within a four-year curriculum in the Music Education degree program with multiple subjects concentrating on learning and teaching music through cultural diversity, one subject in a degree program has great potential to cover many expectations of training music teachers to be aware of the multicultural nature of music education. The learning goals are designed to demonstrate that different cultures have different ways to teach and learn music, and that music pedagogy can be analysed to produce descriptors of culturally influenced teaching methods and learning styles. In this one semester subject, students learn to perform on the instruments of a Balinese *gamelan* (instrumental ensemble), and experience teaching and learning methods of Balinese musicians *in* Bali. There are four main learning goals in this subject, but the most significant one is that through this experience music students will learn to reflect on diversity in how music can be learnt and taught (Karlsen, 2011). This is conceptualised through offering Balinese music pedagogies as a contrast to the Western music learning backgrounds of students, and to encourage students to theorise about music pedagogy from this set of contrasting situations (Dunbar-Hall, 2010).

This subject is delivered in two modes: some students only attend classes at the University and learn using the University's Balinese *gamelan* instruments. Other students undertake the subject in an intensive period of fieldwork in Bali, where they learn from members of a Balinese *gamelan* group while staying in a village where traditional Balinese lifestyles and values can be observed and experienced.

The quality enhancement of the students' pedagogic practice as trainee music teachers is precisely what is described here. They develop in two ways: first in the acquisition and understanding of pedagogic skills and knowledge and second in perceptions of themselves as music teachers (Green, 2011). Through these two areas of development, the fieldwork trip is conceptualised as a catalyst for enhanced learning and teaching, as anti-canonic practice (Kindall-Smith *et al.*, 2011), and as a demonstration of a non-standard application of curriculum. In addition to the stated learning goals are the learning processes that the students engage in. The implications for future curriculum development, teaching and learning practices and strategies therefore, are apparent as students journeyed through the fieldwork. One researcher kept a daily observational fieldwork journal and noted that the curriculum was adjusted and modified by the Balinese teachers to meet students' needs. This was an informal teaching strategy that enhanced the quality of the learning for individual students.

In many ways, living in a Balinese village setting is an important aim of the trip – as is the aim of learning Balinese music and dance and being exposed to Balinese teaching strategies. Quality enhancement of the music students' pedagogic practice, therefore, is also dependent on the socio-cultural aspects of this trip, and on students' abilities to cope with the requirements of living in a traditional village setting. Living in a Balinese village has expectations of personal interactions, linguistic difficulties, adapting to customs (including the need to wear traditional Balinese dress for lessons and attendance at Balinese events), and the need to acknowledge and respect enacted Balinese Hindu religious rites, which are an essential part of daily life and are related to the students' development as music teachers with a broad understanding of pedagogic practices.

The fieldwork trip was conducted in 2011, with 14 students who learnt two pieces of Balinese music; first, a piece of instrumental music, and second, a dance and its accompanying music. The reason for learning both a dance and its music is that Balinese music and dance are inseparable. To dance requires an understanding of accompanying music while to play an instrument requires understanding of the dance that the music accompanies. This introductory concept of the symbiotic relationship between music and dance, and the necessity of learning both, rather than only music or dance as would be the normal practice in Western music/dance study, challenged students' views on music education, and the roles expected of them in it, as their pedagogic skills and knowledge developed. Teaching was delivered by a group of Balinese musicians under the direction of their leader. Such group teaching was another difference for students. Learning is supported by constant contact with Balinese musicians throughout all lessons, and the limited time of the trip (eight days of lessons) results in maximum benefit for students as learners, as potential music teachers, as analysts of pedagogy, as beginning fieldwork investigators, and as holistically formed musicians.

To ensure that students could work with Balinese musicians from their first lesson in Bali, and in this way remove the possibility of important time being wasted on introductory activities, they learnt the basics of *gamelan* playing and supporting Balinese music theory and terminology over the university semester preceding the trip. In these classes they learnt performance techniques and to play a small repertoire of pieces of music. During the trip students not only undertook classes, but also attended and wrote about Balinese cultural performances they attended, visited museums and art galleries, kept a journal about their learning experiences, and wrote journals about the benefits of the trip to themselves as trainee music teachers who were developing pedagogic practice. To assist students to perceive the trip as a source of research, learning and teaching material, they were given video cameras and were required to film aspects of the trip they saw as relevant to themselves. How students utilised these cameras was not prescribed, the intention being that students would self-regulate camera use and utilise some of the material for assessment tasks. Enabling students to immerse themselves in multiple modes of assessment to enhance the learning experience contributes to a personalised learning development of self and skills (Koshy, this volume).

Students training to be teachers in our State are required to meet local State accreditation standards. The mandated graduate teacher standards require 'evidence' to demonstrate the achievement of the standards. Many of the students on the Bali fieldwork trip used the filmed material and their journal reflections as evidence of meeting one or more graduate teacher standards. For example, some of the standards that may have been achieved and evidenced by the students on the Bali fieldwork trip are:

"1.1.2 Demonstrate research-based knowledge of the pedagogies of the discipline";

"2.1.1 Demonstrate knowledge, respect and understanding of the social, ethnic, cultural and religious backgrounds of students and how these factors may affect learning";

"6.1.1 Demonstrate a capacity to critically reflect on and improve teaching practice".

This fieldwork trip to Bali provided evidence of meeting the listed standards stated above and the students used their filmed material and journals (some put video evidence into student ePortfolios) to tell their learning story and development of pedagogic practice. Many other subjects in the degree program provide opportunities to achieve and evidence other stated graduate teacher standards.

Having outlined the process for quality enhancement, in the following sections we present the outcomes of the fieldwork experience from students' perspectives.

Pedagogy: Students Analysing Teaching and Learning

Students' opinions on the influences of learning out of their normal 'comfort zones' were collected through voluntary focus group interviews after their return from Bali. In interviews, students explained their experiences of the teaching from Balinese musicians as different from that they had received in previous learning, in schools, in their histories of private instrumental lessons, and in University. Students noted (often with intended criticism) that Balinese teaching differed greatly from the way their University studies were conducted, especially in the socialised manner of Balinese teaching (i.e. through group instruction) and in the ways Balinese musicians work on a personal level with learners. We planned the fieldwork trip as a quality enhancement and we expected students to develop their pedagogic practice as trainee teachers as a result of their immersion in a non western music learning experience. Students discussed how Balinese teaching practices were to work without notation, relying entirely on aural memory of repertoire. This was very different from anything students had experienced before, and challenged them greatly as learners who were used to Western teaching and learning practices. Students wanted to embrace the new method of learning, but found themselves in conflict with previously learnt music study methods. The building of students as independent learners enhanced the quality of their learning and teaching experiences (Green, this volume).

The Balinese teachers modeled music to be learnt and students copied this and repeated sections of pieces over and over many times until they were assimilated and memorised. Learning strategies in Bali also needed to be 'musically holistic,' and not based on separating components of pieces of music – unlike Western music pedagogy, which tends to atomise music for the purposes of studying it. As the pieces being learnt were repetitive, mistakes could be corrected through repetition of material, and this was something students began to notice during the opening days of lessons. There was a focus on whole group effort, and one student commented, "*everyone was teaching everyone, rather than one person trying to teach everyone*". This removes a sense of anxiety through which learning can be impeded, providing another difference between Balinese learning and that of students' prior experiences of music learning. Learning required intense listening and development of aural skills. There was collaborative learning from student to student, which they were used to in some University subjects, such as workshops and the traditional seminars, but not as individual musicians. The difference, therefore, between the Balinese and the Western pedagogical music approach was obvious to students after the first two to three days. However, students did find this challenging and on Day Three, one student asked if he could arrive early so he could practice the piece by himself before the lesson. One researcher explained to him that although he must have been feeling very frustrated by this different approach to learning music, him going before class to 'practice by himself' was not the pedagogical approach used by Balinese teachers. The challenge of the newly experienced learning strategies encouraged students to examine and question how they had previously learnt music.

Students saw aspects of the teaching practice as an impetus for the development of learning strategies and as a form of problem solving. After the trip, students described their learning as challenging, requiring different ways of learning; that "*we are not used to learning in that way*". One student said that they "*had to figure out how to learn*" and needed to "*let go . . . and have more fun*". Their music learning in Bali was not "*so restricted*", allowing them to "*try things out (without) being ridiculed, blamed or laughed at*".

The implications for a different approach to their previous teaching strategies were becoming clearer to the students and by the end of the eight days they were able to find their own place in adapting to these pedagogical requirements as was evidenced in their reflective journals and focus group interview responses.

Students' Learning Outcomes

Students were interpretative, however, of the experience in various ways as was evidenced in observational field notes, the analysed video material, the focus group interview and the students reflective journals. Some students needed to devise learning strategies in response to Balinese teaching practices and this led one student to comment that *"it gives you insight into learners' problems"*. There was a general discussion about the point at which the music 'clicked', with students agreeing that the beginning of the experience was confusing because it required a different way to learn: *"but on the third or fourth day it clicked . . . and I understood what I was doing . . . all of a sudden I understood . . . what I had to listen for – it just became really clear"*.

One of her student colleagues agreed, saying that once she could *"hear how my part fits"* she could *"relax, have fun ... look around at other people and see what they are doing ... enjoy music as a whole, not just your part"*.

Another student theorised that learning as Balinese musicians do relied on *"development of muscle memory instead of an analytical approach"*, while another discussed links between the music and how it was taught: *"the music directs the pedagogy . . . their (Balinese) methods work because the music works this way"*.

One of the students saw the trip as validation of her identity as a music student, that it made her feel *"appreciated"* because Balinese musicians *"value the essence of music"*. It was noted in the observational field notes that this feeling about herself developed throughout the trip. At the beginning of the trip she had used a *"Western-derived ethos"* but as learning in Bali proceeded she moved to a situation where *"the music came first, it is its own reason"*. Another student commented that in Bali *"you are not playing for yourself, you are playing for everyone – yourself comes last"*.

As a result of working with the Balinese musicians, some of whom were significant composers, there was realisation among students that a hierarchy of music roles (performer – composer – learner – teacher) should not exist. As one student remarked: *"being a teacher, composer, performer is a service – we all serve each other, no-one is on top . . . in Bali . . . this makes sense, and you are not the crazy one"*.

Agreeing with this, another student observed how local people in the village, in markets, shops and cafes were supportive of students in their attempts to learn Balinese music and dance and did not see this as in any way out of the ordinary. She commented that in the West being a musician is often considered *"unusual"*, but in Bali *"that distinction just wasn't there – it was encouraging"*.

One issue that resurfaced a number of times in interview responses was how students appreciated the immersion nature of the experience, with its potential to observe and experience Balinese culture, and also ways in which Balinese musicians explained the religious implications of music and dance. This aspect of the cultural exchange was emphasised by religious ceremonies carried out each day at the beginning of lessons. During these ceremonies the teachers and students were blessed, were sprinkled with holy water, prayed and focused on the spiritual aspects of the experience by an Elder of the village.

True cultural exchange includes all aspects of daily life, and this immersion in Balinese culture enhanced students' learning experiences because the learning took place in authentic Balinese 'everyday' life. This was reinforced by the lessons taking place within a Balinese house compound in a small village where the activities of farmers, artisans, local people and their families could be easily seen.

When asked how the trip had influenced their understanding of pedagogic practice, students listed various outcomes, attesting to the idea that different kinds of teaching can encourage different modes of learning. The embedding of this method of experiential learning into the curriculum meant that students had experienced first hand an alternative pedagogy. As tertiary educators we are meant to encourage critical thinking, to allow students the opportunity to embrace metacognition and to challenge known forms of their discipline – all of these could be demonstrated in this initiative and its outcomes. There are implications for students' learning practices to be altered and enhanced as a result of their experience in Bali.

Social Cognition and Identity

The students' musical identity was challenged during the fieldwork trip in a variety of ways – in particular as they moved from a position of understanding of pedagogic practices and moved away from the cultural questioning of the Balinese musicians' teaching strategies (Rowley &

Dunbar-Hall, 2012). As the Balinese teachers employed a different approach to teaching, and the students needed time to realise that the Balinese teachers were playing *with* the students and not instructing them in the same ways found in standard western contexts. As the social cognition and learning outcomes developed alongside each other it was seen that the experience in identity development for the students was symbiotic as evidenced in the observational field notes, the students journals and the analysed filmed material and focus group interviews.

The unpredictability of the role of musician or performer is a struggle in identifying with one professional role (or the other). Mantei and Kervin (2011) examined the development of professional identity in early career teachers and reported that the participants developed an understanding of their professional role as a teacher after engagement in professional dialogue based on readings on the professional practice of a teacher. This reflection on the professional role of a teacher created a sense of accountability amongst beginning teachers and perhaps gives insight into how professional teacher identity develops. It is not clear how and if the multi-cultural context of the students' learning and teaching experience in Bali contributed toward a negative or positive identity development. Students' comments confirmed that becoming a music teacher not only involves moulding the knowledge of future musicians, it is also a vehicle for professional development in the endeavours of the musician *within* the music teacher (Rowley, 2010).

These issues of analysis of Balinese teaching practices, of students' learning strategies, of students' interpretations of the experience, and of ways that students could identify changes to their own pedagogic practice, are concrete outcomes of the fieldwork trip to Bali. What is less definable, and something students found more difficult to discuss, is ways in which fieldwork in Bali acted as a catalyst in music teacher identity formation.

Aligning Learning in Bali with the Principles of Quality Enhancement

This case study represents an example of quality enhancement that we characterise in Figure 1.

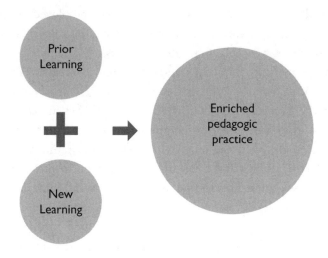

Figure 1: Learning of trainee music teachers.

In Table 1, below, we compare the processes and outcomes of the fieldwork with descriptors for defining quality enhancement in other educational settings. For example, the methodology/process of preparing students, immersing students in Balinese life and cultural expressions, having students reflect on learning and teaching, and defining outcomes as pedagogy, clearly aligns with the Business Excellence Framework used by James Cook University (JCU, 2012) in its definition of quality enhancement.

Descriptors of quality enhancement in educational settings	Fieldwork applications
Focus on learning	The fieldwork experience was planned as an intervention in students' learning styles, as an impetus for reflection on learning, and as provision of a specific style of learning.
Learning as social practice	Learning was conducted in group settings involving personal interaction between teachers, learners and University staff and utilised living in a traditional village setting as one of its strategies.
Focus on professional development	The experience was designed to contribute to the development of trainee music teachers (including identity development) in a professional practice degree program.

Descriptors of quality enhancement in educational settings	Fieldwork applications
Active engagement of teachers during implementation	The experience relied on the work of Balinese teachers and the daily participation of University staff accompanying the students and participating as co-learners.
Flexible, context-sensitive approach based on building knowledge	The contexts of the experience (a foreign setting, a family house compound, a small village, a music group) were contributing factors to building students' knowledge.
Seeks to establish links between teaching and research through reflection on practice	Students were required to research the learning practices and the teaching strategies of the Balinese musicians, and to reflect on these as trainee music teachers.
Respects and values professional autonomy	Students were required to work through their own reactions to the experience in the writing of daily journals focusing on their part in the learning process. The students were given the means to film the experience from their own perspectives according to their own criteria of suitability and potential uses of filmed material. They were encouraged to gather evidence for the graduate teacher standards.
Seeks to increase collaboration between teachers and across disciplines	The trip was a collaborative partnership between the students, the Balinese teachers, and University staff involved.
Emphasis on discussion	Daily discussions with students were held, and the fieldwork was followed by focus group interviews to investigate the issues raised.

Table 1: An alignment of descriptors used by Swinglehurst et al. *(2008) with the Bali fieldwork experience.*

In the JCU model (2012) there is an emphasis on *"self reflection and critical self evaluation"* through: Approach (thinking and planning), Deployment (implementing and doing), Results (monitoring and evaluating), and Improvement (learning and adapting) by which *"quality enhancement builds upon quality assurance processes requiring planned changes to incrementally improve or enhance the quality of our student's learning experience"* (JCU, 2012:1).

Our case study aligns with this JCU definition and has succeeded in quality enhancement of trainee music teacher's pedagogic practice through the mechanisms of experiential learning and immersion. The intention of referring to the JCU model is that in Bali our students' experience was enhanced by continual improvement of resources – such as learning strategies and pedagogic practices. Another example is the definition of quality enhancement at Griffith University, which rests on student feedback, student learning outcomes, consultation and self-reflection (Griffith University, 2012) – all elements of the case study presented here. The Griffith model is committed to professional learning for staff so that the student experience is enhanced through innovative and research-led teaching practices. A core component of the Griffith model is evaluation and feedback from students so that teachers know and understand their students' learning needs. The case study discussed in this chapter relies on feedback from students so that the curriculum for the music education degree program can be evaluated and transformed to meet evolving and changing student learning needs and this is supported by our data. Students wrote reflective journals; videoed themselves whilst engaged in learning and the researchers also participated in the Balinese music and dance training as co-learners.

The clearest agreement between the above stated theories of quality enhancement and our case study, however, is provided by aligning aspects of our fieldwork with the nine descriptors of quality enhancement in educational settings of Swinglehurst *et al.* (2008:390). They posit that there is a difference between quality enhancement and quality assurance by emphasising the importance of reflection on one's own learning and teaching practices. Our students kept learning journals and reflected on their experience as learners and on the observations they made whilst watching performances of Balinese music and dance after their own Balinese music classes. The students looked for relationships between the observed skills, and their own developing skills, knowledge and pedagogic practice as trainee music teachers. Following is a table that aligns the descriptors used by Swinglehurst *et al.* (2008) with the Bali fieldwork experience.

The students experienced a raft of teaching and learning enhancement strategies as they journeyed through the social, cultural, musical, linguistic and cultural world of Bali in tandem with the music and dance classes. The holistic approach to their learning by immersing them in a Balinese village provided an opportunity to practice the customs and culture on a daily basis. As previously noted, there was preparation for this before they arrived in Bali by allowing them to learn how to wear a Sarong, exposing them to some basic language, the custom of bargaining for the market experience etc. The ability of students to analyse Balinese teaching, recognise and develop their own learning styles, and develop individual pedagogic practices was a major feature of this curriculum initiative and drew on the experiential learning involved. Alongside this was a large number of other issues through which students benefitted: living alongside Balinese people; learning how to survive in a setting where language and customs are foreign; confronting explicit religious activity; devising criteria for filming what they saw as relevant and useful; interacting with University staff on a close, personal level; gaining life skills. These issues contribute to and derive from the extensiveness of the short time students spent in Bali and the learning and pedagogic practices they participated in.

Conclusion

The concrete outcomes of this cultural exchange to Bali included enhancement of students' learning, and interpretation of the experience in relation to greater understanding of what is less definable and more difficult for students to discuss. Most importantly, the ways in which the fieldwork in Bali acted as a catalyst to provide insights into quality learning and teaching practices that have assisted University students' learning outcomes and pedagogic practice. Evidence for this process of transformation was extrapolated from student comments. Students agreed that when they adapted a Balinese teaching strategy they had experienced as a learner into their own teaching, they were simultaneously occupying positions as learners and teachers, and this required recognition of multiple understandings of pedagogy. That they had been learning in Bali as a member of a *gamelan* group, had meant learning, as one student put it, "*to be more of a team player instead of an individual*". This indicates a shift in thinking about himself as a learner – and as a trainee music teacher. Realisations about the cultural aesthetics of music pedagogy, the original intention of this immersion, was only one way in which the quality of students' higher education learning was enhanced.

The students had previously struggled to voice their perceptions of themselves as musicians. However, their experiences in Bali assisted them in understanding themselves as musicians through a cultural lens provided by the Balinese musicians' professional pedagogic practice. The learning processes described in this chapter resulted in enhanced quality of student learning as evidenced by the student comments reported that indicated learning practices and understanding of that learning were significantly influenced through this cross cultural curriculum initiative. The demonstrated effectiveness of this multi-cultural experience is in the insight about different and often challenging learning and teaching strategies. The critical perspectives described here illuminate educational practices that demonstrate successful approaches to enhance learners' knowledge, skills and pedagogic practice as trainee music teachers.

The link between the teaching strategies and practices with learners' outcomes demonstrated the development in socio-cultural and historical knowledge of Balinese dance and music that is an affirmation of understanding diverse learning and teaching practices. This equates to quality enhancement of learning and teaching as is evidenced in the figure 1 (presented as an equation). The fieldwork provided an agent of change for students as trainee music teachers and they will have an enhanced journey into their teaching careers as musicians with a broader understanding of self and others. This experience was a powerful tool and a definitive product of experiential learning. The outcome of the students' learning is evidenced in this chapter, where emphasis is on the demonstrated effectiveness of cross-cultural fieldwork in the perception of students' musical development and their development of pedagogical skills, knowledge and practice. This will inform the present curriculum and have an impact on future approaches to learning and teaching in higher education.

About the Authors

Jennifer Rowley is a Senior Lecturer in Music Education at the Sydney Conservatorium of Music at the University of Sydney, Australia. She can be contacted at this email: jennifer.rowley@sydney.edu.au

Peter Dunbar-Hall is an Honorary Associate Professor at the Sydney Conservatorium of Music at the University of Sydney, Australia. He can be contacted at this email: peter.dunbar-hall@sydney.edu.au

Chapter Six

Developing Undergraduate Students' Generic Competencies through Research Activities

Isabel Huet, Ana Vitória Baptista & Carla Ferreira

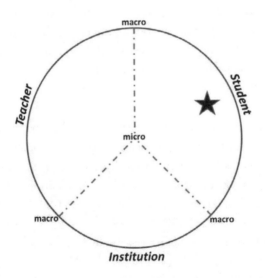

Introduction

This chapter reports a case of quality enhancement at the University of Aveiro in Portugal. The case shows how undergraduate students have improved their learning through engagement in research activities outside their formal curriculum. Working closely together with senior researchers in short-term research (MacDougall, 2012) enabled students to develop generic competencies. In a broader sense, generic competencies can be defined as a combination of abilities, skills and/or capacities (Table 1: 9) providing a strong basis for further learning that can be transferable and developed as a result of both formal and informal learning situations.

In our research we particularly focus on undergraduate students' development of instrumental competencies, interpersonal competencies and systemic competencies (Tuning Project, 2002). We believe that a set of generic competencies can help students to become more independent, autonomous and critical learners able to succeed in a *"transdisciplinary world of learning"* (Jackson & Ward, 2007) and to be prepared to adapt to new conditions of employment and potential career shifts. This is in line with the Europe 2020 strategy (European Commission 2020; Theodoropoulou, 2010) that refers to the need of a strong European skilled workforce that should not only have a sustained knowledge in a specific disciplinary/scientific field but also a set of generic competencies that support sustainable growth. Some such competencies start to be developed in infancy. However, in our view universities have a fundamental role to play in this developmental process. Throughout study programmes at university generic competencies should be developed at different stages and aligned with learning outcomes.

The framework developed at the University of Aviero follows other studies that suggest that higher education should prepare students with an understanding of the need for research skills in society and in their future work (Jenkins & Healey, 2010; Murtonen *et al.*, 2008) and give them the ability to learn in *"complex emergent problems for which there may be a range of possible solutions"* (Jackson & Ward, 2004:427). We strongly agree with Murtonen *et al.* (2008) that research skills are essential to all the learners and not only to future researchers.

> "[It is] *not only researchers who need these skills, but the skills are needed in all kinds of jobs where it is important to constantly follow new knowledge, understand phenomena with the aid of scientific thinking skills, and to be able to act as an active knowledge builder in society."* (Murtonen *et al.* 2008:609)

In this chapter we show how the involvement of students in research activities can promote these competencies and help students to be more confident and motivated in the learning process. The funds granted for these research activities also create the mechanism that make this reflection possible. The grants are funded by the Foundation for Science and Technology – the main Portuguese funding agency for research – to engage selected undergraduate students in research activities outside the formal curriculum. This experience, which is restricted to a small number of students due to the limitations of funding, is the object of our study. The outputs of this study can then be used to reshape the curriculum and/or to lead research centres and laboratories to offer and support similar experiences. Our study follows a straightforward question: "What was the impact of this research experience in the development of students' learning?"

To address this we designed a research study to evaluate and monitor the impact of research experience on the development of the generic competencies which contributed to the students' holistic development as learners in higher education. The research followed an exploratory and descriptive case study at the University of Aveiro in Portugal. The data were collected through interviews with a group of undergraduate students and their supervisors who were involved in research activities and this enabled us to analyse the benefits of undergraduates' engagement in research activities. As we shall show, the data provide clear evidence of the students' development of those generic competencies which are necessary for improving the quality of their learning, not only while at the university but also when starting their working life.

Our examination of the quality enhancement of students' learning gives an indication of how universities can prepare citizens who are able to judge their own decisions in the light of evidence, who are creative and who look for answers in a super-complex society that demands creativity and the ability to deal with complexity and uncertainty (Brew, 2010). In presenting our findings we give examples that represent students' and supervisors' views and perceptions.

In the conclusion, we consider whether experience of research activities can or should be extended to many/all university students.

Undergraduate Research: an Overview of Quality Enhancement of Student Learning

The research experience we report on can be understood as a national/ institutional strategy for quality enhancement of students' learning. Assuring quality of teaching and learning in higher education is a major concern of institutions around the world (Huet *et al.*, 2011; Horsburgh, 2010; Barrie & Ginns, 2007; Biggs, 2001). This cannot be disconnected from a managerial agenda where the achievement/evaluation of quality is strongly connected to accountability. Nevertheless, quality enhancement in higher education should guide the overall goal of quality assurance and be the central element in terms of the processes of evaluation and monitoring (Huet *et al.*, 2010; Ruohoniemi & Lindblom-Ylänne, 2009). This argument raises questions often addressed in the literature (Biggs, 2001), such as: How can we engage teachers to teach better and students to learn better? Are the methods used by teachers promoting autonomous and reflective learners? Do the curricula ensure that students are really experiencing *university* level education? How are universities training students to acquire/develop generic competencies across different disciplinary areas?

We believe that the enhancement of students' learning by means of the development of generic competencies resulting from their involvement in research activities outside the classroom prepares them for applying knowledge to new problems (Ruohoniemi & Lindblom-Ylänne, 2009). Scholars in many parts of the world (Brew & Jewell, 2012; Cuthbert *et al.*, 2011; Wilson *et al.*, 2012; Healey & Jenkins, 2009; Ruohoniemi & Lindblom-Ylänne, 2009; Hunter *et al.*, 2007; Barrie & Ginns, 2007) have observed that developing research activities and engaging students in a research-led environment at undergraduate level enhances the quality of their learning. It promotes an inquiry-based approach to learning which brings major benefits to both students and supervisors/lecturers because they can then better link their roles as 'teacher' and 'researcher/scholar' to high-quality learning outcomes.

Research and evaluation studies on this topic have produced results that begin to throw light on the benefits to students, faculty, and institutions (Barrie & Ginns, 2007; Lopatto, 2007; Russel *et al.*, 2007; Seymour *et al.*, 2004). The types of gains reported are consistent (Lopatto, 2009;

Hunter *et al.*, 2007; Brown & McCartney, 1998) and these include improved retention rates, persistence, and promotion of science career pathways for under-represented groups (Cuthbert *et al.*, 2011; Ruoho-niemi & Lindblom-Ylänne, 2009; Nagda *et al.*, 1998). Moreover, involving students in research activities fulfills one of the Bologna guide-lines; namely that the student is at the centre of the teaching and learning process, is autonomous and is able to appreciate a diversity of research methodologies and approaches.

In the USA, where undergraduate involvement in research has become established, it was originally seen as being for selected, highly-able and committed students in high ranking institutions such as the Massachusetts Institute of Technology; it has now been adopted by a wide range of institutions. A particular stimulus to such programmes has been the perceived need to encourage and prepare highly-able students to enter careers in the sciences. Organisations such as the National Science Foundation and the Howard Hughes Foundation have been especially prominent in supporting such schemes in the sciences and in supporting research into their effectiveness.

As a result there is a willingness in the USA to evaluate undergrad-uate gains from their involvement in research experiences, particularly on their *"learning, cognitive and personal growth, the development of profes-sional identity, and how communities of practice contribute to these processes"* (Hunter *et al.*, 2007:37). Consequently, several projects and research studies are being run in order to:

(i) understand the features of successful undergraduate research and positive motivation to pursue careers in research (Cuthbert *et al.*, 2011; Lopatto, 2003);

(ii) evaluate students' gains from their involvement in research (Hunter *et al.*, 2009);

(iii) analyse the impact these undergraduate research experiences have not only for the student, but also for faculty members and for the institution itself (Barrie & Ginns, 2007; Guterman, 2007; Hunter *et al.*, 2007; Lopatto, 2007; Russel, 2006; Seymour *et al.*, 2004).

Setting the Scene

The promotion of inquiry-based learning and research-led learning has been widely discussed and, in the Portuguese context, is having an increasing impact on policies and practices (Geraldo *et al.*, 2010; Huet *et al.*, 2009). Engaging students in activities that foster their involvement in the learning process is fundamental for increasing their autonomy and motivation to learn. This idea is also discussed by Green (this volume).

One such initiative is a programme of grants, created in 2008 by the Portuguese Ministry of Education (FCT), to promote the engagement of undergraduate students in research activities outside the formal curriculum; these are known as Bolsas de Integração na Investigação or BII (Research integration grants). The beneficiaries of these grants are selected undergraduate students enrolled in Portuguese higher education institutions. Students enrol in research that takes place in research centres/laboratories or departments. The selection of students is made by the institutions they apply to and the evaluation is based on specific criteria, particularly based on students' grades. Students can apply for a one year grant in any institution. A second year grant is possible but cannot be obtained in the same institution or research unit.

Students are supported by a qualified research supervisor. By the end of the grant the student must prepare a report for presentation and discussion in a public session organised by the foster institution. Higher education teachers from the department and students from different courses are invited to this public session to ask questions about the activities carried out during the period of the grant. This debate is extremely important to motivate other students to enrol in similar experiences. The learning outcomes achieved from the involvement of students on a specific research activity can be converted into ECTS (European Credit Transfer System).

This innovative initiative complements others in Portugal in the mainstream or formal curriculum for all students which in part introduce students to the world of disciplinary research. Nevertheless, these sets of grants were designed to foster scientific activity with the purpose of engaging selected students in a research and inquiry-based learning approach outside the classroom. The purpose is that students can be stimulated to develop critical thinking, creativity, autonomy and other important generic competencies which will be applied and developed not only during classes, but also in other research activities, in personal and professional life (Devlin & Samarawickrema, 2010; Jenkins & Healey, 2010; Huet *et al.*, 2009; Brew, 2006; Hunter *et al.* 2007; Lopatto, 2007; Seymour *et al.*, 2004).

Design of the study

As this is the first study in Portugal of these matters we decided to adopt a descriptive and exploratory case study approach (Yin, 1994).

To achieve this goal and gather a more complete perspective, with diverse 'angles' and subjectivities, we analysed the voices of both the undergraduate students (n=12) and their supervisors (n=13) involved in research projects at a Portuguese Research Centre in the area of education in two academic years: 2008-2009 and 2009-2010. The data collected allowed the triangulation of information and sources of data, giving insights into students (self-reflection) and supervisors' voices (hetero-reflection).

Even though small in number, this study served as an exploratory research by testing the method and instruments to monitor the impact of this experience in other Research Centres and Universities. The number of participants represented 80% of the total number of students and 100% of the total number of supervisors engaged in this process. The data sets also allowed an individualistic approach aiming to capture students and supervisors' actual, grounded experience.

The data presented in this chapter corresponds to Phase 3 of the overall study:

- phase 1 focused on understanding the initial expectations and motivations which led students to apply for the grant, and to characterise students' conceptions of research (Huet *et al.*, 2009);

- phase 2 focused on the evaluation of the supervision process, such as the guidance and support offered by the researcher responsible for the student, interaction between student-researcher-student, and the evaluation of the on-going process of students doing research;

- phase 3 came at the end of the grant and focused on the evaluation of the students' final expectations and achievements.

In Phase 3, at the final stage of the evaluation and monitoring process, data were collected through semi-structured interviews conducted shortly after the end of the grant. These enabled us to analyse the participants' reflective and retrospective experiences.

In order to have a richer perspective, to *"triangulate ideas"* (Lopatto, 2009:30), and to capture both students' and supervisors' voices, the interviews were designed to address: (i) expectations, (ii) conceptions of doing research (in education), (iii) undergraduate supervision processes (iv) competencies' development, (v) overall balance of the initiative, and (vi) recommendations/suggestions to enhance further editions.

In this chapter we will focus on the data that emerged from the dimension (iv) – that is, competencies' development. More specifically, we analyse students' and supervisors' conceptions of the benefits and importance of their experience of developing several types of generic competency. Therefore, in the following section we will identify and explore the competencies that have been reported. This analysis took into account the number of students and supervisors that mentioned the development of competencies during the period of the research grants. Table 1 shows the most mentioned competencies, listed in sets.

For the data analyses we used the CAQDAS (Computer Aided Qualitative Date Analysis Software) – N Vivo 7 to support the content analysis of the interviews. This software enabled us to re-organise the data into sub-categories and semantic patterns (Johnston, 2006; Richards, 2002).

Data Analysis

In order to systematise and categorise the data, we envisaged a conceptual parallel between, on the one hand, the competencies students and supervisors highlighted in their discourses and, on the other hand, the Tuning terminology (Tuning Project, 2002). This comparison led us to group the reported competencies in three different types (see Table 1):

(i)   instrumental competencies which are described as a set of cognitive abilities, methodological capacities, technological skills, and linguistic skills;

(ii) interpersonal competencies which are described as a set of individual abilities, and social skills;

(iii) systemic competencies, which are a combination of skills, abilities or capacities concerning the whole system (Tuning Project, 2002:21-22). These competencies presuppose a *"combination of understanding, sensibility and knowledge that allows one to see how the parts of a whole relate and come together"* (Tuning Project, 2002:29-30).

Identification of generic competencies	Students (n=12)	Supervisors (n=13)
1. Instrumental competencies		
Capacity for generating theoretical knowledge	6	9
Capacity for analysis and synthesis	11	10
Capacity for organisation and planning	6	6
Capacity for gathering and analysing data	6	4
Decision-making	4	5
Digital literacy skills (for searching bibliographic resources)	10	11
Software data analysis skills	5	6
Information management skills	5	3
Writing skills for different dissemination purposes	5	6
Academic writing skills	5	4
Oral communication skills	4	4
2. Interpersonal competencies		
Critical and self-critical abilities	4	5
Ability to be receptive/ open to new experiences or contexts	3	7
Responsibility and self-discipline	5	5
Curiosity	5	3
Team work (integration in heterogeneous research teams)	6	5
3. Systemic competencies		
Ability to work autonomously	9	9
Interest and self-motivation	8	6
Capacity and willingness for learning	5	9
Capacity to adapt to new situations and to be flexible	4	5
Capacity for dealing with unpredictability and changes	4	4

Table 1: Competencies identified and number of students and supervisors who referred those competencies.

Table 1 summarises the generic competencies that emerged from the data analysis without considering the frequency of repetitions of the same competency. Most of these competencies are consistent with the Tuning terminology that we have adopted.

Although interviewees' discourses may be characterised as a complex web of ideas and experiences we have observed that the competencies they refer to tend to overlap and to appear together. Therefore, in reporting our findings, we provide representative quotations to illustrate the students' and supervisors' views.

There is a general agreement of ideas and perceptions of students and supervisors with exception of the interpersonal competency ("ability to be receptive/open to new experiences or contexts") and the systemic competency ("capacity and willingness for learning"). In these two cases, supervisors perceived that these competencies were more developed by students than did the students themselves. Further research is required into the difference between these perceptions to understand how they relate to students' evolving self-awareness and meta-learning and to their engagement in the sort of intense and in-depth research experience that we describe in this chapter.

Regarding Instrumental Competencies

In terms of instrumental competencies, one student highlighted several skills which overlap and acquire high importance in her particular learning process. Her example integrates writing skills, information management skills and digital literacy skills. In the students' words:

> "(...) the most evident competence I have enhanced was in terms of writing skills. I had to develop a 'type' of writing, of academic nature, I was not used to. (...) Moreover, I learnt how to create a bibliography, how to search, how to make references... (...) Mainly I learnt to use web tools to search bibliography in specific search engines. I learnt to search in scientific journals and to read academic papers." (Student 1)

Some of the supervisors emphasised that, in the course of doing research and of actively participating in it, students were exposed to an environment that led them to develop a set of competencies that are not properly stimulated in the usual sorts of undergraduate course. In particular, one supervisor stated some important benefits for the students who have engaged in research activities. As the example demonstrates, the supervisor highlights the capacity for organisation and planning as well as the completion of tasks such as literature review (capacity for generating theoretical knowledge), capacity for gathering and analysing data and writing skills for different dissemination purposes:

> "to know how to manage time, (…) to fulfil different [research] tasks (…) and evolve throughout the entire process that starts in the (short) literature review, passes through data collection and then analysis and also through the writing and publication of a short article and/or final report." (Supervisor 5)

Regarding Interpersonal Competencies

In terms of interpersonal competencies we found that the enhancement of individual abilities and social skills was essential for the students' holistic development. Students stressed the importance of being in contact with other researchers and of being integrated into research teams. The next example illustrates the intersection between the individual and social aspects of the learning process through team work, even though the focus is on the social factor:

> "(…) the contact with (…) those who are involved in research activities, namely those senior researchers who work in the area for quite some time… It's incredible." (Student 3)

Supervisors have not only underlined the social aspect of the process of doing research but also the benefits of this experience on individual abilities – particularly considering critical and self-critical abilities, responsibility as well as openness to new experiences. For example, one supervisor said:

> "She [the student] had a great integration and has a great potential: she is very reflexive, receptive and open to new things, (…) responsible. (…) There are several personal competencies that also facilitate team work: sharing, being receptive, questioning, reflecting on the task she is

doing (...) And this student has clearly demonstrated and enhanced these competencies. (...) The quality of her work and reflections is undeniable within the work she has developed while participating in the research and receiving the grant (...)" (Supervisor 4)

Regarding Systemic Competencies

In terms of systemic competencies, it is evident that this initiative had great importance for students from many perspectives. For instance, the development of autonomy was one of the factors frequently referred to. Nevertheless, as the next example demonstrates, the experience characterises itself by being a process that stimulates the enhancement of competencies which cannot be considered as isolated from each other:

"I recognise that the concept [of the initiative] lies on stimulating the beginning of scientific activities and the development of critical awareness, creativity and autonomy of the students through the process of doing research (...)" (Student 12)

Supervisors also reinforce the latter perspective. However, they go beyond it by stressing the enhancement of the capacity, willingness and openness to learn – an aspect that underlines the holistic nature of involving students in research activities. Two supervisors share similar views:

"(...) this experience [of exposing undergraduate students to a process of research] has (or should have) an impact (...) They become more mature, more responsible (...)" (Supervisor 3)

"After the conclusion of the work and the grant, he [the student] keeps the desire of continuing to collaborate with the same team (...) and interested in continuing to learn. (...) This also shows that he developed competencies, and truly learnt that it [the research process] was important for his development (...)" (Supervisor 13)

To sum up, the relevance of these research grants was generally confirmed by both students and supervisors. In view of the individual context where students' learning took place it was emphasised by the interviewees that this initiative was extremely important for students. It brought them into contact with research cultures and environments which were quite different from the teaching and learning strategies inside the mainstream curriculum, particularly by promoting an intense learning process through research. Therefore, this was considered an opportunity for undergraduates to develop generic competencies required in academic and professional settings.

Conclusions on the Research Evidence

The Portuguese initiative in launching research grants for undergraduates follows international trends which aim to enhance selected students' learning experiences and to equip them with appropriate competencies to face the world – personally, academically, cognitively and professionally.

The impact of students' engagement in research activities was elicited through the perceptions/understandings of students and supervisors as part of a three-phased study of monitoring. The objective was to identify the advantages or limitations of this initiative for the enhancement of students' competencies.

The evidence we have reported shows that new skills, capacities and abilities are being learned and developed. We believe the set of competencies presented in this chapter equips students to be successful learners, to cope with the unpredictable world of workplace, and to succeed as lifelong learners. The sense of belonging to a research community as well as of being able to participate in research projects and to develop generic competencies that are not often developed during conventional courses. In the future this may lead students to be more motivated to learn, to be more self-confident, to act more as active learners and truly engaged professionals.

We believe that this experience promoted students' empowerment and that this can lead to transformative changes in the way students approach learning ('deep learning'). Supervisors and students then become active agents in implementing transformational change (Middlehurst, 1997) contributing to the improvement of students' learning quality in higher education.

Accordingly we propose that initiatives such as the one described in this chapter are needed not only outside the formal curriculum but also integrated into the curriculum. Therefore, we hope to follow up this research by analysing the long term impact (if any) of this intervention on issues such as drop-out rates, degree results and future employment.

To conclude our analysis we feel there are three aspects that should be stressed:

- this Portuguese case study further demonstrates the validity of the growing international research evidence of the positive impacts of special undergraduate research programmes/curricula for selected students. Thus, they reinforce the arguments of George Kuh's analysis of the US National Survey of Student Engagement (NSSE) data: *"There is growing evidence that (…) some programs and activities appear to engage participants at levels that elevate their performance across multiple engagement and desired outcomes measures such as persistence."* (National Survey of Student Engagement, 2007:7);

  Regarding the impact of such selective undergraduate research programmes in the Sciences, Laursen *et al.* (2010:33-34) conclude that: *"In sum, the literature converges on a broad set of benefits as arising from the students' engagement in authentic research. Notably congruent are gains in confidence and establishing a collegial working relationships with faculty and peers; increases in students' intellectual and practical understanding of how science research is done; students' greater ability to work and think independently from faculty (…)"*;

- undergraduate research projects are extremely relevant because they have an enormous impact on students' holistic growth and promote an environment for learning. This learning is not only more personalised, leading to greater intentionality, but also more authentic, 'real', more concrete and less abstract (Cuthbert *et al.*, 2012). In particular, when analysing Table 1, we notice the design of the generic profile that a recent graduate must demonstrate to be prepared to work and/or to engage in further studies (namely at postgraduate level). This goes in line with the findings of Laursen *et al.* (2012:34): *"Gains in career preparation reflected students' readiness to undertake work in their field as employees or graduate students, while increased career clarification addressed students' better understanding of whether or not they wished to pursue a research career or attend graduate school (…)"*;

- the study further demonstrates the potential links that may exist between teaching, learning and research, being the research process not only an intense process of learning, but also a way of 'refining' the teaching process, with potential benefits for faculty researchers. As Lopatto (2009:12) emphasises, research and teaching are "*two forms of creative work*" and particularly "*undergraduate research mentoring may be viewed as the purest form of teaching' with benefits to the mentor as a researcher and as a developing teacher.*"

Final Reflections

This research has been important in stimulating efforts to make undergraduate students more aware of research done by academic staff and in directing greater attention towards making students explicit participants in research and inquiry.

While this Portuguese case study adds to the international research evidence on the potential positive impacts of selective undergraduate research grants, it would be more speculative to say they point to the value of such forms of *curricula* design for all students. One provisional judgement might be that in a context of a mass higher education system and where research is often highly concentrated, such grant schemes while valuable are best reserved for selected students in selected institutions, either through special summer enrichment programmes or specially designed curricula for 'honours' students.

Looking more widely, scholars such as Healey and Jenkins (2009) draw on evidence from international examples which range from the level of the individual course to national interventions, such as that of the QAA Scotland on 'graduate research attributes'.

> "We are convinced that US-derived conceptions of undergraduate research offer ways forward for universities worldwide to hold onto the Humboldtian ideal of the university as an institution where teaching and research are interconnected. The strength of undergraduate research is that the spotlight moves from the traditional focus on individual academics, being effective as both researchers and teachers, to a focus on students and realising the Humboldtian ideal through the undergraduate curriculum. The task then for national systems, institutions and departments is to

> *reinvent and reshape the overall curriculum and other aspects of university structures to support students engaging in research and inquiry".* (Healey & Jenkins, 2009:123)

Institutions and national systems that seek to intervene in the curriculum, and in how students learn, need strong research-based evidence to judge the impact of such interventions. The engagement of students in funded research activities offers perspectives and guidelines that may lead to other, more effective interventions.

About the Authors

Isabel Huet is a researcher in higher education in the Laboratory for the Evaluation of Educational Quality at the "Didactics and Technology in Education of Trainers" Research Centre, Department of Education at the University of Aveiro, Portugal. She can be contacted at this email: huet@ua.pt

Ana Vitória Baptista is a PhD student in the Laboratory for the Evaluation of Educational Quality at the "Didactics and Technology in Education of Trainers" Research Centre, Department of Education at the University of Aveiro, Portugal. She can be contacted at this email: ana.vitoria@ua.pt

Carla Ferreira is a PhD student in the Laboratory for the Evaluation of Educational Quality at the "Didactics and Technology in Education of Trainers" Research Centre, Department of Education at the University of Aveiro, Portugal. She can be contacted at this email: carlasusana@ua.pt

Chapter Seven

Using Computer Supported Collaborative Learning to Enhance the Quality of Schoolteacher Professional Development

Andrea Raiker

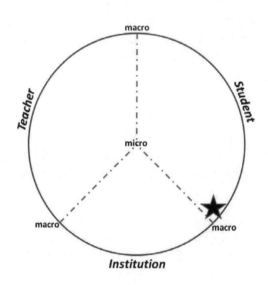

Introduction

This chapter is written from the premise that quality enhancement (QE), as a practice or paradigm, does not exist merely in service to itself. Rather, QE is enacted in the service of wider change. Furthermore, where QE is focused on students, it is related to transformational learning whereby new effective pedagogic practice leads to the development of people who are better able to make a positive difference in the world. This is the ultimate purpose of QE in Higher Education (HE) – progressively to enhance universities' capabilities to prepare people for their lives and professional roles.

Within this context, I offer a case of quality enhancement relating to the professional development of schoolteachers (who work in England) with the aim of helping them to become reflective practitioners who are able to engage confidently in the socio-political discourse of their profession to the extent that they may be able to influence policy change.

By combining seminars in traditional university locations with online collaborative software, university academics and schoolteachers and experts in Information and Communications Technology (ICT) from five European countries took part in two events designed as an action research project. The project's aim was to investigate if computer-supported collaborative learning (CSCL) enabled schoolteachers to overcome barriers in developing their professional selves through reflection on practice. A further aim was to ascertain if the resulting collaboration encouraged the emergence of theory as a step towards generating policy. This could then be used to brief local and regional management, with the potential to influence the UK government's Department for Education (DfE).

Socio-political Context

Currently, English schoolteachers perceive that their professionalism is being eroded. Their regulatory body, the independent General Teaching Council, has been abolished and replaced by the Teaching Agency (TA) which is controlled by the government's Department for Education (DfE). In England, schoolteacher education is in the process of been taken out of universities and put into schools. The results of the action research project demonstrated partial success with clear indications for a third cycle of research.

Some years ago Carr and Kemmis (1986:221), in their work integrating Habermas' (2001) conceptions of communicative action with schoolteacher education, proposed that schoolteachers could *"organize themselves as communities of enquirers, organizing their own enlightenment"*. In my opinion the aim of in-service higher education for schoolteachers in England is not 'enlightenment'. Enlightenment involves insight, the result of personal and purposeful critical reflection and evaluation. Insight in higher education involves growing awareness and understanding of the epistemological and ontological underpinnings of pedagogy (Raiker, 2010).

At first glance, this appears to resonate with the definition of continuing professional development (CPD) given by the TA: *"Professional development consists of reflective activity designed to improve an individual's attributes, knowledge, understanding and skills. It supports individual needs and improves professional practice"* (TA, 2012).

However, 'reflective activity' takes place in an education system controlled by government through imposed standards, inspection and competition stimulated by the publication of league tables. League tables rank schools' performances in national examinations. Performance is the only indicator taken into account. The socio-economic background of the students, their mother tongue, levels of parental support and resourcing are not considered. The outcome is that HE courses for schoolteachers, focused on improving their practice through reflective activity, become aligned with and conform to a customer-centric paradigm.

This interpretation of quality enhancement is predicated on the TA managing the process on the Government's behalf. The TA's role is to encourage improvement through conformity which does not resonate with improvement construed as the deepening of personal insight into the factors that underpin pedagogy. Indeed, the TA's definition of professional development does not even include the term pedagogy. This suggests to me that the TA does not consider knowledge and understanding of theory as an important aspect of improving practice. If so, it is unlikely that the TA would support schoolteachers using the insights gained through relating theory to practice to develop their professional selves and their power to influence high level educational change. It appears that quality enhancement of schoolteachers as postgraduate professional development has more than one interpretation, dependent on the meaning given to 'improvement'.

Developing Notions of Professional Development

The term improvement implies effectiveness; without effectiveness improvement is unlikely. Statutory conditions of service in the UK (England, Wales and Northern Ireland. Scotland has different arrangements) require that teachers be available on five days per year for non-teaching activities, including professional development. Professional development is focused on practice and can be delivered by university lecturers, consultants or teachers with specialised knowledge. Sessions can be via face-to-face workshops or online courses. In this chapter I focus on quality enhancement of schoolteacher professional development in HE delivered by university academics. In my university, the University of Bedfordshire, an academic chooses both the content and mode of delivery of the postgraduate courses. S/he is considered to be an 'expert' and is given control of the learning experience and its assessment against norms laid down by government agencies such as the Quality Assurance Agency (QAA) for Higher Education. However, research by Patall *et al.* (2010) into the effect of learner choice has shown that choice improves intrinsic motivation, endeavour, engagement with task and perceived confidence. Furthermore, according to self-determination theory, autonomy and relatedness improves motivation and performance outcomes (Ryan & Deci, 2000). In other words, the quality of learning is enhanced when control of learning is given to the learner and the content to be learnt and the learning methods are chosen by the learner. This suggests that in professional development, control of content and methods should be given to the learner. This is at variance with commonly found practice (see Bartholomew *et al.*, this volume).

It is acknowledged that socially agreed norms for teacher performance are necessary; teachers have a responsible role in society, passing on systematic knowledge compiled over centuries and supporting the construction of understanding. Teachers completing HE courses should provide evidence that they have met socially-agreed norms so that their achievement can be communicated with confidence. However, there are different ways of meeting socially-agreed norms; for example, in Finland there are no government imposed teacher standards or inspection, and no league tables. The quality of professional development is decided by the profession working in partnership with the universities and municipal authorities, with guidance and financial support from government (Hämäläinen *et al.*, 2011). Also there is emphasis on student teachers acquiring knowledge and understanding of philosophy and its impact on pedagogy (see Mäensivu *et al.*, this volume). Yet Finnish teachers are highly regarded and are trusted because their pupils perform well in international tests such as the Programme of International Student Assessment (PISA). This heightens the status of teaching, resulting in more young people wanting to become teachers. Universities are able to select the best students in terms of academic achievement and motivation to study and they achieve good results as teachers (Heikkinen & Huttunen, 2004). Finnish teachers clearly satisfy their society's expectations. In my view this demonstrates that improvement, or quality enhancement, can be achieved by supporting teacher autonomy and pedagogical development rather than by imposing prescriptive central control or league tables.

Teachers usually attend professional development courses led by university academics in their own schools or at their local university. This is valuable because they contribute, in a social constructivist sense, to a shared pot of expertise and take away their enhanced portion for future practice. However, this has the effect of creating local silos of knowledge, particularly if the learning event takes place at a school. I suggest that improved or enhanced quality in professional development could be achieved more effectively by teachers coming together to engage online with educators in other areas of the country and in countries abroad. This chapter describes and evaluates data collected from two HE professional development events. Educators were brought together physically and virtually through a website. The aim was not only to enhance knowledge gained from practice in a focused area, but also to construct conceptions of the underlying theory through a computer supported collaborative approach. I propose that in doing so, teachers would be demonstrating the higher order thinking skills associated with critical thinking - reflection, analysis and evaluation leading to synthesis of new learning - commensurate with postgraduate study. In addition, they would become aware of their professional selves and their potential to create policy for their institutions and to brief the wider community, even Government; Figure 1 illustrates this process as a framework.

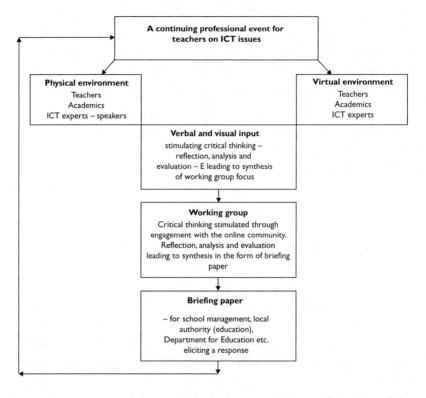

Figure 1: An action research framework for developing teachers' critical thinking and their awareness of their professional selves.

Earlier professional development activities led by the author's co-researcher had tested the notion that participating teachers, working together in physical and virtual social spaces, could generate both curriculum and theory. The ideal outcome would be that, having abstracted theory from their various experiences, teachers would take their transformed conceptions into their classrooms to inform their pedagogy and practice. I propose that the activities would show that these conceptions, rooted in prior knowledge and understanding, could be enhanced through enquiry (Carr & Kemmis, 1986). This would involve reflection upon, and analysis of, presentations by ICT experts and contributions from educators who attended physically or online. Predictions of the outcomes of applying conceptions to practice could then be tested, for example, through action research. The quotation on enlightenment from Carr and Kemmis (1986) at the beginning of this chapter arose from their discussion on action research in education. Professional development, involving the generation and testing of theory by teachers, could result in enlightenment as both process and product. In the UK, teachers could use their insights in practices bounded by UK government prescriptions and requirements. However, it can be argued that the community of enquirers established virtually (or 'in the digital habitat' as Wenger *et al.* (2009) term it) establishes a public sphere for communicative action (Habermas, 1991). An outcome of enlightened interactions from diverse educators from across the world could result in the questioning of, and ultimately opposition to, ideological conformity. So quality enhancement could come at a price to government ideologies of what is deemed to be appropriate 'process', 'product' and, indeed 'curriculum'.

In these preliminary activities, my co-researcher acted as a participant observer and facilitator. She encouraged the externalisation of teacher conceptions through the collaborative construction of a communal online mind map. The mind map, which focused on educational blogging, drafted a curriculum for further investigation through its reorganisation into themes. Because the participants were able to edit the map by adding and amending, grouping and regrouping concept labels, it could be construed that theory on educational blogging had been generated. For the purposes of this chapter, theory is defined as generalised, socially-agreed proto-knowledge. However, not all participants contributed to the editing, nor was there evidence that the passivity displayed by the non-editors simply denoted congruency of personal knowledge with the socially agreed proto-knowledge constructed by the rest of the group. Furthermore, and importantly, there was no evidence that the participants either understood that they were participating in the generation of theory or that they could use the theory so generated to influence policy and practice.

Acknowledging that the activity fell short of catalysing the aspirations of activism that underpins action research paradigms, I decided to progress from informal 'testing of a notion' to a more highly structured investigation of the potential of this HE experience in order to enhance the quality of in-service teacher education. Specifically, the potential of such activity to develop teachers in such a way that they felt empowered to challenge policy and to pursue change actively as a member of an enlightened, inquiring community.

As I placed my investigations on a more structured footing I came to realise that with its focus on physical and virtual communities of enquirers my research interest lay within the domain of co-located CSCL.

Why use CSCL as a Method to Support the Development of these Learners?

My previous research (Raiker, 2010) suggested that an aim in this research should be to ascertain the degree to which co-located CSCL environments enabled teachers to transition their personal 'liminal spaces' in learning. Although the term 'liminal space' has emerged from my previous work, it is closely related to the well-understood concept of knowledge construction. In my writing, I have described liminal space as a mental tunnel connecting two knowledge areas, one area being existing knowledge and the other new knowledge. Some learners pass through the tunnel to access an enlarged area of extended learning. Others pass into the tunnel but find the new knowledge troublesome and counter-intuitive; these learners cannot apply the knowledge of one area to another area because the relationship is meaningless to them (Lather, 1998; Perkins, 1999). A learner finding knowledge troublesome would be 'stuck' in the tunnel of liminal space. However, the research described here is related to the potential of working in a community rather than learning in solitude. Hence the metaphor of a tunnel is no longer appropriate – there is no guarantee that learners' inabilities to integrate new knowledge relates to the same troublesome concepts or shared notions of what is counter-intuitive. Thus 'shared liminal space' could be conceptualised as formless, with learners' misconceptions, misunderstandings, or simply their lack of knowledge, interacting with each other without a common framework of underpinning, constructed knowledge. The aim of the CSCL environment that I report here is to allow for exploration of the shared liminal space – to locate its boundaries and to provide opportunities for learners to socially construct shared knowledge that will assist in making sense of their personal troublesome knowledge.

In the environment created by the co-located CSCL, teachers, academics and ICT experts could act in the Brunerian sense (Bruner, 1986) as scaffolds to support each other as they traverse liminal space together to reach shared and individual enlightenment and transformation. Applying terminology used by Habermas, the co-located CSCL environment forms a public sphere in which communicative action can take place.

A second, equally important aim was to consider the degree to which personal reflection on practice in co-located CSCL environments encouraged the emergence of theory (as defined above). I propose that this is a step towards influencing policy generation at various levels. I also suggest that, if liminal space is traversed and socially-generated theory emerges, an educational transformation in both the learning and teaching of professional development will have occurred. Transformation is described by Freire (1978) in his definition of 'praxis' as the evidence that the professional as the agent has forged together theory and practice. Praxis is a high-level mode of professional operation where the practitioner possesses skills and deep knowledge and understanding of the theories that underpin practice. This can lead to a profound change in teachers' understanding of their professional selves, giving them the power to take greater control of their profession. For me, this is the true nature of quality enhancement in teacher education.

In this research CSCL is aimed at the quality enhancement of school-teacher professional development. However, the methodology for using co-located CSCL synchronously is very new and so we decided to supplement the tool with the more established approach of action research. As Cohen *et al.* (2005:226) remark, it *"...is a powerful tool for change and improvement at the local level"*. It is also, when applied to education, concerned with critical *praxis*, action informed by disciplined inquiry aimed at developing evidence-based knowledge and theory (Habermas, 1984; Elliott, 1991). It focuses on practical issues identified by practitioners as being problematic but capable of being changed (Elliott, 1991: Zuber-Skerritt, 1996). However, there can also be a social dimension to action research, essential for an investigation predicated on co-located CSCL. According to Kemmis and McTaggart (1992:16), action research involves: *"...changing individuals, on the one hand, and, on the other, the culture of the groups, institutions and societies to which they belong"*. [Furthermore, action research is] *"...a form of collective self-reflective inquiry undertaken by participants in social situations in order to improve the rationality and justice of their own social or educational practices..."* (Kemmis & McTaggart, 1992:5)

Although my co-researcher and I undertook the research in the spirit of 'teachers-as-researchers' as advocated by Stenhouse (1975) and Whitehead (1985), and 'researchers-as-participators' (Weiskopf & Laske, 1996), colleagues were and will be included throughout the research process. Altricher and Gsettner's (1993) model of action research was adopted as being appropriate for the context. Their four steps of finding a starting point (the outcomes of 'testing a notion'), clarifying the situation (countering any lack of awareness of the deeper purposes of the activities undertaken), developing action strategies (arising out of evaluated professional development events) and putting them into practice, and publicising the results, allows clarification and putting actions into practice to occur in parallel. This was ethically essential because, to maximise teacher development, actions based on findings had to be put into practice when proven to increase the effectiveness of the CPD process in terms of quality enhancement. However, action research is goal-orientated; this research was not. It was testing a proposed framework (Figure 1) and therefore can be considered as an adaptation or development of Altricher and Gsettner's model. We used mind mapping software as a means of mediating language misinterpretations, misunderstandings and supporting knowledge transfer. We also employed content analysis of word clouds and analysis of discourse generated through physical and virtual interaction. Transcripts of the data generated through the collection methods outlined above were subjected to qualitative content analysis (Hsieh & Shannon, 2005).

Together, these enabled us to explore the following questions:

- can teachers "organise themselves as communities of enquirers, organising their own enlightenment" through a co-located CSCL environment?

- can enlightenment be regarded as traversing shared liminal space?

- can the enlightenment achieved be used to brief policy makers?

Data Collection, Analysis and Discussion: First Cycle

The first cycle of data collection took place at my university in May 2012. The professional development session was entitled *Assessing the value of physical and virtual spaces in enriching learning*. The physical session was attended by 32 teachers, academics and ICT experts from schools and university departments, and also by IT consultants and technicians. They were joined online by eight teachers, academics and ICT experts from Germany, Czech Republic, Ireland, Slovakia and other sites in England. The physical environment was a large lecture room for 200 students, from which most of the seating had been moved so that the session's technology could be accommodated. At the front of the room was the speaker's space on which various cameras were focused. Behind the speaker's space were four large screens. The first displayed the footage being streamed out to a website; online participants could see and hear the session by accessing the website. They could also see themselves and send messages on a second screen via FlashMeeting software. A third screen displayed a Twitter feed and a fourth contained the emergent mind map, again accessible through the website (http://www.mirandanet.ac.uk/mirandamods/events/). All participants had wireless mobile technology so that they could interact with the website and each other. In this way, something resembling Wenger *et al.*'s (2009) digital habitat was created.

The format of the session had two distinct parts, a presentation part and a discussion part. The presentation part involved an introduction by the professional development event's host. This was followed by a series of ten-minute presentations by nine ICT experts in fields related to the session's focus - such as social-networking and education, and copyright and web publishing. During this part nearly all interactivity was via Flash Meeting, Twitter and the mind map; even those present in the physical space 'talked' with each other through the technology. It appeared that the digital habitat was assuming elements of 'public sphere' (Habermas, 1991). However, only 16 of the 40 participants were engaged in the online exchanges. The longest exchanges, consisting of observations, rhetorical questions and statements were made through Tweets that rarely could be construed as conversations. Content analysis showed that there were some exchanges on topics generated by speakers' topics such as Twitter (6 exchanges between 5 participants (6/5)), cyber-bullying (4/4), children staring at screens all day (2/2) and social media in schools (5/4). However, analysis also revealed that there was very little interaction signifying intention to discuss theory or practice in any depth. For example the exchange on cyber-bullying, which was interspersed in the conversations on social media in schools and Twitter (these have been removed), was as follows:

"So the data was flawed, only asking teachers who were being bullied if they had been bullied online". Participant 2 (P2).

"It occurs to me that a cyber bully never gave me a bloody nose." (P7).

"The internet has not led to an increase in bulling, just seems a bigger problem as it is more visible." (P6).

"Bullying is about people's behaviour. Technology [is] *not the cause but does amplify."* (P9).

Discourse extract 1: discourse generated virtually on a connected topic.

Interestingly, these exchanges took place approximately an hour into the two-hour session. Earlier exchanges took the form of information exchange about the difficulty of getting personal technology to work followed by disconnected observations exemplified in the following continuous discourse:

"The mobile device is with you (til the battery is flat :-(( )." (P2).

"It's Derek off of Coronation Street: he's got an iPad, an iPad, I tell you!" (P2).

"Is no-one scared about the vision that kids are staring at a screen the whole day?" (P10).

"Watching a demo of kosuMobile learning platform. Sweet!" (P7).

Discourse extract 2: discourse generated on disconnected topics.

For the first hour 'Tweets' principally took a form similar to what Vygotsky (1987) termed 'collective monologues' or individual learners' utterings expressed during social events (Discourse extract 2). According to Vygotsky these marked a transitional stage between two types of activity: regulative communication which is *"… spontaneous, involuntary and nonconscious, while the other* [spoken language as a tool of thought] *is abstract, voluntary and conscious"*, (Vygotsky, 1987:43). Just like Vygotsky's learners, the Tweeters appeared to be rehearsing thoughts as speech rather than initiating interaction.

During this discussion part of the seminar, a mind map was created online and was visible to all on the fourth large screen. At certain times, when activity stopped, a lead facilitator would add some words or a phrase to stimulate participation. However, there was no attempt by any participant to edit it. This was discussed in the second part of the session when I explained that it was hoped that the data from the session would demonstrate application of higher order thinking skills as an indicator of the quality enhancement of the professional development process. I suggested that the group might consider editing, and that this would involve reflection, analysis and evaluation (Raiker, 2010). The edited map would present a synthesis of thinking, and even the generation of theory, through the process. In the silence that followed this, P7 interjected:

> *"Why can't it stand as it is? The thinking's already happened, the reflection, in the map there. What you have there is the synthesis of each person's thinking".* (P7).

This important insight was supported by analysis of the data from the latter half of the second part of the session, which was for participants in the physical space only. A discussion began, facilitated by one of the authors with reference to the discussion on Twitter and FlashMeeting; as might be expected, it was more focused and in greater depth with 30 of the 32 participants contributing to a greater or lesser extent. The most important finding from analysis of the transcript of this conversation was that participants felt that the online contributions during the first part of the session had stimulated and formed their thinking on the topic. There was agreement that the co-located CSCL interaction had helped them bring disparate nuggets of knowledge to the forefront of their thinking, enabling them to consolidate a perspective that could be shared in the face-to-face interaction, As P28 expressed it: *"You know, like a pre-wash so that the end product is more whitey-white than grey"*. However, P28 admitted that she had not engaged with the virtual community. When asked by the facilitator why not, she replied:

> *"Well, there was the technology to begin with. I couldn't get into the wifi. It was ... thanks, P3, it was thanks to you ... but by then there was stuff going on all the screens and Speaker 1 had started on...well, you know, how education can tap into the internet and it was deep stuff. I was listening to Speaker 1 and waiting for him to take a breath, then trying to get on the website. I was missing what he was saying. I...they... the kids at school, they have Facebook open and are listening to their music with headphones on and into websites and writing their coursework...but I can't do that. I could listen to Speaker 1, or get onto the website but not both. It's too much for me!"*(P28).

P28's response to the value of physical and virtual spaces in enriching learning was therefore not straightforward. P28 was a teacher; other participants were university academics, consultant technicians and speakers specialising in educational technology. Analysis of their discourse showed that their assessment of the professional development experience in terms of enhancing learning was generally positive, but in different ways. For example P4, an academic in university secondary teacher training who regarded himself as *"...a bit of a technophile..."*, enjoyed the virtual interactions and did not find the multitasking of media difficult. He did however find the lack of response to his observations and questions in Twitter frustrating and realised that the nature of Twitter - discourse limited to 140 characters - prevented in-depth conversations:

> *"What did I tweet? Let me see... yep,... 'Is the BBC trying to entertain or educate us about the dangers of FB and teachers? Reithian principles compromised.' I'm passionate about this! What about you guys?"* (P4).

Despite the varying reactions to the technology and interpretations of the nature of the learning experienced, session evaluations were positive. However the aims of the research were not achieved. We did not ascertain the degree to which a co-located CSCL environment enabled teachers to transition shared and individual liminal spaces in learning, and we did not consider the degree to which personal reflection on practice stimulated by social interaction in a co-located CSCL environment encouraged the emergence of theory as a step to generating political activism. Analysis of the first cycle of data suggested that none of the three questions could be answered positively. Our critical reflections resulted in the insight that we had been unrealistic in expecting participants to 'invent the wheel' of autonomously understanding liminal space and its role in enlightenment. We were naive in thinking that participants could deduce for themselves that an aim of the process was to generate theory and, ultimately, policy. Also we recognised that for some participants there was too much technology. It was decided that for the next professional development event, to be held at in a university in the Czech Republic, the technology and the process would be simplified and that there would be a presentation by one of the authors on *Traversing together liminal spaces in learning.*

Data Collection, Analysis and Discussion: Second Cycle

The topic to be investigated at the Czech Republic event was *What does the 21st century teacher need to know about digital technologies, why, and how, will their prowess be assessed?* Twenty-five participants from Bulgaria, England, Germany, Slovakia, the Czech Republic and the Netherlands met to share experiences and to listen to a range of speakers on various aspects of technological innovation and issues affecting professional development in digital technology. Like the UK event, participants were academics and practising teachers supported by ICT innovators and technicians. I followed the speakers with a presentation designed to synthesise key messages from their inputs. The presentation showed how theory and policy could be generated from teachers' reflections and evaluations of what they had heard related to their own experiences and expectations. The key messages of the presentation concerned collaboration through digital technologies to support individual and social learning, collaboration through digital technologies to generate, amend or confirm theory, and *"turning up the volume of professional voice"*. I explained how individuals had to *"come out of their silos"*, and share their different personal, national and socio-cultural perspectives to identify common interests, and that a co-located CSCL environment could support this endeavour.

Only five participants from the UK joined the discussion online, which was disappointing. Also, the technology at the Czech university caused issues with the interface generating the mind map. So the principal data collection came from the discussion in the physical space at the university. A transcript of the discussion resulted in the word cloud depicted in Figure 2.

Figure 2: Word cloud from transcript of Czech event discussion.

The focus on technology in the discussion is clear. 'Digital', 'technologies' and 'online' have a strong presence, as does those who use technology- 'teachers' and 'educators' who are engaged in 'professional' and 'working' activities connected with 'learning'. Also strongly represented, though less so, are 'research', 'knowledge', 'development' and 'group'. This suggests that my presentation on the underlying purpose of the Czech event may have had an impact. However 'liminal' does not appear at all. It would appear that for this group, understanding of liminal space was meaningful, in terms of 'research', 'knowledge' and 'development'. However it is possible that individuals had passed through some form of liminal space to reach understanding of the relevance of 'research', 'knowledge', and 'development' to their professional selves. This is supported by the generation of five areas of interest by participants in the co-located CSCL environment:

- continuing Professional Development: multimedia resources and training for teachers;

- developing effective professional communication models using technology;

- sustaining collaborative professional learning and research through technology;

- digital professional identity/digital e-wellness (link with digital safety);

- theories of learning underpinning digital technologies in education.

All participants linked themselves to one of the groups; some participants wanted to be involved in more than one group. It was decided that meetings would be held online through an educational community website already established by one of the group (a higher education professor) for communicating and engaging in research practices. The group decided that there should be another co-located CSCL environment event later in the year where each sub-group would speak about their progress and findings. In other words, the sub-groups would take the place of the expert speakers. They would become autonomous in taking their learning forward. It was not suggested at this event that the findings of the sub-groups could be construed as creating theory or working towards establishing policy. However, this could be the aim for the co-researchers as participators and facilitators at the next event as the third cycle in this action research project.

Conclusions

The aims of the research were to ascertain the degree to which a co-located CSCL environment enabled schoolteachers to transition shared and individual liminal spaces in learning, and to consider the degree to which personal reflection on practice stimulated by social interaction in a co-located CSCL environment encouraged the emergence of theory as a step towards the generation of policy. To do this, three questions were identified. Conclusions to the research carried out so far will be discussed under each.

Q1) Can schoolteachers 'organise themselves as communities of enquirers, organising their own enlightenment' through a co-located CSCL environment? Findings from the second cycle but not the first suggest that, with facilitation, they can. It is clear that they needed to be given clear messages on the various levels of purpose of co-located CSCL events. They also needed to be given time to get to know each other, the technology and the format of the events in terms of what was expected of them. However, the question has to be asked - could the same result have been achieved with the events taking place in a physical environment only? Further research is needed on this. However, the integration of various multimedia technologies and the virtual presence of contributors created an environment that provided cohesion for the topics being discussed and the interests of the group. In other words, the co-located CSCL environment defined, focused and united the community of enquirers working within it and the outputs they produced in terms of sub-groups.

Q2) Can enlightenment be regarded as traversing shared liminal space? Findings from the two events demonstrated progression from individuals working principally in isolation to individuals working within a community of enquirers as demonstrated by the emergence of sub-groups focused on learning in defined areas. It was proposed that individuals will progress from one learning state to another through shared liminal space and that there must be elements allowing this to happen, including a sense of containment or boundedness. The findings suggest that boundedness was established by the community of enquirers and that the co-located CSCL environment supported the focusing and defining of the community. The co-located CSCL environment community supplied a democratised space that supported purposeful reflection, criticality and evaluation. In the introduction, I suggested that enlightenment involved insight, the result of personal and purposeful critical reflection and evaluation. From this I deduce that not only can it can be said that enlightenment can be regarded as traversing liminal space; it can also be regarded as the product of traversing liminal space.

Q3) Can the enlightenment achieved be used to brief policy makers? The findings from the second event suggest that participants working in a co-located CSCL environment demonstrated their enlightenment by their self-determination to develop sub-groups as communities for inquiry. This is not in itself sufficient to produce outcomes that could be used to brief policy makers. However, each of the sub-groups formed created an agenda around which to collect data. It is intended that the research should have a third cycle, a co-located CSCL event to be held later in the year as outlined above. At this event, we intend to signpost the participants towards the data that they have collected in their subgroups in terms of organising it to influence policy-making in their schools or professional organisations.

I proposed earlier that quality enhancement, when enacted with a student focus, concerns the facilitation of transformative learning experiences that develop people who can make a positive difference in the world. The action research process presented in this chapter sought to create conditions that could precipitate community-desired change. Change was made possible because sub-groups of enquirers, of their own volition, identified areas for further investigation. I have stated that for my co-researcher and me, attainment of praxis and changes in teachers' understanding of their professional selves is the true nature of quality enhancement. We are on the journey but have a distance to travel yet.

About the Author

Andrea Raiker is a curriculum enhancement developer at the University of Bedfordshire, UK. She can be contacted at this email: andrea.raiker@ beds.ac.uk

Chapter Eight

Quality Enhancement through the Peer Review of Teaching for Learning and Learning for Teaching - a Process and an Outcome.

Christopher Klopper and Steve Drew

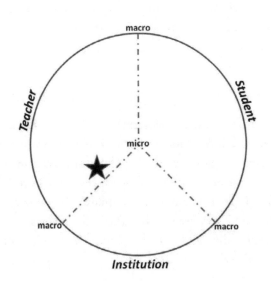

Introduction

This chapter is about quality enhancement of university teaching and learning. Confronted by regulatory systems, the increasing competitive climate of burgeoning knowledge economies and the over-reliance of student evaluations of teaching as sole arbiters of teaching quality, a process for peer observation of teaching quality (teaching for learning) and academic staff development (learning for teaching) has been investigated. We contextualise and report a case study of quality enhancement originating from a larger University wide initiative (PRO-Teaching) explicitly focusing on the enhancement of quality in teaching. The reason for this is the underlying argument that quality in teaching improves students' learning outcomes. We follow this line of argument throughout the chapter. In relation to the enhancement of quality in teaching we do argue that student evaluations, although holding important information about students' perception of quality in teaching, should not stand alone as an indicator of quality in teaching. We collate data from multiple observers together with the students' evaluations and learning outcomes from the observed episodes to create a data set from which defensible evidence of quality teaching for learning is inferred. We therefore propose peer review of teaching as both a process and an outcome towards quality enhancement in university teaching and learning.

Quality Enhancement: Context and Need

Higher education in Australia consistently ranks in the country's top four export earners (Hall & Hooper, 2008). However, for more than 15 years there has been a rapidly expanding global marketplace for higher education to service burgeoning knowledge economies in many regions (Marginson, 2007). In such a competitive climate it is imperative that the education products and services can be clearly differentiated to market needs globally, regionally, and locally (Jones & Oleksiyenko, 2011; Marginson, 2011); and that they are of an outstanding quality in terms of access (Morley, 2012; Rizvi & Lingard, 2011), processes and outcomes (Wong, 2012). To maintain a national competitive advantage it is also imperative that there is a quality agenda supporting the development of higher education from the national level (Lomas, 2004) through to the provider organisation (Barnard *et al.*, 2011; Becket & Brookes, 2006), disciplines (Healey, 2000), and individual teachers.

For many universities there is a reliance on student fees to subsidise the operations and growth of the organisation. Thus, in any region there is always competition amongst universities for student enrolments with public image, position, product differentiation, and transparent representations of quality highly important to its success. Various national surveys provide data that is made available to institutions and their stakeholders, including potential students to make informed choices. In Australia the *MyUniversity* website (Australian Government, 2012) provides data about courses of study and each university. The Good Universities Guide (Good Universities Guide, 2012) has variants around the world as an independent vehicle, popular with students and parents that provide similar information for comparing and ranking organisations. Improving university ranking on these open and transparent information systems is becoming an effective quality driver (Alderman, 2010; Shah & Nair, 2011).

The recent introduction of a prescriptive regulatory system administered by the Tertiary Education Quality Standards Agency (TEQSA) is of particular importance to Australian Universities as the framework provides and develops standards relating to the nature of learning underpinning the awarding of qualifications, quality of teaching and learning, quality of research, and quality of information provided to stakeholders (TEQSA, 2012). This broad standards approach combined with government funding policy and the uncapping of student numbers places pressure on regions, organisations, departments, and individuals each to align their own quality agendas (Sachs *et al.*, 2011). As a result there is increasing pressure for universities to exhibit quality processes that enhance the quality of teaching as this has explicit links to student success and retention (Biggs, 2003; Tinto, 1993; Gibbs, 2010).

Boyer (1990:23) describes teaching as: "*a dynamic endeavour involving all the analogies, metaphors, and images that build bridges between the teacher's understanding and the student's learning*" and observes that: "*great teachers create a common ground of intellectual commitment. They stimulate active, not passive learning and encourage students to be critical, creative thinkers, with the capacity to go on learning*".

In order to achieve this goal Boyer advocates a scholarly approach to good teaching. This in turn contributes to professional development through the benefits of the observation process by learning for teaching (Bell & Mladenovic, 2008; Martin & Double, 1998; Shortland, 2004; Swinglehurst et al., 2008).

Fincher and Work (2006) construct a pyramid derived from Boyer's writing that articulates the progression from teaching to scholarly teaching and, finally the scholarship of teaching. Teaching includes the design and implementation of activities that promote learning, and includes direct classroom teaching, course design, development of instructional materials, and development of formative and summative assessment. Scholarly teaching provides the link from teaching to learning such that academic teaching staff consults relevant educational literature as well as the pedagogical content knowledge to consistently enhance their teaching practice (Shulman, 1986, 1987). Scholarly teaching and undertaking a scholarship of teaching do not necessarily indicate excellent teaching for learning but they signal an approach that has the capacity to enhance teaching practice and inform others as they seek to improve their own practice through learning for teaching. In this context, defensible evidential claims enhancement and of excellence in learning and teaching should be derived from a range of sources (Jahangiri et al., 2008; Nygaard & Belluigi, 2011; Shah & Nair, 2012).

Most Australian universities have adopted student evaluations as a mechanism to appraise the performance of teaching. These evaluations can be understood as providing a 'customer-centric' portrait of quality; and, when used as the sole arbiter of teaching performance they do not instil confidence in the system of evaluation by academic teaching staff (Langbein, 2008; Clayson & Haley, 2011). Providing peer perspectives as counterpoint, whether in a developmental or summative form, goes some way to alleviating this imbalance and is the impetus for the resurgence of interest in peer review of teaching. Alternative sources of data that complement the now ubiquitous student evaluations for quality of courses and teaching include:

- peer evaluation or observation of teaching (Barnard et al., 2011; Bennett & Santy, 2009; Chamberlain et al., 2011; Ginns et al., 2010; Lomas & Nicholls, 2005; Smith, 2008; Swinglehurst et al., 2008);

- structured reflection on teaching practice (Askew, 2004; Bamber & Anderson, 2012; Biggs, 2001; Boud, 1999; Healey, 2000); and

- student learning outcomes (Biggs & Tang, 2011).

The peer review of teaching is recognised (Bell, 2001; Donnelly, 2007; Lomas & Nichols, 2005) as an effective method for assessing quality enhancement from a range of sources and generating professional development for incremental improvement of teaching.

A process for quality enhancement

The case study reported here originates from a University-wide initiative, known as 'PRO-Teaching', that explores the potential for the peer review of teaching to enhance teaching practice and the learning outcomes of students. The PRO-Teaching project aimed to develop a flexible suite of peer review processes and resources to support a range of peer assisted teaching activities.

A participatory action research methodology was employed to cyclically evaluate the question: "How can peer review of teaching be used to enhance the quality of teaching within the University?". Participatory action research is cyclical in nature and the relationship between action and reflection can be understood as a self-reflective spiral that involves "multiple cycles of reflecting, planning, acting and observing" (McTaggart, 1997). In order to operationalise the project administrative hubs were created to facilitate staff engagement, training and foster an institutional culture of professional development and quality enhancement opportunity. Creswell (2012) explains that participatory action research strives for: "*open, broad-based involvement of participants by collaborating in decisions as consensual partners and engaging participants as equals to ensure their well-being.*" Creswell (2012:583). Over time, the methods and modes of action are formed through a "*dialectic movement between action and reflection*" (Kidd & Kral, 2005:187).

The design of the PRO-Teaching process (Figure 1) involved an observee, two observers (a discipline expert from the same school as the observee, and a teaching and learning expert from a different school), and students, in two sequenced teaching episodes of the same course. The mix of relevant discipline knowledge and recognized teaching and learning expertise provided a balanced range of views and ideas when generating the observation reports.

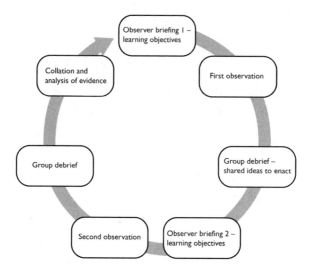

Figure 1: The design of the PRO-Teaching process.

A developmental approach to the observation instrument design was utilised. This involved adapting Nulty's (2001) dimensions by gaining feedback from 128 academic teaching staff observers to create a hybrid instrument for recording and analysing observations of teaching. An important finding from the trial of the first incarnation of the instrument was the need to find an appropriate shared language amongst academic teaching staff. To this end, research informed aspects of the constituents of good teaching (Biggs, 2003; Chickering & Gamson, 1987; Nulty, 2001; Ramsden, 1992; Young & Shaw, 1999) were used to create and re-create a set of dimensions that were descriptive and indicative of a shared teaching for learning language. During episodes the observers take notes about what they see as evidence of each of the dimensions prompted by focus questions for which appear in Table 1.

1	Does the teacher clearly define explicit, realistic and challenging yet achievable aims and learning objectives?
2	Does the teacher demonstrate advanced content knowledge to create clear explanations and address student questions?
3	Does the teacher demonstrate a teaching style supported by appropriate strategies for creating interest and effectively engaging students in learning activities?

4	Does the teacher exhibit a generosity of person, benevolence toward students, humility in their role, interest in teaching, and availability to students to render assistance?
5	Does the teacher engage with activities in class that test student understanding and adapt or adopt teaching strategies to further develop that understanding?
6	Does the teacher encourage students to reflect and share what they already know about the topic, discuss how it relates to other things that they know, and hypothesise about its implications for particular problems and cases?
7	Does the teacher organize learning activities and assessments in a structured and coherent manner that assists students to achieve the stated learning objectives?
8	Does the teacher make effective use of the available features of the environment to enhance their teaching and the student learning experience?
9	Does the teacher use appropriate teaching materials and aids and make use of them in an appropriate manner that assists students to reach the learning objectives?
10	Does the teacher reveal a scholarly approach to teaching and seek to improve teaching performance?

Table 1: Dimensions of evidence for observed teaching.

After the first episode a report was generated using peer, student, and self-reflection data. This was then returned to the observee to consider strategies to implement in a following episode. The second episode was an identical process. The feedback report however was now accompanied by a compilation of student evaluations from both episodes. This was correlated with the peer observations and self-reflection data for the development of ideas.

In relation to the enhancement of quality in teaching we do argue that student evaluations, although holding important information about students' perception of quality in teaching, should not stand alone as an indicator of quality in teaching. Table 2 highlights the complementary perspectives of teaching performance gathered by a range of distinct data sources for increased reliability and validation which promotes increased confidence in the evidence.

	Learning and teaching objectives	Student evaluations of teaching	Student learning outcomes (one-minute paper)	Peer observations
Constructive alignment within lessons	✔		✔	✔
Student perceptions of teaching quality		✔	✔	
Observer perceptions of teaching quality	✔			✔

Table 2: Mechanisms to observe aspects of teaching quality.

The PRO-Teaching mechanism collected data in order to create developmental ideas to improve teaching performance. The observee implemented developmental ideas agreed collaboratively with the observation team and in conjunction with their own reflections on their teaching performance and available student evaluation data. Three aspects relating to observed teaching performance were analysed and reported: constructive alignment within lessons, student perceptions of teaching quality (including summary of student learning outcomes), and observer perceptions of teaching quality.

Constructive alignment in the context of a lesson is the alignment of class learning objectives with learning and teaching activities and effective assessment to measure how well the objectives were met (Biggs, 1996). For this to occur the learning objectives stated in the briefing document are matched against representative phrases in the student responses to the learning outcomes using a one-minute paper:

- what was the most important thing you learned today?

- what questions do you still have?

Where there was a match between the stated objectives and the student learning outcomes then it was reasonable to suggest that the learning and teaching activities in that class were effectively aligned to reach the desired objectives for those students. Where students had questions related directly to the stated objectives then it indicated that there might be a requirement for learning and teaching activities that are better aligned or better designed to reach the intended learning objectives for those students.

As a simple indicator, constructive alignment was represented as a percentage value for each learning objective stated in the briefing document. This was expressed as the number of representative phrase matches, counted manually, between objectives and student-learning outcomes realized in the corresponding one-minute paper, divided by the number of respondents to the one-minute paper. The higher the percentage value the better the constructive alignment attained. For this particular case the constructive alignment measures, presented as a percentage value representing the proportion of the class that realized each stated learning outcome were 81% and 92% respectively. There was a slight improvement in student perception of the academic teacher making use of feedback to improve the teaching for learning. An indication of the level of constructive alignment for each class that was observed is contained in Table 3.

Student responses to the evaluation of teaching were uniformly high for each dimension across both observed episodes. Lesson objectives and student learning outcomes were compared to gauge how effective the lesson's activities were in helping students achieve the knowledge outcomes set in the lesson objectives. The survey questions and information derived from the responses to a five point Likert scale (Likert, 1932) for the observed episodes are presented in the Table 4.

Stated Learning Objectives – Session 1	Matches n=27	Questions	Alignment
Learning objective 1: Students aurally and visually recognize and respond to core content in music they hear and perform	22	0	81%
Learning objective 2: Students read and write short musical patterns containing core content	22	0	81%
Stated Lesson Objectives – Session 2	**Matches n=26**	**Questions**	**Alignment**
Learning objective 1: Students aurally and visually recognize and respond to core content in music they hear and perform	24	0	92%
Learning objective 2: Students respond through movement and/or percussion instruments to selected repertoire	24	0	92%
Learning objective 3: Students describe and express their responses to music using appropriate vocabulary.	24	0	92%

Table 3: Constructive alignment.

Key

Mode: These are the most popular responses to the Student Evaluation of Teaching (SET) for this episode with values in the range (1 - 5)

Resp.: The total number of responses to each question on the SET for this episode

Average: These are the averages of response values (1 - 5) to each question on the SET for this episode. They are comparable to the average SET score for this question on end of semester student surveys

d Mode: This is the *change in most popular response* value for each SET question between observation 1 and observation 2. A positive number shows improvement from student perspective.

d Average: This is the *change in the average value* for each SET question between observation 1 and observation 2. A positive number shows improvement from the student perspective.

How effective is this teacher in: Mode		12/09/11 Resp. = 27		19/09/11 Resp. = 26		Change	
		Ave	Mode	Ave	dMode	dAve	
1	Making clear the objectives of this lesson?	5	4.70	5	4.81	0	0.1
2	Using approaches that helped you to learn?	5	4.85	5	4.85	0	-0.01
3	Motivating and inspiring you to learn?	5	4.81	5	4.81	0	-0.01
4	Highlighting the relevance of what you were to learn?	5	4.73	5	4.77	0	0.04
5	Assessing your prior knowledge before explaining new material?	5	4.70	5	4.65	0	-0.05
6	Ensuring that you received feedback which helped you learn?	5	4.67	5	4.81	0	0.14
7	Explaining the requirements and standards of work for excellence?	5	4.81	5	4.77	0	-0.05
8	Helping you to extend your knowledge, understanding and skills (i.e. challenging you)?	5	4.81	5	4.85	0	0.03
9	Teaching in an organised, coherent and well-ordered manner?	5	4.93	5	4.92	0	-0.01
10	Using feedback to improve his/her teaching?	5	4.59	5	4.88	0	0.29
11	In helping you to learn overall?	5	4.81	5	4.88	0	0.07

Table 4: Student responses for the observed sessions.

In this case the data indicated that the teacher is a highly engaged and an engaging teacher as evidenced by the uniformly high scores for each student evaluation question at each observed lesson. The only small but significant change in student responses indicated that more students felt that the teacher was responding to feedback in order to improve his teaching. As the presence of peer observers was apparent in the classes and as student input was considered in the second observation then this change is considered reasonable and understandable.

During observation episodes the observers attending each class took notes about what they saw during the execution of each lesson. With these notes in mind the observers then determined how much evidence they perceived of each of the 10 dimensions appearing in Table 4. Dimensions are framed slightly differently depending upon whether the focus is on the teacher or the students participating in the class. During each episode the observers assigned a value to the level of evidence that they perceive to be supporting each observable dimension. The level of evidence is given a numerical value between 0 and 3 where the actual value did not reflect on teaching performance but related to that which was observed.

Between the two episodes the observers and observee identified feedback ideas to enact. The observed change was witnessed through the level of evidence of each dimension perceived by the observers. A positive value suggests an increase in perceived evidence relating to a particular dimension while a negative value suggests a decrease in that perception. Evidentiary data collated from the observed episodes are presented in Table 5.

Observer Data – Observing the Teacher		Observation 12/09/11	Observation 19/09/11	Observed Change
1	Clearly conveying the learning aims and objectives?	3	3	0
2	Demonstrating and advanced level of content knowledge?	3	3	0
3	Using effective pedagogical techniques for the teaching and learning activity?	3	3	0
4	Demonstrating personal charac-teristics that engage, stimulate, encourage, inspire, etc?	3	3	0
5	Demonstrating concern for indi-vidual students and their learning needs?	2.5	3	0.5
6	Implementing effective forma-tive assessment techniques or procedures?	3	3	0
7	Explaining the requirements and standards of work for excellence?	1.5	1.5	0
8	Encouraging students to engage with learning activities?	3	3	0
9	Demonstrating effective curric-ulum design that is structured and coherent?	3	3	0
10	Revealing a scholarly approach to teaching and seeking to improve teaching performance?	2.5	3	0.5

Observer Data – Observing the Students				
1a	Appearing to understand the learning aims and objectives?	2.5	3	0.5
2a	Responding positively to or seeking examples from the teacher's content knowledge?	2.5	3	0.5
3a	Responding positively to or engaging effectively with peda-gogical techniques employed?	3	3	0
4a	Responding positively to the teacher's approach by being engaged, stimulated, or enthused?	3	3	0
5a	Demonstrating confidence in approaching the teacher for their individual learning needs?	3	3	0
6a	Appearing to be learning through formative assessment techniques or procedures?	3	3	0
7a	Appearing to understand the requirements and standards of work for excellence?	1	1.5	0.5
8a	Actively engaging with learning activities in a manner that will aid understanding?	3	3	0
9a	Appearing to perceive curriculum structure and use it to develop their understanding?	2	2.5	0.5
10a	Engaging in activities to provide data for course, teaching or assessment improvement?	2.5	2	-0.5

Table 5: Observer responses for the observed sessions.

Quality Enhancement Suggested by Evidence

After both observations were completed and short reports for each observation episode had been returned to the observed teacher, a final report relating the changes in data between observations was compiled. In order to create a consistent structure and provide adequate explanatory notes for non-education academic staff a report template was constructed into which data and analyses could be edited. The following section reflects the final reporting format and content (PRO-Teaching Project, 2012).

As per the student evaluations of the teacher's teaching in the two episodes, the peer observers indicated high amounts of evidence supporting nearly all of the dimensions of good teaching. Key aspects of teaching for which observers recognized consistently high levels of evidence were:

- 1: clearly conveying learning aims and objectives;

- 2: demonstrating advanced levels of content knowledge;

- 3: use of effective pedagogical techniques;

- 4: personal characteristics that engage and stimulate students;

- 6: using effective formative assessment techniques;

- 8: actively encouraging students to engage with activities; and

- 9: demonstrating structured and coherent curriculum design.

It appeared to the observers that student behaviour supported similarly high levels of evidence in:

- 3a: responding positively to pedagogical techniques;

- 4a: responding positively to the teachers approach by maintaining engagement with learning;

- 6a: appearing to learn through formative assessment techniques, and 8a: actively engaging with activities in a purposeful manner that develops understanding.

A consistently moderate level of evidence was seen for only one dimension (7, 7a) which related to explanation and understanding of requirements and standards for excellence. For conceptual learning this was appropriate for the particular stage of the course. However the effective modelling of student behaviour and professional expectations in the conduct of each of the lessons was apparent.

Observation of the teacher revealed a slight increase between the first and second observation in evidence of dimension 5: demonstrating concern for individuals' learning needs. This was reflected in the enactment of some of the development ideas gleaned from the first observation. Observation of the students indicated some other slight increases in apparent evidence relating to:

- 1a: appearing to understand the learning aims and objectives;

- 2a: actively seeking examples from the teacher's content knowledge, 7a: appearing to understand the requirements and standards of work for excellence; and

- 9a: appearing to perceive curriculum structure and use it to develop understanding.

All of these small improvements related directly to the development ideas that were shared at the debriefing after the first observation. An increase in evidence is usually a good thing but can be tempered by different teaching context, difficulty of concepts being taught, level of engagement that relevant activities engender, and many other things. As all other things did not change between observation episodes it may be reasonable to assign increase in evidence to the successful implementation of the collaboratively derived developmental ideas.

The only reduction in evidence occurred in 10a: the apparent student engagement in activities relating to the provision of data for course, teaching or assessment improvement. A decrease or nil change in evidence could be due to various influences relating to the differences in content, activities and difficulty level experienced. It may also be that developmental ideas did not have further effect on that particular dimension or were not executed effectively given the teaching and learning context.

Generally speaking the observers were more critical than the students but appreciative of the uniformly high level of excellence of teaching demonstrated. Observers were able to discern micro-pedagogical increments between first and second episodes as feedback ideas were successfully enacted.

An Outcome of Quality Enhancement

Responses to the learning outcomes test question seeking the most important thing that the student learned indicated that in the first lesson 81% (22 out of 27) of students' responses matched the teacher's stated learning objectives. In the second lesson this figure was increased to 92% (24 out of 26). This can be interpreted as a slight improvement in the constructive alignment of learning objectives, learning and teaching activities, and assessment (Biggs, 1996). Supporting evidence from student evaluations or peer evaluations might indicate that the objectives were made clearer, or that engagement with activities was higher, or that formative assessment reinforced the attainment of learning objectives.

In this case both the students and peers observed increments in the student perception of clarity and understanding of learning objectives between episode one and episode two. Students also perceived that they received better formative feedback and were more highly challenged in the second lesson suggesting higher levels of engagement (Kuh, 2003). All of which confirms that enacting improvements based on feedback between episode one and two assisted in improving constructive alignment.

Analysing the frequency distribution graphs of each semester's mark allocations has the capacity to track relative performance of each student group. Improved student engagement with learning should be reflected in an elevated median mark indicating that more students achieved better learning outcomes; and, a reduction in the number of failures in the tail of the distribution indicating better outcomes for students experiencing limited levels of achievement. In this particular instance, a comparison of student mark distributions indicated that the median mark rose from 64% (a Pass grade) to 69% (a Credit grade) and the standard deviation (spread) of marks fell from 15.85 to 13.70 indicating a shorter tail to the distribution. At the same time the number of failures fell from 23 (11.1% of class) to 3 (2% of class) students, all of which suggests higher levels of student engagement enhancing learning outcomes as designated by the National Survey of Student Engagement (NSSE) data analysis (Carini et al., 2006). The comparative frequency distribution of marks is represented in Figure 2.

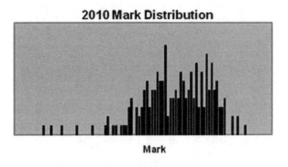

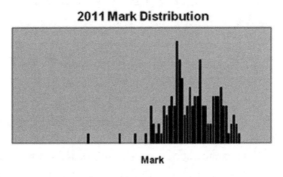

Figure 2: Comparative frequency distribution of marks.

There are limitations on the differential analyses between observed episodes and between offerings of the course. Between episodes there is relatively small room for movement indicated numerically in the quantitative domain. Between course offerings there were different student cohorts. However social systems sampling suggests that inter-cohort differences are averaged out over large population numbers. To make the leap from the use of PRO-Teaching to improve academics' learning about teaching to evidence the enhancement of student learning we compared the student evaluation of teaching in the previous year where the process was not used. The comparison confirmed incremental improvement of overall satisfaction on the course from 4.1 to 4.2 on a scale where 5 is the highest. All other areas pertaining to the student evaluation of the course revealed correspondingly incremental improvements across the board. The comparison of the student evaluation of teaching revealed incremental improvement in four of the six areas, while two areas received a decrease in incremental change. This decrease could be attributed to any array of influences relating to the differences in content, activities and difficulty level experienced by the students in the particular cohort. The comparison of student evaluations of teaching and the course appear in Table 6.

	2010	2011
Student evaluation of teaching		
This staff member presented material in a clearly organised way.	4.8	4.9
This staff member presented material in an interesting way.	4.8	4.7
This staff member treated students with respect.	4.4	4.7
This staff member showed a good knowledge of the subject matter.	4.9	4.9
Overall I am satisfied with the teaching of this staff member.	4.7	4.9
Overall, how effective was this lecturer/tutor in helping you to learn?	6.6	6.5
Student evaluation of course		
This course was well-organised.	4.2	4.4
The assessment was clear and fair.	3.9	4.0
I received helpful feedback on my assessment work.	3.8	4.1
This course engaged me in learning.	4.1	4.3
The teaching (lecturers, tutors, online etc) on this course was effective in helping me to learn.	4.2	4.4
Overall I am satisfied with the quality of this course.	4.1	4.2

Table 6: Student evaluations of course and teaching.

Teaching for Learning through Learning for Teaching - a Process and an Outcome

The PRO-Teaching mechanism recollected in the case study demonstrates the capacity to collect data to inform the constructive alignment within teaching episodes, student perceptions of teaching quality and observer perceptions of teaching quality enhancement. Effective implementation of the PRO-Teaching is contingent upon collegial support, trust and respect administered by accompanying guidelines, resources and supportive advice.

This process of quality enhancement is applicable to teachers with a range of content knowledge classroom proficiency. In this case the data indicated that the teacher is a highly engaged and an engaging teacher as evidenced by the uniformly high scores for each student evaluation question at each observed lesson. Even though the teacher is recognised to be highly proficient the data has still shown incremental enhancement in teaching quality. This highlights the benefit of the PRO-Teaching process to bring about enhanced learning outcomes for both the teacher and the students.

The wider PRO-Teaching project has involved 160 academics in training and the observation of more than 240 teaching episodes. Variants of the process have been developed for a range of teaching contexts including lectures, tutorials, workshops, 1-to-1-studio teaching and on-line course delivery. Over the duration of the project many participants have been awarded teaching citations and awards at group, university and national levels using PRO-Teaching evidence of impact on teaching and learning quality enhancement. Direct impact of peer observation has been gauged against student evaluation of courses and indicates for example, that in the Science, Engineering, Environment and Technology group 71% of staff engaged with PRO-Teaching elicited an incremental improvement in their student evaluations.

We contend that teaching for learning through learning for teaching is both a process and an outcome for multiple stakeholders participating in the sequenced episodes of peer observation of teaching. Figure 3 illustrates the participatory action research guided quality enhancement process that participants in PRO-Teaching undertake. With a directing question of how peer observation of teaching can be used to improve teaching quality data informed interventions are executed to improve both teaching and through this students' learning outcomes.

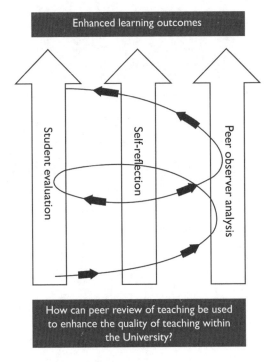

Figure 3: A guided quality enhancement process.

Through the presentation of this case study using data from multiple sources the link between PRO-teaching and the enhancement of student learning outcomes is explicitly evidenced when data from multiple sources is used. We conclude that the peer observation of teaching for learning that enables learning for teaching is both a process and an outcome of quality enhancement.

About the Authors

Christopher Klopper is Senior Lecturer in the School of Education and Professional Studies at Griffith University, Gold Coast Campus, Australia. He can be contacted at this email: c.klopper@griffith.edu.au

Steve Drew is Senior Lecturer in the Griffith Institute for Higher Education, Griffith University, Australia. He can be contacted at this email: s.drew@griffith.edu.au

Chapter Nine

Quality Attributes and Competencies for Transformative Teaching: a Theory of the Transformative Teacher

Sigrídur Halldórsdóttir

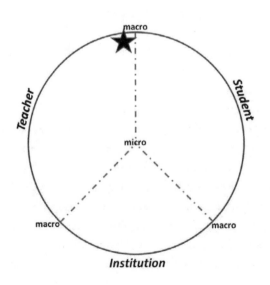

Introduction

In this chapter I present a theory of the transformative teacher. By the transformative teacher I mean a teacher, who is able to create a culture of quality, actively pursues quality as transformation and is, therefore, instrumental in student transformation. In my view transformative teaching (and the transformative teacher) is an important part of quality enhancement in Higher Education (HE). One of the overall objectives of HE is that students receive education of excellent quality. Quality assurance and quality enhancement have, therefore, become central activities at most universities and as Harvey and Williams (2010:4) have noted *"a genuine culture of quality is necessary"* (see also Nygaard *et al.*, this volume). In a rare paper where the teacher is included in a discussion about quality in HE, Andersson *et al.* (2009) rightly point out that quality in HE is produced at the confluence of students, programme content, the teacher, the planned teaching activities, and the teaching culture and traditions of the university. They claim that understanding the processes in this conflated domain is imperative if we are to enhance quality in HE. They further assert that if quality is to be enhanced every part of an HE institution needs to develop an awareness of how to support student learning effectively and efficiently. They state that such awareness can be developed by teacher educative programs, rewarding teaching competencies and enhancing dialogue about teaching and learning. The theory presented in this chapter can be used as a basis for such dialogue. Before I present the theory however, let us look at what is meant by 'quality' and 'quality transformation'.

'Quality' is difficult to define since it is a multidimensional and complex concept (Andersson *et al.*, 2009). In an excellent paper, 'From quality assurance to quality enhancement in the European Higher Education area', Gvaramadze (2008:445) claims that quality is a continuous process concerned with values, internal processes and effectiveness rather than input and/or output. Here, he sees two important concepts: *"quality as transformation"*, a process of changing individuals; and *"quality as enhancement"*, a process of changing institutions. Quality as enhancement, he claims, focuses on *"the continuous search for permanent improvement"* which is, according to Vlasceanu *et al.* (2004), a primary responsibility of HE institutions where quality enhancement occurs through structured enhancement measures for the improvement of quality. Harvey (2004) contends that HE institutions develop quality enhancement mechanisms within an internal quality culture in accordance with their institutional mission and objectives.

In line with many contemporary HE scholars, Gvaramadze (2008) stresses the importance of placing the learner as the central figure in 'quality as transformation'. In his view, education should enhance students' educational experience and empower them as critical, reflective and lifelong learners. This requires complementing value-added measures of enhancement with empowerment mechanisms. Empowerment in this sense means *"giving power to participants in order to influence their trans-formation"* (Gvaramadze, 2008:446). Transformation is not just linked to learner self-empowerment but also leads to increased awareness, confidence and critical reflection (Roper, 1992 cited by Gvaramadze, 2008). However, many academics hold on to content-oriented didactic models of teaching and, as a consequence, find it challenging to adopt forms of teaching that embrace approaches leading to active student engagement, in spite of the reported effectiveness of such forms of learning (Kember, 2009). This pedagogic inertia may inhibit or delay such transformation in students (Harvey & Knight, 1996).

Long after Keller's (1968) influential paper 'Good-bye, teacher' was published, teachers' influence on students has remained a well-debated issue (Halldorsdottir, 1990; Schuck *et al.*, 2008). While I agree with Kember (2009) that we need to shift from teacher-centred forms of teaching to student-centred approaches, I want to challenge the assumption implied in the discourse on quality in HE that a transformative teacher is unimportant. My aim in this chapter is to present a *Theory of the Transformative Teacher in HE: an Essential Aspect of Quality as Transformation* and thus the facilitation of students' self-development of higher-order thinking skills and transferable competencies as well as an improvement in overall student learning outcomes.

Development of my Theory

The question I am answering is: *"What kind of personal attributes and competencies are needed for a teacher in HE to be able to participate in a process of empowering and changing students within the framework of quality as transformation?"*

I start by describing the method I use for theory development, then theory in general and finally the personal attributes and the competencies of the transformative teacher in HE according to the theory.

Method

The method I used for the theory development was theory synthesis as described by Walker and Avant (2004) (see Table 1).

STAGE	ACTIONS AT EACH STAGE
Stage 1	**Key concepts and key statements, on which the theory was based, were specified.** The theory is based on more than 30 years' experience as a teacher and administrator in HE; listening to students about what empowers and dis-empowers them as students; as well as published research papers and scholarly works. In this first stage of the theory development, the above-mentioned research papers were critically evaluated and used to construct analytical frameworks as the basis for the theory on *The Transformative Teacher in HE: an Essential Aspect of Quality as Transformation*.
Stage 2	**The literature was reviewed to identify factors related to the key concepts or key statements and the relationship between these.** At this stage I reviewed numerous research papers to compare the analytic framework from stage one to the literature, using the constant comparative method for confirmation and clarification. Many of the papers reviewed were directly or indirectly connected with *The Transformative Teacher in HE: an Essential Aspect of Quality as Transformation*.
Stage 3	**Concepts and statements about *The Transformative Teacher in HE* were organised into an integrated representation of it.** Having collected a representative listing of relational statements pertinent to one or more key concepts, these were organized in terms of the overall pattern of relationships among variables. In *Figures 1, 2* and *3* there is an overview of the different aspects of *The Transformative Teacher in HE: an Essential Aspect of Quality as Transformation* as it was constructed from the papers and scholarly works used as the basis for the theory development.

Table 1: Summary of Principal Stages in Construction of the Theory (after Walker and Avant (2004).

Walker and Avant (2004) claim that more theory synthesis is needed to advance practice disciplines. Since teaching is a practice discipline, I looked for and found a defensible fit. In theory synthesis, the theorist combines isolated pieces of information that hitherto may be unconnected and then constructs a theory from various (and possibly multitudinous) sources such as the findings of studies and scholarly writings. It enables theorists to organise and integrate a large number of findings into a single theory. Theory construction using theory synthesis comprises three principle stages. Table 1 highlights the three stages and how each stage was carried out. Although a full description of the theory synthesisation process is outside the scope of this book, this method can be compared with painting a picture. During Stage 1 the picture is drawn. In Stage 2 other frames of viewing (the literature in this case) are used to compare the 'picture' drawn with other similar 'pictures' for confirmation and clarification. In stage 3 the 'picture' is presented.

Description of the theory

Teachers in HE face the complex challenge of bringing together many different factors in their work. According to my theory, the transformative teacher is personally and professionally developed, succeeds in making students feel cared for as learners, communicates with them in an empowering manner, and has a positive partnership with them aimed at their learning and transformation. Who the teacher is, as a person, and the teacher's personal attributes and core competencies combine into a whole (see Figure 1). I postulate that when HE teachers are transformative, students benefit from their competence by being transformed. This empowers them as learners to do their best in their studies; it increases their self-development of higher-order thinking skills and transferable competencies as well as improving overall learning outcomes.

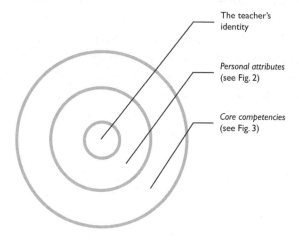

The teacher's identity

Personal attributes (see Fig. 2)

Core competencies (see Fig. 3)

Figure 1: Overview of the theory of the Transformative Teacher.

In my theory, a transformative teacher is like a gardener nurturing students; a sculptor shaping students' thinking and moulding the way in which they become members of a particular professional community; and a personal guide, who steers students through their studies and whose guidance is adapted to the study needs of the students during their transformational learning journeys. The teacher utilises all appropriate communications to empower the students – for instance, by providing information, facilitating discourse and supporting the construction of appropriate knowledge – all with the objective of empowering the students to pursue excellence. The teacher enhances the educational experience and improves student engagement in their studies and their overall learning outcomes. Hence, the transformative teacher in HE creates a culture of quality and actively pursues quality as transformation.

Personal Attributes for Transformative Teaching

According to the theory, the transformative teacher's personal attributes and competencies are necessary to transform students and empower their self-development of higher-order thinking skills and transferable competencies in HE. Figure 2 is a schematic representation of the personal attributes of the transformative teacher in HE. I assert that each of these personal attributes affects the other attributes.

In my theory, personal attributes needed for transformative teaching are: critical thinking, caring, authenticity, self-knowledge, assertiveness and creativity (see Figure 2).

Figure 2: Personal Attributes for Transformative Teaching.

Critical thinking. The transformative teacher is a critical thinker. I postulate in my theory that critical thinking develops through the interplay of knowledge and experience. The transformative teacher also knows how to help students develop critical thinking and reflective judgement – for example, through case-based teaching with complex, real-life scenarios.

Caring. The teacher really cares about students' learning within the professional domain and cares for each student's individual learning and transformation. This caring lies at the heart of teaching according to the theory; to want what is best for students as learners. It prompts the teacher to pursue excellence in teaching and strive to find creative ways to contribute to students' learning and transformation.

Authenticity. The transformative teacher is authentic, trustworthy and genuine. According to the theory, authenticity is essential in teaching because being authentic is at the heart of all interpersonal relationships.

Self-knowledge. The transformative teacher has insight into his/her self and has knowledge and understanding of his/her own nature, abilities, and limitations. Self-knowledge is fundamental for virtue and essential for ethical and meaningful life. It is a critical component of my theory.

Assertiveness. The transformative teacher is assertive and has the courage to affirm his/her own point of view without either aggression or submission; neither aggressively assuming a position of dominance nor permitting another to ignore or deny one's right or point of view. The transformative teacher respects boundaries for self and others.

Creativity. The transformative teacher is creative and unafraid to use innovations in teaching and study methods in order to increase student learning and transformation. The teacher raises student awareness of what creativity means in different contexts and encourages forms of learning that will enable students to develop the forms of creativity most appropriate for their field of study and future careers.

As an essential ingredient for achieving quality as transformation, the transformative teacher in HE must be multifaceted. This is explained by the following exploration of the core competencies required to be a transformative teacher.

The Core Competencies for Transformative Teaching

According to the theory, the transformative teacher has seven core competencies. These are: interpersonal competence, teaching competence, caring competence, existential competence, ethical competence, competence in empowering students and competence in self-reflection and self-development as a person and as a teacher (see Figure 3). The teacher is capable of empowering communication and partnership with students. For many students this partnership is the difference between perceived empowerment and disempowerment. The teacher's message is: *"let's work together towards your learning and transformation"*. Figure 3 is a schematic representation of the core competencies of the transformative teacher in HE. I postulate that each of these core competencies affects the other competencies.

Figure 3: Core Competencies for Transformative Teaching.

Interpersonal competence. The transformative teacher is socially competent and has interpersonal competence. This involves two inter-related aspects: communication competence and connection competence. In *communication competence* the teacher is competent in initiating communication, in appropriately communicating with students in HE, and in active listening. In *connection competence* the teacher is competent in connecting with students and building a partnership based on mutual trust. The teacher is competent in building a 'bridge' between teacher and students and in creating mutual trust where the students feel free to reveal to the teacher hindrances to their learning and transformation. This enables the teacher to do his or her best to remove the perceived barriers with timely and targeted interventions. Finally, the teacher is competent in keeping an appropriate distance so that the connection or partnership is kept at a professional level.

Teaching competence. The teacher has knowledge of the subject matter and is competent in facilitating students' learning and transformation that improves student learning outcomes. Through the teacher's creativity, self-knowledge and critical thinking, the teacher is unafraid to use innovations in HE teaching and is able to inspire students to do their best in meeting learning outcomes. The transformative teacher creates a culture of quality and actively pursues quality as transformation.

Caring competence. The transformative teacher is competent in conveying his or her caring for the students' learning and transformation, both collectively and individually. Caring competence also includes being attentive to the individual student, giving professional and honest feedback, and being interested in the student's future. The transformative teacher is warm and open to students and cares about their learning needs. The teacher displays understanding, can demonstrate good will and has the courage to give of him- or herself and thus be a partaker in the transformation of students.

Existential competence. The teacher has existential competence within the professional domain. This means that the teacher is able to be present in the moment, the here and now, really listening to the students and being present in a situation and in a dialogue. The teacher has emotional competence, is emotionally literate and is competent in giving undivided attention to students when needed.

Ethical competence. The transformative teacher is ethically mature and respectful of students and their right to self-determination. The teacher is morally responsible and discreet about all confidential matters and is able to take into consideration the culture of the students. The teacher has integrity and is professionally responsible and accepts responsibility for any decisions s/he makes. The teacher is capable of being the spokesperson and advocate for students when this is necessary and appropriate.

Competence in empowering students. The teacher is able to empower students as learners. This increases their motivation to learn and transform and facilitates learning and transformation in students by creating an empowering atmosphere of study and by increasing their knowledge of what is expected of them. In turn, the teacher will use various creative ways to inspire students to pursue excellence. The teacher is also competent in decreasing unnecessary stress in students and is competent in creating a learning environment that is collegial, thereby providing a sense of control.

Competence in personal and professional reflection and development. The transformative teacher is reflective and knows and nurtures him- or herself, both personally and professionally. The teacher knows his/her own strengths, weaknesses and limitations and is competent in managing personal stress. The teacher knows his/her own attitudes and feelings, has a clear self-image and sufficient self-confidence and professional confidence. The teacher is competent in maintaining his or her professional development – for example, by making use of information technology, by being open to constant knowledge development, and by constantly constructing new knowledge. Finally, the teacher is competent in doing research, thus contributing to his/her own ability to construct new knowledge to share with the profession (see also Huet *et al.*, this volume).

The Effects of the Transformative Teacher

The influence of the students' encounters with a transformative teacher is best described as *empowering and transformational*. It is postulated in the theory that the transformative teacher motivates students in an important way to learn and grow, both personally and professionally. The students develop increased interest in the subject and their learning and growth gives them a sense of accomplishment and achievement. The students feel accepted, develop positive self-image as learners, and develop a sense of security that they're on the right track by getting positive feedback on a job well done. The transformative teacher is able to give students hope and optimism and this encourages and challenges them to do better.

Discussion of Findings

Schools exist to change people (Sizer & Sizer, 1999) and the theory presented here is developed to answer the question: What kind of personal attributes and competencies are needed for teacher in HE to be able to participate in a process of changing students within the framework of quality as transformation? According to the theory, the personal attributes of the transformative teacher include critical thinking, caring, authenticity, self-knowledge, assertiveness and creativity and the core competencies include interpersonal competence, teaching competence, caring competence, existential competence, ethical competence, competence in empowering students and competence in self-reflection and self-development as a person and as a teacher.

Personal Attributes for Transformative Teaching

The concept of teaching as praxis being supplanted by notions of greater centrality of the student learning experience, with the teacher's role transformed from 'instructor' to 'facilitator', has been discussed by many authors (Gordon & Fittler, 2004; Schuck *et al.*, 2008). Andersson *et al.* (2009) rightly point out that, in order to enhance student learning, teachers need competencies in teaching and learning, enabling them to make the right choices to support student learning effectively and efficiently. I believe that empowerment of students and promotion of student learning and transformation is the goal and measure of quality teaching. Korthagen (2004) reminds us of the complexity of teaching and refers to Hamachek's (1999:209) wise words *"consciously, we teach what we know; unconsciously, we teach who we are"*. In line with this wisdom, my theory attempts to delineate who the teacher is as a person and what personal attributes and competencies s/he has. As Korthagen (2004) asserts, the question 'what is a good teacher?', and the complexity of this question, seems to be overlooked by policy-makers.

Being self-analytical is part of the process of being a teacher (Cambone, 1990). We have to understand ourselves if we are to understand others (Moss, 2005). The world needs people who can combine their knowledge, skills and capabilities in creative and innovative ways to find and solve complex problems (Jackson, 2006); creativity is important for our well-being. Higher education needs to embrace and nurture creativity in order to instil propensity for it in our graduates. This is crucial if universities are to succeed in fulfilling the important role they play in preparing people for an uncertain and increasingly complex world of work; a world that requires people to utilise their creative as well as their analytical capacities (Jackson, 2006). Kristjánsson (2006) asserts that the emotionally intelligent person – that is, the person who has mastered 'self-science' – has learned the arts of cooperation and negotiating compromise and has 'emotional vigour' in which creativity, originality and assertiveness play important roles.

Kristjánsson (2006:49) reminds us of Goleman's (1995) assertion that the study of emotional intelligence gives rise to an educational science of the self. This involves 'self-awareness' combined with mindfulness and the ability to recognise one's own feelings and learn to handle difficult emotions with non-judgmental self-observation. It also involves 'self-control' through self-regulatory strategies. However, as Kristjánsson (2006) points out, Goleman fails to realise that through his account of self-control, he ignores his own Aristotelian rhetoric about the need to synthesise head and heart. It can be argued that we often ignore the reality that some professions can be emotionally challenging. In the health sciences, for example, one may be attending to people who are under great stress and are filled with sorrow and deep, unexpressed suffering. We have to teach them emotion-regulating virtues such as courage, which regulates fear. But as teachers we have to start with ourselves. Brownlee (2004) advises that teachers, like all knowledge workers, need to be self-regulated, critically reflective, lifelong learners.

Core Competencies for Transformative Teaching

In my theory, the transformative teacher has to have interpersonal competence. Bartlett (2005) points out that Freire (1990) argues that educators should reject a 'banking' model of education, in which the teacher 'owns' knowledge and 'deposits' it in students. Instead, she asserts, Freire promoted a 'problem-posing' method in which teachers and students learn together, through dialogue. His problem-posing education relies on a transformed and transformational, respectful relationship between teacher and student. For Freire, all learning is relational; knowledge is produced in interaction.

Knowledge emerges through invention and re-invention resulting in the inter-subjective 'synthesis' of new knowledge where student autonomy is respected and the teachers build upon student knowledge (Bartlett, 2005). Freire also promoted authentic caring and mutual respect between teacher and students and building emotional connections. He also asserted that relationships be prioritised over things and ideas (Bartlett, 2005). Lundberg and Schreiner (2004) found in their study (n=4,501) that effective relationships with teachers were stronger predictors of learning than student background characteristics. Noddings (1988:218) sees morality as an educational aim and calls for "relational ethics" rooted in and dependent on natural caring. Witmer (2005) is among those who have concluded that relationships are the foundations of effective education. Ramsden (2008) claims that we need to enable students to find resources of courage, resilience and empathy that traverse national boundaries and that quality systems have to be developed which realise a vision of HE as an engaged partnership between students and providers (see also Bartholomew *et al.*, this volume).

Many books and papers have been written about teaching competence in HE (for example Halldorsdottir, 1990; Noddings, 1988). Typically, this literature highlights the need for professional knowledge and experience, professional presentation of teaching material, high standards for self and students, academic fairness, and caution to avoid impersonal grading and the overuse of lecture without discussion. Smeyers (2005) reminds us that Socrates claimed he was ignorant and denied being a teacher. He did not tell his students the answers he knew; instead, he led them to discover answers for themselves. His ironic insistence that he neither knew what virtue was nor was capable of teaching it disappears into a mechanism for motivating otherwise unenthusiastic students. This is in line with Heidegger (1968) who claimed that teaching is more difficult than learning because what teaching calls for is 'to let learn' (cited by Dall'Alba, 2005).

According to my theory, the transformative teacher not only cares but has caring competence and is able to build a caring community (Bruce & Stellern, 2005) and foster growth in 'the other' (Mayeroff, 1971). Nel Noddings has been untiring in reminding educators of the importance of caring within the educational context. Noddings (1986:497) asserts that 'natural caring' – the sort of response made when we want to care for another – establishes the ideal for 'ethical caring'. Ethical caring imitates this ideal in its efforts to institute, maintain, or re-establish natural caring, steadfastly promoting both the welfare of the other and that of the relation. She suggests that all human beings will benefit from a heightened *"moral sensitivity"* and states that from the perspective of an ethic of caring, development of the whole person is necessarily our concern. Furthermore, she claims that teaching requires caring for the individuals we teach. Like many other educators, she quotes Aristotle saying of the teacher-learner relationship that it is a *"moral type of friendship"* not on fixed terms: it makes a gift, or does whatever it does, *"as to a friend"*. Noddings states that an ethic of caring guides us to ask: What effect will this have on the person I teach? What effect will it have on the caring community we are trying to build?

In my theory, emotional competence is an essential part of existential competence. Goleman (1995) asserts that academic intelligence, as measured by IQ tests and carefully nourished in the typical school curricula, offers virtually no preparation for the turmoil of life. He claims that cultivating emotional intelligence at home, in schools and in workplaces can serve as an effective antidote to the historic overemphasis on purely cognitive skills. This notion is also supported by Kristjánsson (2006:41). Goleman emphasises the importance of interpersonal and intrapersonal intelligences as well as 'emotional intelligence', defined here as: *"the capacity to process emotional information accurately and efficiently, including the capacity to perceive, assimilate, understand, and manage emotions"* (Mayer *et al.*, 2000, cited by Kristjánsson, 2006:41).

My theory emphasises that the transformative teacher has ethical competence and is a moral person. By the term 'moral', I am referring to *"normative considerations about the enhancement of other people's good or well-being, as well as of one's own"* (Kristjánsson, 2006:45). I am not alone in believing that a teacher has an ethical function. Noddings (1986:509) claims that teaching is a *"constitutively ethical activity"*. She asserts that it is a *"moral type of friendship"* in which teachers and students work together to construct and achieve common ends and those who enter classrooms become part of this ethical activity. Tarc (2006:287) argues that educators can be seen as those who *"dare to respond to the call to the ethical"*. However, she claims, educators often heed this call without fully realising its metaphysical heritage and may unwittingly engage in ethical teachings that violate the uniqueness of 'the other'.

Kristjánsson (2006:52) claims that, for Goleman (1995), the key to the link between emotional intelligence and morality lies in the emotion of empathy. Furthermore, emotional intelligence skills, in particular self-awareness, breed empathy and empathy leads to caring, altruism, and compassion. Schuck *et al.* (2008) claim that it is the teacher's responsibility to ask what students should learn, in what context, and with what goals. They suggest considering ethical practice in HE as encompassing professionalism and remind us that ethical considerations are intrinsically contextual and have to do with relationships in specific contexts. Ethical practice, they claim, means reflecting on and revising the assumptions that underpin our teaching. It should be our goal in all of education to produce caring, moral persons (Noddings, 1986). Lundberg and Schreiner (2004) found that satisfying relationships with faculty members and frequent interactions with them, especially those who encourage students to work harder, were strong predictors of effective learning.

Student Involvement in Quality as Transformation

Schuck *et al.* (2008) have called for a broader understanding of teaching quality and assert that using students as 'critical friends', and encouraging their input at a deep level, is a valuable way to enhance teaching – even if it can be a challenging task. Ramsden (2008) claims that student involvement in quality processes should start from the idea of building learning communities. He points out that universities and colleges are increasingly positioning students as 'engaged collaborators' rather than subordinate associates in assessment, teaching, course planning and the improvement of quality.

Hindrances to Student Transformation

Korthagen (2004) rightly points out that a 'good teacher' will not always show 'good teaching'. Although someone may have excellent competencies, an inspirational self and mission, the type of the environment – for example, a hostile student group – may put serious limits on the teacher. Moreover, it is hard to see how further progress in enhancing student transformation can occur if attention is not given to amending the fact that many teachers in HE feel that, in comparison with research, high quality teaching is under-rewarded and unrecognised by universities and colleges (Ramsden, 2008). I agree with Rodgers and Raider-Roth (2006) about the present devaluing of the teaching profession, which is leading to an educational climate in which teaching is defined through lists of behaviours, standards and measures, while the intangible aspects of effective teaching are largely ignored. I worry with them that we are in danger of losing sight of what it means to teach. Therefore, through my theory, I am offering an alternative paradigm.

Benefits from being a Transformative Teacher

The influence of the students' interaction with a transformative teacher is best described as empowerment and transformation. I am aware that empowerment is a term that has been open to criticism. My understanding of empowerment is that the teacher strengthens a student's self-confidence by helping the student to recognise his/her own strengths and capacities. Student learning can include students' factual knowledge, critical analytic skills or engagement in the topic (Schuck *et al.*, 2008). Furthermore, transformative teachers, as framed by Gvaramadze (2008), support individual learners in their learning experiences to develop as autonomous learners. They encourage students' reflexivity, critical thinking, self-reflection. They make students aware of the teaching-learning processes and institutional culture, and they promote student identity and membership in the institution and its community. All of this has a positive effect for creating an effective communicative learning environment through which universities can orient themselves towards continuous quality as transformation.

Application of the Theory

Teachers in HE can use the theory for self-reflection and as a basis for dialogue with other teachers about quality as transformation. It will thus be possible to identify factors which could be improved, with the objective of achieving student transformation as well as enhanced teacher well-being and job satisfaction. It could also be used by managers as a tool in personnel interviews aimed at enhancing quality as transformation or by academic staff development units to support academic development. I agree with Nye *et al.* (2004) who maintain that it is fundamental to educational research to define whether individual teachers differ dramatically in their effectiveness in promoting students' academic achievement.. They rightly claim that if differences in teacher effectiveness are large, then identification of more effective teachers and the factors that cause them to be more effective is important, both for basic research and for educational reform.

Conclusion

Current approaches are reorienting the focus from quality assurance towards contextualised quality enhancement and quality as transformation. The processes of transforming individuals and institutions are becoming the primary responsibility of universities and their stakeholders as they search for sustainable improvement. Within that vision is a commitment to create internal quality cultures since such cultures contribute to vibrant educational and intellectual attainment and enhance learners abilities to move towards self-empowerment, increased awareness, confidence and critical reflection. Such transformation enhances students' educational experience and empowers them as critical, reflective and lifelong learners. Even the mere discourse of quality has the potential to broaden the quality agenda and make it more critically self-reflective. I see the theory presented here as a platform for further research and theory development as well as an aid in the improvement of an HE institution's teaching and learning mission, with a clear focus on the transformative teacher as an essential factor in quality as transformation.

About the Author

Sigrídur Halldórsdóttir is a Professor and Dean of Graduate Studies, School of Health Sciences, at the University of Akureyri, Akureyri, Iceland. She can be contacted at this email: sigridur@unak.is

Chapter Ten

Enhancing the Enhancers: Action Research as a Quality Enhancement Tool

Lesley Lawrence and Helen Corkill

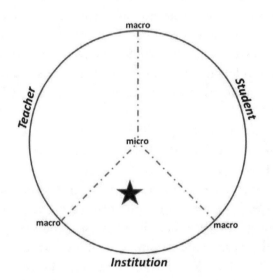

Introduction

This chapter examines *"action research as a quality enhancement mecha-nism"* (Kember, 2000:23). The case presented focuses upon introducing an assessed action research project into the curriculum of a part-time Postgraduate Certificate in Academic Practice (PgCAP) at the

University of Bedfordshire, UK. This university-wide programme is primarily intended for staff in the early stages of their academic career and therefore inexperienced in teaching in higher education. In a University where the curriculum is driven to a large extent by professional and vocational demands, participants teach in a variety of disciplines ranging from Art and Design to Computing, Education, Nursing and Biomedical Science. The PgCAP programme supports participants' development as capable and creative higher education academic practitioners, competent to enhance the student learning experience. At any one time, there are typically around 75 staff drawn from across all faculties of the University undertaking one of the two 30 credit modules which comprise the PgCAP.

The first module, Effective Academic Practice, addresses the key elements and issues that affect participants' professional practice and development. The second module, Enhancing Learner Development, promotes a more strategic and evidence-informed approach to evaluating students' learning. It was into this second module that an assessed action research project was introduced in 2009. As described in this chapter, this intervention was followed by a process of continuous and review and change within the programme, akin to an incrementalist model (Allen & Layer, 1995).

The participants on the PgCAP programme face an intriguing scenario, assuming the dual identities of staff and student thus providing a noteworthy dimension to this case (see Figure 1). In adopting the persona of first-year student, staff-as-students often develop a heightened sense of empathy with their own students as they struggle to master new technologies, manage group work or submit assessed coursework on time. Ultimately, the staff-as-students are aiming to meet the learning outcomes of a postgraduate award, one key outcome being the ability to demonstrate an evidence-informed, self-reflective approach to the continuous development of academic practice. Concurrently, as individual members of staff, participants are expected to fulfil their responsibilities as enhancers of quality, not only developing and enhancing their own practice, but also actively evaluating its effectiveness. Further, it was intended that the dissemination activities embedded into the action research approach would support the development of participants' departmental and faculty practices as well as help inform the future enhancement of institutional teaching and learning strategy. All participants in the PgCAP are therefore encouraged to present the findings of their action research at the University's annual conference.

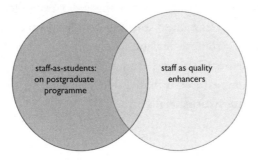

Figure 1: Dual identities of PgCAP programme participants.

A further dimension (represented in Figure 2) concerns the key role played by the programme leader of the PgCAP. The programme is delivered by staff within the University of Bedfordshire's Centre for Learning Excellence (CLE), a central strategic department responsible for promoting and supporting effective teaching and learning across the whole University. The Head of Academic Professional Development, one of the authors of this chapter, is based within the CLE. She holds a cross-institutional quality enhancement role, including that of taking the academic leadership for the PgCAP as a whole and specifically for the module around which the intervention in this chapter is based. Thus the PgCAP sits centre stage within the University and is ideally placed to act as a conduit for quality enhancement.

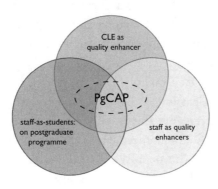

Figure 2: Quality enhancement at the intersection.

Whilst offering readers an insight into a specific initiative in one institution, this case may be sufficiently generalisable to have application to similar settings. As we found, the evidence-informed nature of action research can empower staff to make changes, for example: designing an alternative technology-enhanced learning activity; expecting students to self-assess work to promote real understanding of assessment criteria; and engaging students with developing presentation skills. Before focussing upon the action research initiative itself, the chapter situates the case both nationally and institutionally.

Situating the Case

The University of Bedfordshire, like all UK universities, has experienced a period of rapid expansion and change over the past twenty years, leading to concerns about maintaining and enhancing standards and quality within a widening participation imperative. The Dearing inquiry into higher education in England (NCIHE, 1997) recommended that all permanent staff with teaching responsibilities should undergo a programme of training on an accredited programme. The Institute for Learning and Teaching in Higher Education (ILTHE) was established in 2001 in order to support and inform the professional development and recognition of staff and was superseded by the Higher Education Academy (HEA) in 2004. The PgCAP, like many similar HEA-accredited programmes in the UK, has a curriculum aligned to the UK Professional Standards Framework (UK PSF) (UK PSF, 2011). The Higher Education Statistics Agency's (HESA) remit to record and monitor teaching qualifications of staff from 2012-13 coincides with an incremental rise in student tuition fees. Alongside other external factors, this heightens the pressure on delivering a curriculum which offers a quality learning experience and added value to the student.

Within the new UK Quality Code for Higher Education (QAA, 2012), the section on learning and teaching refers to the twin bedfellows, assurance and enhancement. The Quality Assurance Agency for Higher Education (QAA) defines enhancement as *"the process of taking deliberate steps at institutional level to improve the quality of learning opportunities"* (HEA, 2008:20). Quality enhancement is ultimately the responsibility of individual higher education institutions; the institutional sub-culture likewise requires enhancement to be a responsibility of the individual academic. Institutional programmes such as the PgCAP are designed to assist the induction of new staff into such a culture. As Trowler and Bamber (2005) note, a programme must be properly resourced and measured, and aligned to institutional policy. The University of Bedfordshire's Education Strategy 2008-13 states that: *"The effective delivery of our curriculum to a diverse student body in an ever-changing world requires staff who are knowledgeable and flexible facilitators of the learning process"* (University of Bedfordshire, 2008:5).

Not only should staff to be flexible, but: *"The curriculum must no longer be made uniform and fixed for long periods by means of degree programme regulations, but be variable and adaptable to current needs, for example, in professional life"* (Peters, 2000:12).

In 2008, the University undertook a whole-institution curriculum review focusing on enhancing quality by promoting and incorporating into the undergraduate curriculum what it termed as personalised learning, realistic learning and employability (Atlay et al., 2008). The PgCAP was aligned with this curriculum model during 2009. All programme teams across the University had been given a degree of structure and direction whilst being encouraged to be creative in application (Lawrence, 2010). This philosophy clearly resonates with a view of quality enhancement that: *"relies on the ability to...promote a culture of transformation in which innovation and change are valued; explore alternative approaches to doing things, rather than relying on tried and tested methods; undertake self-evaluation"* (Brown, 1999:46).

Such an ethos underpinned the approach adopted by the programme team during institutional periodic review and HEA re-accreditation in 2008-09. A key outcome of this activity was the action research intervention which is described in this chapter. This was aimed at encouraging participant staff-as-students on the programme to adopt a similar ethos in their own practice.

The Case Study

Largely aimed at inexperienced teaching staff, the PgCAP espouses the five key concepts in higher education teaching and learning to be found in similar postgraduate certificates in Australia and New Zealand as well as in the UK: constructive alignment; student approaches to learning; scholarship of teaching; assessment-driven learning and reflective practice (Kandlbinder & Peseta, 2009). On reviewing the programme however, the team was acutely aware of the common criticism of reflective practice, namely, that of reflection not being followed by action (COBE, 2005). Indeed, specifically relating to higher education programmes underpinned by reflective practice, the literature has pointed to "*inconclusive evidence as to the effectiveness of programmes for new academic staff that promote 'reflective practice'*" (Kahn et al., 2008:162). This was reaffirmed by the programme's external examiner who advocated the need for: "*the reflective elements in the programme to be more related to 'so what'? How for example, does reflection lead to learning and/or action, and ultimately to enhancing the student learning experience?*" (University of Bedfordshire, 2009a).

Such deficiency was addressed through adding a key learning outcome, namely that participants should be able to demonstrate: "*an evidence-informed, theoretical, self-reflective approach to the continuous development of your academic practice*". It was hoped that doing so would foster the development of "*a reflexive, critical, inquiry-based approach to learning and teaching ... [providing] an impetus for change*" (Brew, 2006:xii).

The programme team hypothesised that enabling participants to meet the additional programme learning outcome referred to above was achievable through incorporating action research into the curriculum, with an assessment that required participants to: *produce a report ...articulating your action research project findings and to be reflecting upon the process you underwent when critically reviewing the one aspect of your work-based practice you had opted to examine*" (University of Bedfordshire, 2009b:5).

Action research offered an appropriate solution. From numerous descriptions, perhaps action research within an education context can be succinctly viewed as: "*a method used for improving educational practice. It involves action, evaluation and reflection and, based on gathered evidence, changes in practice are implemented*" (Koshy, 2010:1).

Introducing Action Research into the Curriculum: the Need for Action rather than Unconnected Reflection

Action research has enjoyed a substantial revival since the late 1990s and is widely used in a variety of professional workplace and educational settings. Diverse private and public sector organisations including the World Bank and UNESCO now employ action research techniques within the workplace. Continuing professional development schemes increasingly link to evaluative practices, projects, participatory training and personal development planning, thus beginning to link higher education curriculum and practices more closely to the wider workplace. Action research has often been applied to the development of teaching and became widely used in the school sector as a means of investigating teacher quality enhancement. Stenhouse (1975:142) claimed that *"curriculum research and development ought to belong to the teacher".* Within higher education, the use of action research as a *"quality enhancement mechanism for learning and teaching"* (Kember, 2000:23) is less extensively used though not new (for example, Swann & Ecclestone, 1999; Dexter & Seden, 2012). More associated with school teacher training programmes, action research plays a less significant part within the curriculum of a HEA-accredited programme.

The use of action research process models are useful in introducing inexperienced university staff to the notion of building cycles of continual improvement in practice together with a commitment to bring about change. In the case of the PgCAP, participants were directed to Norton's (2009) ITDEM model, a five-stage process consisting of: Identifying a problem/paradox/issue/difficulty (Step 1); Thinking of ways of tackling the problem (Step 2); Doing it (Step 3); Evaluating it (actual research findings) (Step 4); and Modifying future practice (Step 5). The programme team had deliberated over whether what was being introduced was action research or action learning (Revans, 1982) and in choosing action research, drew on constructive comparisons of the two concepts (McGill & Beaty, 1995; Kember, 2000).

The action research assessment task became part of a re-developed module, Enhancing Learner Development, designed and successfully re-validated and re-accredited to encourage participants to act as change agents to enhance student learning. The module adopts a blended learning approach, delivered in blocks of structured online learning using the University's virtual learning environment, and supported by occasional face-to-face workshops. Underpinned by assessment for student learning (Tennant *et al.*, 2010), a clear relationship between learning outcomes, online learning blocks, workshops, and assessments was articulated. The introduction of action research into the PgCAP programme in September 2009 was followed by its continuous review and change over a period of three years (2009-2012). The main changes are summarised in Table 1 and outcomes are then discussed.

Cohort	Impetus for change →	Main and/or planned changes
2009-10 (1)	Critical review of programme (2008-09). Changing higher education environment. Innovative institutional curriculum framework.	Design of action research assessment element in Enhancing Learner. Development module (50% weighting) approved during institutional review/ HEA re-accreditation.
2010-11 (2)	External examiner feedback. Participant engagement concerns and feedback.	Greater personalisation and flexibility in the action research task. Weighting increased to 70% in the module.
2011-12 (3)	Programme team and participant feedback.	Further negotiation of task outcomes. Group tutorials introduced. Justification of project as action research.
2012-13 (4)	Content analysis of final assessment (July 2012). Writing this chapter.	Greater encouragement to publish work – share and disseminate. Extending peer support element.

Table 1: Action research and the PgCAP: summary of key changes.

As this action research intervention was not conceived as a research project back in 2009, no substantive numerical data collection can be reported. Adding to views of participants and the external examiner, however, we also draw upon findings from content analysis undertaken on the 2011-12 cohort's final Learning at Work assessment submissions. This analysis entailed dividing the text into content areas (Graneheim

& Lundman, 2004). For example, within any source of learning stated, was learning from action research specifically mentioned, and what did this entail? Acknowledging that *"a text always involves multiple meanings and there is always some degree of interpretation"* (Graneheim & Lundman, 2004:106), was there a sense of the participant grasping the essence of action research and the notion of an evidence-informed approach to continually evaluating and changing practice? If mentioning action research, did participants have plans to disseminate their findings and continue their action research in the future?

The first year of implementation

The programme team was uncertain of success during the first year of implementation (2009-10). From the end-of-programme evaluations, however, variable feedback was received from programme participants, for example:

> *"Although it seems a lot of work I have read some excellent articles and it has made me quite motivated on this topic. I know I have made a difference!"* (Participant 1/ Cohort 1 (P1/C1))

> *"I have found this task very enjoyable on the whole. However, it has also been very frustrating due to the lack of time, both in terms of the overall timeline offered and in my ability to dedicate time to it".* (P2/C1)

Pinpointing the main issue, the external examiner commented:

> *"The action research project provides participants with an authentic learning experience in terms of undertaking scholarly research into their practice. However, the feasibility of this appears to be problematic in relation to them being able to complete it to a meaningful level...Is the emphasis here the product or the process? ...it may be more helpful to the students to let them identify their own research approach, define their outputs and evaluate how far they have got with them".* (University of Bedfordshire, 2010)

In preparing for the second year of operation (2010-11), assessment weighting was increased to 70%. The balance between outcome and process shifted towards the latter. In line with the University's new curriculum framework (see Atlay *et al.*, 2008), a more personalised learning approach was adopted with negotiated task outcomes. Allowing participants to focus on the early stages of an action research project became an option, allowing some to focus on clearly identifying or justifying a problem, and designing an appropriate intervention. Shifting the emphasis from the product to the process of action research seemed to produce more positive feedback and improved learning outcomes. One participant who did not complete a full cycle of action research revealed:

> *"The action research project has allowed me to experiment with research ideas and processes in a comfortable environment where I have not felt judged or exposed".* (P1/C2)

Feedback from those completing a cycle was consistently positive, for example:

> *"I have been enthused by many of the outcomes resulting from my action research, one being the monitoring of the successful impact of group work upon the students' learning".* (P2/C2)

> *"In hindsight the action research process combines my affinity for reflection and review/action planning. The action research conducted seems to evidence improved learning and has also given me a framework to develop my practice".* (P3/C2)

According to the external examiner, developing participants' teaching approaches:

> *"was enhanced by the element of choice in some aspects of the assessment. The benefits for students were clear. It supported them to review and change specific aspects of their practice which were of concern to them in their own context".* (University of Bedfordshire, 2011a)

The programme team further enhanced the personalised learning element of the curriculum for the 2011-12 cohort through a requirement that participants identify a personal developmental outcome in their action research proposal. Potentially linked to their personal outcome, participants were then required to add an assessment criterion (to the tutor-derived criteria) against which they wished their submitted report to be graded. To enable those participants not completing a full cycle to structure their report as a research funding bid, the programme team also extended the element of negotiation. All six participants who chose this option welcomed the opportunity to do so, particularly well-illustrated below by participant P1/C3 reflecting on her final assessment. Her action research focused on peer mentoring.

"The idea for a peer mentoring project emerged through discussions with students about ideas for placement related workshops. Students mentioned how useful they had found meeting Level 2 students in induction week…Discussing this idea in more detail via PgCAP tutorials and group workshop led me to realise there was scope for action research that tested peer mentoring as a model for addressing elevated anxiety of students. What also emerged, however, was again that timescales might preclude this idea. I felt frustrated at this point, as I felt strongly that the action research should be meaningful to my learning as a practitioner and to the student experience. I was worried that I would not feel committed to a problem area chosen just to fit within the timescales. Being able to present my action research as a proposal therefore has allowed me to engage with the topic that I feel is really relevant to current themes in social work education and has emerged from reflection on my own teaching experience. I am at the stage of having gathered initial data to better understand the nature of anxiety experienced by students. I have presented the proposal to demonstrate where I am in terms of the planning stage and the next step for me: 'doing it'. Based on feedback, my next step will be to discuss implementation with the department during the forthcoming academic year". (P1/C3)

One successful change introduced, and alluded to above, was peer support through the advent of participant-led group tutorials:

"we shall be encouraging and expecting you to share what you are doing with colleagues on the programme and receive and give peer support and encouragement more formerly during group tutorials." (University of Bedfordshire, 2011b)

Introducing small group tutorials seems to have been beneficial, for example:

> "I have gained useful feedback from other students and from X (tutor). In turn, I've found that giving feedback to others has, in fact, helped to clarify my thoughts about my own research". (P2/C3).

> "The enlightenment for experimental interventions came from the discussions with my PgCAP peers and tutor, as we all seemed to struggle with our personal aims, outcomes and experiences as PgCAP students (and action researchers). Being able to share and link our personal thoughts with the failure/success of the interventions made the project more manageable, and perhaps even made the pedagogic maze look more like an immense, but understandable, map". (P3/C3)

One issue to have emerged from action research submissions in the previous year suggested the essence of action research was still not being grasped by everyone. Thus, in progress reports submitted a few months prior to their final submission, participants were specifically asked if they could 'easily justify what you are doing is action research rather than any other form of research?' A typical response in the progress report was:

> "I think it is the fact that my research project opens itself up to be modified and re-evaluated in a cyclical manner year-upon-year. The project itself involves a direct intervention into teaching practice with a measurable outcome on learner development". (P4/C3)

Discussion in subsequent group tutorials helped to reinforce and clarify, for example:

> "Have learnt from others that it is helpful to have a clear focus from the outset, and to ensure that it is action research and not some vaguely reflective attempt to improve teaching and learning". (P5/C3)

Enhancing the Enhancers

For the final reflective assessment (15% weighting), participants had to critically review their learning on the PgCAP programme within a wider learning at work context. Not specifically directed to reflect upon their action research in the assessment brief, 86% (n=29) of participants mentioned learning from undertaking their action research project. Of these, 56% did so substantively and such learning was reassuringly accompanied by stated plans to follow-up their action research project. For example:

> "I've decided to redesign two of the assessment points [in a module] ... overall I found the process of action research really useful and will continue this project to evaluate the changes". (P6/C3)

> "I believe my role as a developing teacher is to continuously review and modify my teaching and learning practice. I recognise that this is part of my professional accountability, to question current practices and consider alternatives with the outcome to improve student learning and self-assessment. For me, this is just the beginning of action research with the anticipation that my report is published; I will continue further cycles of the ITDEM process". (P7/C3)

Stated intentions to follow-up on specific action research projects initiated during the PgCAP were naturally welcome to see from a quality enhancement perspective. Many participants expressed plans to use structured evidence-informed approaches to enhance learner development, for example:

> "I believe that the PgCAP programme has allowed me to develop as a HE practitioner, although, this development has not occurred as I thought it would. Use of a self-reflective approach and action research has led me to understand that in this, as with any profession, I am unlikely to get it right first time. As a professional learner I will constantly be developing my practice and so the tools of reflection and the cycle of action research will allow me to do this in a structured fashion". (P8/C3)

The PgCAP programme team were themselves in a similar position as participant P8/C3 as they developed and refined the action research initiative for 2012-13.

Further Enhancing the Programme

An important characteristic of action research is the imperative to share and disseminate (Lewin, 1946; Norton, 2009), thus adding to the notion of a professional learning community (Jackson & Tasker, 2003) or learning organization (Senge, 2006). During 2011-12, a greater emphasis had been placed on dissemination and, encouragingly, one third of those completing projects in 2012 presented their action research at the University's annual conference. This was a significant increase from the previous year.

The University's innovative curriculum model promotes collaborative learning, "*students learning with and through peers, tutors and others creating and sustaining a learning community*" (University of Bedfordshire, 2011c). Given the benefits of the optional group tutorials introduced for 2011-12, as described earlier, it was decided to make these compulsory for 2012-13 to maximize participation. This has increased attendance to 100%. The team has also explored options drawn from a range of peer-based HE practice (Falchikov, 2001) and learning groups (Tennant *et al.*, 2010). As a result of this, peer support has now been extended, as described by one participant in feedback:

> "*I, in particular, benefitted from the discussion with others who simply asked me "how is this action research"? Maybe the sessions themselves may not need improvement, but you should encourage more interaction between the group participants to discuss their action research project also beyond the group sessions*". (P9/C3)

Constructing a Quality Enhancement Framework

In reflecting on the changes made to the programme over several years, it is possible to situate these within an emerging quality enhancement framework. This chapter has described the quality enhancement of inexperienced teachers' professional practice and the ongoing development of the PgCAP programme which facilitates this. The mechanism which enables the enhancement of quality was the introduction of an assessed action research project into the second of the two modules, resulting in parallel cycles of continuous improvement being undertaken by the programme team and staff-as-students.

This framework is based on the concept of an incrementalist model of quality enhancement. As described by the American Society for Quality (ASQ), an incrementalist model relates to a cyclical system of continual improvement, with specific or radical interventions breaking up a linear pattern of change, thereby providing discontinuous improvements. The identification of a problem within the PgCAP programme, the resultant decision to make an intervention, followed by an iterative development process, subsequent evaluations and changes acknowledges a model of incremental change based on the Deming cycle of continual process improvement (Deming, 2000:88).

The quality enhancement framework for this case study utilises Deming's Plan-do-check-act (PDCA) cycle (Figure 3) identifies four distinct steps for improvement or change: recognise a need and plan for change, make the change in a small way, check the results and identify what has been learned from them, and take action based upon what has been learned, using these as a basis for entering the next phase of the improvement cycle.

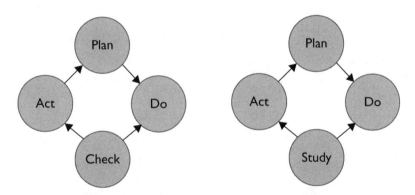

Figure 3: The PDCA cycle.   *Figure 4: The PDSA cycle.*

At another level, the actions taken within this case study are in themselves reciprocal and display similarities with an action research cycle, the focus of the specific intervention within the case study. Scott (1999) acknowledges that the introduction of such a radical intervention can trigger a chain reaction of consequences, both intended and unintended. Concurrently, therefore, for the staff-as-students undertaking the PgCAP, an interaction of cycles commences. Two variants of the

Deming cycle apply, the Plan-do-check-act (PDCA) (Figure 3) and Plan-do-study-act (PDSA) (Figure 4) models. The inclusion in the PgCAP programme of a cyclical model of action research relates directly to the PDSA cycle (Figure 4) and to the staff-as-student persona. When the parallel persona as member of teaching staff is resumed and the principles of an action research approach are applied directly to practice, the PDCA cycle (Figure 3) comes into play, in a similar way to that adopted by the programme team when introducing action research into the curriculum.

Becket and Brookes (2008) argue that there is considerable diversity as to what enhancement means within a higher education context and therefore the means by which it can be measured are also variable. From the case we can conclude provisionally that the action research intervention has helped to engender conceptual and behavioural transformation among many of the participants. The action research intervention has therefore resulted in positive changes in participants' attitudes, knowledge, skills and thinking, applying Scott's (1999:64) framework of success indictors. This in turn is beginning to lead to change across their own programmes and departments, an example of functioning bottom-upwards improvement.

As a learning organisation, the University's processes for the enhancement and assurance of quality are intended to be two-way, informing top-downwards and bottom-upwards cycles of improvement. Arguably the PgCAP sits centre stage within the quality enhancement processes within the institution, while governed by those of quality assurance (Figure 5). McKimm (2009:186) notes the necessity to provide a context within which:

"... lecturers can develop their understanding of quality issues in higher education, and consider their roles and obligations in relation to maintaining and enhancing quality and standards."

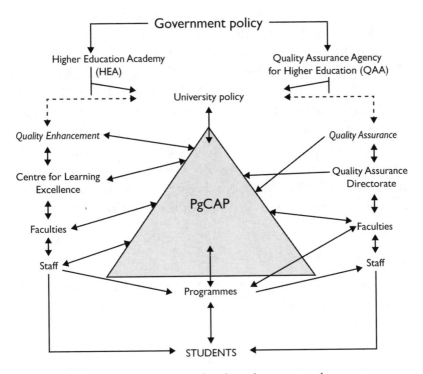

Figure 5: PgCAP as central to institutional quality enhancement and assurance.

There are increasingly encouraging signs that the PgCAP's action research initiative refined over a period of four years has provided this context by enabling staff to experience for themselves the benefits of employing an evidence-informed approach in their teaching practice and localised classroom contexts. For example, admitting to being *"sceptical at first"* where studying teaching and learning in HE was concerned, one participant (P4/C3) later confessed that his attitude had *"changed enormously"*. For his action research project he had investigated the impact of a guided instructional description of assessment criteria and video examples on first-year undergraduate students' understanding and confidence ahead of an oral presentation assessment. The problem identified (as in stage one of the ITDEM model, Norton, 2009) was a noted lack of student understanding and confidence and as such, the learning activity was amended. Results demonstrated that understanding and confidence relating to the assessment had significantly improved. The intervention is being extended to further modules in the next action research cycle and he has disseminated the results to his peers across the University with plans for wider dissemination through publication.

Ultimately, as the Cooke Report (TQEC, 2003) suggests and as evidenced in this chapter, individual change may foster longer-term systemic change across the institution as a whole resulting in enhanced student engagement and learning. As demonstrated, parallel cycles of continuous quality enhancement can be employed in tandem. Just as the programme team were able to develop a process of continuous quality enhancement, so staff-as-students were enabled to make the transition to become the enhancer, in turn to enhance the student learning experience.

About the Authors

Lesley Lawrence is Head of Academic Professional Development, Centre for Learning Excellence, University of Bedfordshire, UK. She can be contacted at this email: lesley.lawrence@beds.ac.uk

Helen Corkill is the University Co-ordinator for Part-time Provision, University of Bedfordshire, UK. She can be contacted at this email: helen.corkill@beds.ac.uk

Chapter Eleven

Course Evaluation Systems for Open-ended Quality Enhancement

Jesper Piihl and Jens Smed Rasmussen

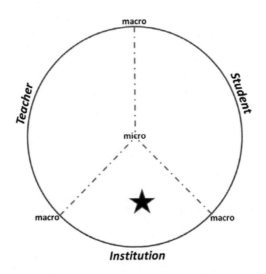

Introduction

For quality enhancement in higher education, quality control and evaluation systems play significant roles. Students' evaluation of courses and teachers in the form of performance measurement through questionnaires has become a widespread concept (Hofman & Kremer, 1980). In designing such measurement based systems for quality control, different ideas turn up as to definitions of quality (Middlehurst, 1995) and the role of a university, the role of management, curriculum design, concepts of learning, teaching and study methods, student engagement and the freedom of the individual teacher. In some instances course evaluation systems play significant roles in the decision-making regarding resource allocation to courses and the promotion of teachers. In other instances evaluation systems seem to be decoupled (Meyer & Rowan, 1977; Røvik, 1998) from the daily activities in the classroom.

This chapter addresses the questions: How can course evaluation systems be designed to play an active role in strategic quality enhancement at universities despite the many contradicting forces? Or more specifically: How can course evaluation systems be designed in ways that fulfil the need for legitimacy and managerial control whilst simultaneously being open to different conceptions of curriculum development, learning, and teaching and study methods? How can course evaluation systems be designed to form a valuable tool for quality enhancement instead of being an empty decoupled ritual serving legitimacy purposes only?

The main purpose of this chapter is to lay out and illustrate a theoretical framework for course evaluation systems addressing these questions. This is done by working theoretically on different perspectives drawn from accounting theory and theory on strategic performance measurement, and at the same time by participating in actual discussions regarding the development of course evaluation systems at the Faculty of Social Sciences at University of Southern Denmark. Experiences and evidence derived from this involvement during a period of 10 years provides the empirical case inspiring and challenging the theoretical work in the chapter. Therefore the methodological framework resembles action research (Jönsson, 1996) in which we develop this theoretical model simultaneously with engaging actively in developing the course evaluation system at the specific university.

Inspired by Dewey (1986), it is our ambition to avoid building a new perspective on evaluation based on opposition to old paradigms. Instead, it is our ambition to focus on the problems in the real world and discuss how inspiration from different paradigms can support the development of evaluation models that address these problems. However, in doing so it is essential to be aware of differences between paradigms and viewpoints which can broaden our perspectives on evaluation as well as make the way in which we discuss evaluation systems more specific.

The phrase *open-ended* in our title emphasises the need to build course evaluation systems that do not freeze quality definitions into specific standards, but actually promote multiple dialogues amongst Faculty management, faculty members, course directors, teachers and students regarding quality in academic endeavours.

Current Debates on Course Evaluation Systems for Quality Enhancement

Course evaluation based on students' evaluation of teaching has a long history and serves a role in giving feedback to instructors to help improve teaching and to give feedback to students and administration to inform decisions regarding the course and instructors (Hofman & Kremer, 1980).

However, the use of and benefit from course evaluations based on student feedback is highly contested. Jiang (2009) argues that it is more complex to introduce accountability systems in higher education than in traditional for-profit organisations for at least two reasons. First, there is a long tradition among academics that they treasure and value high levels of independence in their work. Secondly, institutions of higher education face competing objectives and stakeholders (Sarrico *et al.*, 2010) that vie for priority. Hofman and Kremer (1980) find that course evaluations are influenced by students' prior attitudes towards higher education. These attitudes compete with evaluation of the actual teaching in which the students have taken part. Thereby they question the validity of the systems. Valsan and Sproule (2008) critically argue that student evaluation of teaching is an effective way to 'mollify' tax-payers and other donors of funding to universities by giving an impression of accountability, while pointing towards conflicts of interest when student responses play a role in promoting the teacher.

This discussion points towards a need for design of course evaluation systems that allow for some level of governance and at the same time are open to issues regarding multiple objectives and concepts of learning, academic freedom and problems of reliability and validity in student responses regarding quality.

Performance Measurement and Accounting

Contemporary accounting theory offers multiple perspectives on performance measurement and control systems such as the widely used Balanced Scorecard (Kaplan & Norton, 1996) or the 'Levers of Control' framework (Simons, 1995). Although both frameworks offer comprehensive guidance and understanding of the role and purpose for performance measurement and management control, there are also important differences between them. The 'Levers of Control' framework suits our purpose well as it blends seemingly opposing and contradictory perspectives into the same framework of controls. This framework characterises two different perspectives of the use of measurements as either diagnostic or interactive controls. It incorporates cultural and managerial contexts and empowers actors to develop local quality definitions. Furthermore, Simons (1995) suggests that the interactive control lever is amenable to emergent strategy, which matches our interest in an open-ended quality control system while retaining elements of governance. In the following sections we first elaborate on ideas of diagnostic and interactive controls. Then we elaborate on the influence from cultural and managerial contexts through the systems of beliefs and boundary rules and finally how these levers of control interact during practical use.

Diagnostic and Interactive Controls

In the 'Levers of Control' framework, Simons (1995) balances two very different perspectives on performance measurements and management control. He divides performance measurement into two main purposes; diagnostic controls and interactive controls. Diagnostic control systems are grounded in the concept of known criteria against which performances are to be measured and evaluated. In contrast, interactive control systems are grounded in strategic uncertainty and the need to enable the organisation to develop strategic answers to strategic uncertainties.

Diagnostic control systems are based upon the ideas of cybernetic systems: The first step is to determine which actions lead to production of quality. Secondly, actual performances are measured against these standards. Based on variation between standards and actual performances corrective actions can be initiated to make performances meet the predetermined standards. That is, when the strategic priorities are well-known and the recipe is known, performance measurements can be utilised as a very efficient control to diagnose deviations and make appropriate corrections.

Diagnostic control systems are organised inside hierarchies. Consequently, the organisation risks acting as a filtering mechanism for valuable information, comprehended knowledge and emergent strategy conceived in action and practice whereby improvements get lost (Jönsson, 1996). Diagnostic control systems are the target of criticism put forward on the wide spread use of performance measurement. Based on a longitudinal case study in professional organisations Townley et al. (2003) suggest that what starts out as an invitation to start new accountability discourses by introducing measurement systems easily ends up being dominated by only an administrative logic. The saying: "You only get what you measure" is often mentioned by critics (many examples are given in Ahrens & Chapman, 2006).

However, Simons (1990) found from longitudinal field research that managers also use their formal control systems interactively to form new and innovative strategies. Additionally, measurements can also be carried out to reduce strategic uncertainties and to develop emergent strategies.

The interactive use forms a different perspective on measurement. Interactive control, is constituted by its 'style of use', characterised by managers engaged in face-to-face conversations and dialogue concerning measurements and strategic uncertainties (Simons, 1995). The control system thus becomes amenable to emergent strategy.

In Table 1, a diagnostic control paradigm is contrasted with an interactive paradigm on dimensions relevant to quality enhancement in higher education. The terms 'performance measurement' and 'control system' are used synonymously for the terms 'course and teaching evaluation' and 'quality control system'.

	Diagnostic course evaluation systems	Interactive course evaluation systems
Definition of quality	Clear.	Multiple and evolving.
Application	Low degrees of strategic uncertainty. Causalities are known and built into the system.	High degree of strategic uncertainty. Causalities are unclear or vary.
Initiation of quality enhancing activities	Based on variance analysis. When measures are different from expectations, correcting actions can be initiated.	Activities are initiated based on dialogue between the parties involved in quality production.
Criteria for a solid quality assurance system.	Known causalities. Validity and reliability in measures.	Increased dialogue regarding quality enhancement among people involved in the activities.
Style of use	Hierarchical control of performance and corrective actions.	Challenging dialogues on strategic direction and specific actions.
Terminology regarding questions in evaluation questionnaire	Measures: To emphasise measuring actual performance against a standard model for quality.	Indicators: To emphasise that questions serve as indicators initiating and mediating debates around quality issues between different groups of stakeholders.

Table 1: Diagnostic and interactive controls contrasted.

Cultural Context: Systems of Beliefs and Boundary rules

The 'Levers of Control' framework focuses on belief systems and boundary rules as elements from the cultural context forming part of the overall control system. The belief system gives meaning to actions and exploration of opportunities. The boundary rules informs members of the organisation negatively by explicating which actions they must avoid.

To understand the whole package of control (Otley, 2005) the organisation's systems of beliefs and systems of boundary rules must be explicated and considered as two separate levers of control. The organisation's systems of beliefs and boundary rules can influence empowerment and thereby contribute to spreading or stopping the use of the interactive systems in larger parts of an organisation.

These qualitative domains are thus interconnected to the diagnostic and the interactive systems. The four systems act, each by their own special role and purpose in the framework, as levers of control in mutual interconnections to form the overall package of control.

Control Systems in Use

Bisbe *et al.* (2007) made a detailed conceptual analysis of the nature of interactive control and found five constitutive dimensions: (1) Intensive use by senior management, (2) Intensive use in operative management, (3) Pervasive face to face challenges and debates in the interaction, (4) Focus on uncertainties, and (5) Non-invasive but facilitating involvement by senior management.

Ahrens and Chapman (2006) elaborated on the fifth dimension - facilitating involvement – by counter-posing on the one hand *coercive* and on the other *enabling* bureaucratic control systems. Ahrens and Chapman (2006, 2007) suggest that members of an organisation can actively draw on the measurement and control systems as shared resources in their construction of meaning; however, they also reconstitute the system by their actions.

The theory of management accounting as practice gives centre stage to the practising of control systems and the actions taken by those who are operative and implicated in the practice.

This theoretical background suggests both benefits and caveats in moving from diagnostic towards more interactive use of course evaluation systems. In the following sections we discuss the case of changing evaluation systems at the Faculty of social sciences at University of Southern Denmark which reveals shifts in balances between diagnostic and interactive controls. The case presents changing designs and increasingly enabling styles of use, which contribute to the development of increasingly interactive and open-ended course evaluation systems. Furthermore, the evidence presented reveals how these shifts in balances interact with existing systems of beliefs at the university.

Evaluation for Quality Enhancement: an Illustrative Case

The scene for this case is the Faculty of social sciences at University of Southern Denmark. The Faculty of social sciences covers disciplines such as business and management, political science, economics, journalism, and law. The Faculty is organised with eight departments and 14 study boards. The Dean's office is in charge of the day-to-day management of the Faculty as well as the long term strategic development. Heads of departments are in charge of the day-to-day management of departments including responsibilities of the staff related to teaching.

Day-to-day management of study programmes in the hands of Heads of Studies and study boards. Heads of Studies have academic responsibility for programmes but no formal managerial authority regarding staff. Each study board comprises equal numbers of representatives from the academic staff and students. The study board shall ensure the organisation, realisation and development of the study programme and teaching. Each study programme is a collection of courses led by a course director. In some instances the course director also teaches the course and in other instances other faculty members or external teachers teach the course.

The case runs through three phases with different approaches to evaluation systems. The first phase can be described as a centralised control system, the second phase as a decentralised system at the level of study boards. The system in the third phase can be described as a layered system with both centralised and decentralised elements.

Phase I: Centralised Control System

In the first phase the evaluation system was based on a centralised model with two open and four closed questions with possible comments to each of the closed questions (see Table 2). This was followed by a talk with the head of the department in cases where results did not meet the prescribed threshold. In principle, the system was built in a way that made it possible to extract data in order to follow a specific teacher's "progress" over time.

Question	Scale
State three positive elements of this course until now?	Open question.
State three elements, which could be improved?	Open question.
What is your evaluation of the teachers' pedagogical level in this course?	Very positive to very negative (6 point scale).
What is your evaluation of the teachers' academic level in this course?	Very positive to very negative (6 point scale).
How will our effort in this course be evaluated by others?	Very insufficient to Very sufficient (6 point scale).
How relevant is this course in the overall curriculum?	Very relevant to Very irrelevant (6 point scale).

Table 2: Questionnaire in phase one.

This model is to some degree close to the idea of diagnostic controls. The questionnaire has no specific ideas regarding the content of quality. However, it promotes a focus on the teacher as responsible for the course and that good courses need a knowledgeable teacher with pedagogical abilities as determined by the student. This model highlights two issues to be discussed here.

First of all, it is a consequence of the focus on the individual teacher that the answers are regarded as being a personal thing to be discussed in the study board and in special circumstances with the head of department who is responsible for hiring specific teachers. However, in many courses it is not the person responsible for the course programme who is teaching, and in several courses more teachers are involved. In these instances, none of these teachers were allowed to see the evaluations of each other's teaching, since it was regarded as personal information. This means that the dialogues on quality improvement could only address issues concerning the individual teacher's pedagogical and academic performance. Broader issues regarding quality as for example the quality of the overall course design, collaboration amongst teachers if more teachers are involved, the students' engagement in the activities etc. could not be addressed.

Another consequence is that it tends to incorporate the student in the role of customer in the teaching process (Dobozy, 2011). Bringing matters to a head, it can be said that this questionnaire forms an alliance between students and management pointing towards the individual teacher as the one to be held accountable for the quality of a given course.

Phase 2: Decentralised Evaluation Systems

In the second phase, the evaluation system was opened for local adjustments at the level of study boards. At the Faculty of Social Sciences there are 14 study boards. In this phase many different procedures emerged as reactions to shortcomings in the procedures in the first phase.

One study board argued that a growing dissatisfaction had been found with the relatively mechanical procedures which meant the students did not experience changes in courses as a consequence of their responses. Therefore the response rate became low and unrepresentative. Instead, the study board turned towards a model based on dialogue in which teachers and students were given more responsibility for the course. The idea being that the dialogue initiates a more interactive process where teacher and students avoid many frustrations resulting from different expectations regarding teaching. At the end of the course the teacher produces, in collaboration with the students, a short report documenting the experience gained – with specific emphasis on experience regarding new teaching and evaluation forms, which can inspire others.

Another study board chose to use the evaluation system as an opportunity to initiate new types of dialogue for teaching and learning. Instead of posing questions about the qualities of the teacher, the focus of the evaluation was directed towards students' learning from the teaching/ learning activities organised and performed within the course. The ambition was to change focus away from the teachers' qualifications towards the learning processes.

This change in focus had several consequences. First, one teacher argued that the validity of the measures might fail. In the first version, questions were framed like "to what degree do *the activities of the course design* contribute to your academic development". A debate emerged as to whether the students would know what was meant by "activities of the course design", since students tend to have expectations regarding teaching at a university as something resembling traditional lectures. As a result the question was framed like: "did the *teaching* contribute to your academic development"?

In this example the question interfered with existing belief systems and ended up being framed within the ambition of diagnostic controls with an emphasis on validity in measures. If this debate was instead framed within a paradigm of interactive control, the 'style of use' could have been to take the evaluation questions as an opportunity to open discussions of teaching/learning quality with the students prior to putting the questionnaire to them.

By changing the focus from the teacher to the teaching or learning processes, the issue of personal data inhibiting dialogue on quality among teachers and course directors for specific courses was overcome in principle. This opened several new opportunities for discussions of quality among faculty members. It turned out that the students answering the open sections of the questionnaire still commented on personal performances of individual teachers – and these comments were now available not only to the teacher but also to the person responsible for the course and other teachers of the course. Some teachers found this uncomfortable and asked whether these data could be omitted from the data sent to others than the specific person him/herself? However, instead of omitting these data, a broader discussion was opened as to the coordination among teachers in courses and how more experienced teachers can help less experienced teachers to handle these kinds of comments and actually improve the quality of the teaching and student learning. Thereby these discussions, initiated by the change in the evaluation system, played a role in breaking down elements of the existing belief systems which strongly focus on the individual teachers' personal responsibility of teaching.

The change in focus from teacher to teaching also opened up new alliances around who should be held accountable for problems in courses. Whereas the system in phase one tended to construct an alliance between students and management against teachers, the new system also constructed an alliance between students and teachers against management. Based on evaluations teachers and students could side against curriculum planners in discussions regarding how the specific course interplayed with other courses and regarding resources allocated to carry through the learning activities in the courses. Thereby the new system opened several new avenues for debates on quality improvement among head of study, study board, head of department, course directors, teachers and students.

Phase 3: Layered Quality Enhancement System

In developing the model for the third phase, different forces influencing the evaluation processes were identified and, as proposed by Rasmus (2011) they were balanced against each other. This led to identification and discussion of the following issues (among others):

1. quality enhancement is prioritised above quality control. Evaluation is used actively to address future development needs;

2. evaluation of student learning is prioritised over student's perception of the teacher;

3. quality enhancement ambitions at various managerial levels (Dean, study boards, course responsible, teachers and students) must be addressed.

The first balance promotes a shift in prime emphasis from diagnostic control to interactive control. However, it is only a push in a direction; the model is still open to diagnostic control. The second balance promotes a shift in prime emphasis away from focusing on the role of the teacher towards focusing on the students learning processes. The third balance is translated into an evaluation model with three different levels in a layered structure. At the overall Faculty level, three to four indicators are constructed to cover all courses within the Faculty of Social Sciences. These indicators support strategic issues at the university and Faculty levels. At present these indicators aim at promoting debates around teaching and learning methods, which make the students more active in the processes.

At the middle level, a number of indicators or measures can be constructed by the study boards to maintain their possibility to support specific developmental needs regarding a specific study programme. Finally, at the micro-level each course director can – when the system is fully implemented – develop specific questions to support the special needs and concepts of learning of each course. Potentially, these measures can be developed in collaboration with the actual students following a specific course.

This layered structure opens several arenas for quality enhancement dialogues, without necessarily defining quality in specific ways. At the top level, Faculty management can decide on which strategic issues to emphasise opening up possibilities for debates between Dean and Heads of Study/study boards regarding the way in which to interpret and operationalise these issues in a questionnaire form. At the next level, each study board must decide on the way in which they will work with quality enhancement within their specific area and take these ideas to be debated with course directors – who again should discuss with specific teachers and students which measures/indicators would be relevant at specific courses. In this way, the system promotes construction of a chain of dialogues regarding quality, ranging from the Dean to individual students on specific courses.

As an example showing how this course evaluation system opened up new dialogues, representatives from a student organisation sent a letter to the Dean. This letter both acknowledged the ideas in the system and raised some concerns. One of the concerns focussed on the ideas of students participating in the teaching and learning methods as co-producers of the curriculum and teaching activities. The letter argued that not all students necessarily liked these new teaching methods and, due to the way the questions were formulated, students were unable to state their dislike of these teaching methods. Therefore, the students argued that their responses would not be valid.

From the perspective of diagnostic controls this response from the students is of great concern. However, from the perspective of interactive controls, this kind of reaction is very valuable since it created an arena within which we could debate quality enhancement issues directly with the students in an engaging way. A meeting was set up with the representatives of the student organisation. At this meeting the pedagogical arguments regarding promotion of students activating teaching and learning methods were discussed and a new alliance on quality enhancement involving the student organisation was initiated (see also Bartholomew et al., this volume, for discussions regarding engagement of students in quality enhancement at an institutional level).

Controls and measurement across the phases

The key changes in the designs of course evaluation systems and styles of use is summarised in Table 3.

	Phase 1: Centralised control system	Phase 2: Decentralised evaluation system		Phase 3: Layered quality enhance-ment system
		Study board 1	Study board 2	
Strategic Performance measurement perspective	Questionnaire constructed as diagnostic control system.	Unstructured evaluation dialogues of each course.	Questionnaire promoting discussions on quality amongst faculty members and students.	Setting focus on strategic issues. Giving part in quality definition and enhancement to multiple actors.
Who is controlling	Heads of departments and study boards control teachers.	Study board controls existence of evaluation dialogues of each course.	Study board controls learning processes.	Dean, study boards, course directors, teachers, and students control learning processes.
Validity and reliability	Important: System may potentially be a foundation for sanctions.	Validity and reliability is constructed in local dialogues of each course.	Varies: Less important since system empha-sises dialogue on criteria.	Less important since system is based on dialogue as a foun-dation for quality enhancement.

	Phase 1: Centralised control system	Phase 2: Decentralised evaluation system		Phase 3: Layered quality enhancement system
		Study board 1	Study board 2	
Arenas for quality enhancement dialogues	Fewest arenas	Few arenas	More arenas	Many arenas
	Teacher and head of department will have a dialogue regarding needs for competence development if evaluation results are critical. Course directors have no access to teacher evaluations.	Between teachers and students. Between study board and teacher.	Dialogues in study board regarding evaluation questions and procedures. Relation between evaluation and continuous development of course descriptions. Course directors and teachers can discuss improvements inspired by evaluation results.	Faculty management and heads of studies regarding strategic key variables. Study boards regarding study wide priorities and quality definitions Course director and teacher regarding course specific priorities and quality definitions. Teacher and students regarding mutual expectations regarding quality.
Object controlled	Teacher.	The existence of course specific dialogues.	Students learning processes.	Learning activities constructed in collaboration between teacher and students.
Style of use	Control.	Local dialogue.	Setting direction for dialogues. Interactive.	Strategic direction and quality enhancement in students' learning.

Table 3: Summarising the phases.

The overall package of control (Otley, 2005) for a course evaluation measurement and control system saw fundamental changes between the three phases of the case. The changes can be traced and categorised inside the 'Levers of Control' framework (Simons, 1995) as they finally end up as implicated in situated functionality (Ahrens & Chapman, 2007).

As situated controls they are sometimes characterised by local dialogue regarding learning, teaching, and curriculum as well as new performance measures. Sometimes they are characterised as practical resources for skilful manipulation. And sometimes they can even be characterised as signalling intentions by the rules, against the rules or to show achievements.

The course evaluation and measurement system ends up being implicated in constituting its own context in an enabling (Ahrens & Chapman, 2007) and potentially quality-enhancing way. The criteria for quality in teaching thus get constructed in dialogues regarding criteria and measures. In interactive use of measurements and communication through more than one channel the context is implicated in the sense-making devices in particular ways (Jönsson, 1996). This kind of accounting talk in different local contexts began in phase 2.

Over time, local differences in belief systems developed into different notions about systems design, measurements and 'style of use' amongst different study boards. These different notions of evaluation systems and control designs were eventually supplemented in phase 3 by a set of central strategic quality issues. However, when compared with the diagnostic use of centralised hierarchical quality metrics seen during phase one, the new central layer of indicators more clearly resembles interactive controls. Lively conversations and debates can now take place between study boards and the Dean's office concerning the nature of the quality issues and the meaning attached to these central performance measurements.

In phase 3 we now see a three layered course evaluation system at the Faculty characterised more or less by elements of enabling controls made live by different interactive 'styles of use'.

Furthermore, the later phases in this case are open to more and more involvement of students in the evaluation process – in the first instance by focusing on how the activities of the course promote student learning and in the third phase by potentially engaging students as partners in constructing the measures for quality teaching and learning. Thereby the evaluation system can potentially play a role in resisting the idea of students as consumers and instead promote the idea of students as producers (Dobozy, 2011).

Conclusion

In this chapter, course evaluation systems were made synonymous with quality control and performance measurement systems. How can an open-ended teaching quality enhancing measurement and control system then be designed to play an active role at enhancing dialogues on teaching and learning quality at a university? We chose the 'Levers of Control' framework which left us with two different perspectives on the uses of quality measurement – diagnostic and interactive measures – together with contextual aspects – systems of beliefs and boundary rules – regarding controls and empowerment inside the control framework.

From our engagement in the case including several of the theoretical concepts we were able to see changes in the teaching quality control system at Faculty level and we could trace these changes inside the chosen framework. At the end we saw how the situated functionality, by engaged actors, was leading to new and useable meanings on good quality in teaching. Furthermore we give example of evidence regarding how a shift from diagnostic towards more interactive measures interferes with and challenges existing belief systems regarding teaching and learning.

We thus offer a case description with implications for management and teaching practice as to the important engagement that we have witnessed at the Faculty in terms of constitution, use and reconstitution of the measurement based teaching course evaluation system.

In this case the measurement and control system became more enabling and open-ended over time. This potentially makes the interactive use of controls more widespread and open for more dialogue and experimentation from those who are involved in the teaching practice – including the students. This opens up opportunities for enhancing learning and experimentation at relevant situated places concerning quality in teaching. The accountability discourse can start anew and shift from teachers being held accountable to standards of quality imposed on them towards enabling stakeholders to actually take responsibility themselves for defining and developing quality.

The balance between diagnostic versus interactive and enabling control is intimately connected to the boundary and belief systems. In other words, context matters. Differences in local context can enhance the situated sense making and the different use of devices. In turn, this led to more than one system layer and localised but engaged and enabling design changes in the system. Eventually, a third central layer was initiated. The point is, though, that the interactive control can potentially dominate the diagnostic controls in every layer of the measurement system during time.

Management and designers of teaching quality measurement and control systems should therefore pay attention to the practising of such performance measurement based control systems. If open-ended construction using this approach will enhance teaching quality is eventually a matter of how the professionals in teaching engage with the measurements and control systems and how they are enabled to engage interactively.

The enabling and interactive control systems cannot be made by design only. The enabled interactive *use* of the measurement system by all participants – ranging from Dean to first year students – holds the key to the quality enhancing capability.

About the Authors

Jesper Piihl is Associate Professor at the Faculty of social sciences, Department of Entrepreneurship and Relationship management at University of Southern Denmark. He can be contacted at this email: jpi@sam.sdu.dk

Jens Smed Rasmussen is Teaching Assistant Professor at the Faculty of social sciences, Department of Entrepreneurship and Relationship management at University of Southern Denmark. He can be contacted at this email: jpi@sam.sdu.dk

Chapter Twelve

Quality Enhancement through Student Engagement

Paul Bartholomew, Stuart Brand and Luke Millard

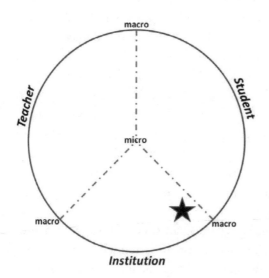

Introduction

This chapter presents an institution-wide case of enhancing the quality of academic provision at an English University through a coherent strategy that broadens the interface between students and academic staff (faculty). We describe how new relationships are building a sense of 'belonging' characteristic of a learning community; and we demonstrate how this in turn leads to enhancement of 'dimensions' of academic quality as described by Gibbs (2010).

Gibbs (2010) discusses how attempts have been made to measure academic quality for the purposes of comparing institutions; although the report questions the efficacy of such comparisons, it does nonetheless usefully identify a number of dimensions of quality organised according to the 3P model (Biggs, 1993). These dimensions are categorised as either one of presage (institutional context), process (learning and teaching practices) or product (student performance or educational gain) variables. For the most part, this chapter describes an enhancement agenda that is focused upon a process quality variable – and more specifically the student engagement dimension, with particular reference to the extent and quality of student-faculty interaction.

The United Kingdom's Quality Assurance Agency for Higher Education (QAA), in a handbook of its process for auditing higher education institutions (QAA, 2006), defined quality enhancement as *"the process of taking deliberate steps at institutional level to improve the quality of learning opportunities"*. This definition resonates well with our work as we have sought to take such deliberate institutional steps by putting in place a suite of initiatives that have utilised the agency of students to improve the quality of learning opportunities and their sense of belonging to a learning community. It is important to add that these steps, though conceived by and driven from an institutional level, are made manifest through the agency of faculty and students at the points of curriculum design and delivery.

Previously, although mechanisms that supported quality enhancement as an activity have been manifested within the action plans relating to annual cycles of quality enhancement at all levels of our institution, the involvement of students in these processes was limited. Although diligent in-gathering of student perceptions was commonly carried out, and formal student representation at boards and committees was in place, for many students the outcome was only witnessed as the reporting back of decisions made. However, it is of course possible to use such in-gathered student data in much more effective ways in relation to quality enhancement (Klopper & Drew, this volume).

In recent years, however, student engagement has become a crucial issue for UK higher education. Debates that contrast conceptions of students as customers or as active partners are prevalent and have gained prominence. One reason for this is the shift of funding emphasis, moving from the state to the student with a threefold rise in undergraduate fees for many programmes. A notable feature of this new focus on student engagement has been the inclusion in the new UK Quality Code of a chapter on student engagement (QAA, 2012). Within that chapter, the overarching expectation expands on the QAA's 2006 definition of quality enhancement to advocate articulation with the student engagement agenda: *"Higher education providers take deliberate steps to engage all students, individually and collectively, as partners in the assurance and enhancement of their educational experience."*

So this concept of students as partners in the delivery of quality assurance and enhancement agendas extends the notion of faculty-student interaction to include an expectation for student engagement with the quality bureaucracy of universities. Notions of the meaning and scope of student engagement have been fluid for some years. Like other dimensions of quality, some constructs of student engagement are just about quantifiable; for example Kuh (2009) equates student engagement with notions of the time and effort students invest in the pursuit of measurable learning outcomes. A less measurable approach may also be helpful here; a number of authors have referred to a 'sense of belonging' as central in consideration of results from student engagement (Goodenow, 1993: Baumeister & Leary, 1995). This 'sense of belonging' seems more likely to arise from a student/faculty active partnership paradigm than one that conceives students as customers.

Certainly, for us, the notion of a sense of belonging is an important dimension of quality and we would contend that such a sense emerges from the construction of a broad and deep interface between faculty and students. It is this central philosophy of broadening the interface through the development of a learning community that underpins all of the initiatives described in this chapter.

Underpinning Philosophy

The notion of students as customers has been critiqued for many years and the social constructivist model of learning acknowledges the importance of students taking an active role in their learning. Far less examined is the role students play in the shaping of the opportunities to learn that universities place in front of them; less examined still is the role that students may play in supporting the academic quality infrastructure to help deliver a student-shaped quality enhancement agenda.

Our institutional journey towards developing a learning community through student engagement began as far back as 2005 when institutional review of our university by the UK Quality Assurance Agency acknowledged the strength of university quality assurance processes but also recommended a greater focus on enhancement. Data from student surveys also demonstrated a student learning experience that could be characterised as one of a relatively transient student population attending just for scheduled teaching sessions and not remaining engaged on campus outside of these fixed periods of time.

By 2008, the university had started to develop a series of activities with the intention of fostering greater levels of student engagement through the purposeful creation of a learning community. This has since manifested itself at multiple points in the 'curriculum design and delivery life cycle' (JISC, 2009) and, indeed, through a nascent student employment scheme outside of the curriculum.

Taking such a broad-brush approach to student engagement has evolved from a philosophical position that notions of 'community' and 'belonging' are not confined to the curriculum elements of a university education. Universities are entrusted with three years or more of a student's life and, as such, this time represents an opportunity for personal development and growth. We believe that only by supporting a holistic conception of the university learning experience can institutions hope to connect with students to the degree that learning communities thrive and thus create a fertile environment to support the faculty/student interactions required to sustain a learning community. Thomas (2012) connects 'belonging' with student success and we sought to embrace that ideal through the initiatives described in this chapter.

There is sector-wide evidence, such as that summarised by Zhao and Kuh (2004) and echoed in our own institutional experience, that such engagement leads to a variety of positive outcomes for students ('product variables' under Biggs' 3P model nomenclature) – including enhanced performance at the point of assessment, improved progression and higher levels of social development. Our premise is that as we (faculty/

staff) broaden our interface with students so they do the same with us; student/faculty discourse becomes more extensive, more involved and crucially more reciprocal. As a consequence, we see a greater sense of community and joint responsibility to enhance the learning experience of all students; such communities of mutual learning are well discussed in Raiker (this volume). Only with this willingness, even expectation, to be involved can the student body as a whole become influential to such a degree that they are able to co-deliver institutional enhancement agendas. We have sought to make such student/faculty discourse a cultural norm.

Of course, a philosophy alone is not sufficient to drive the step-change in culture required to realise the 'learning community' and so co-deliver a shared quality enhancement agenda with our students. As a result we have attempted to deliver our aims through three parallel, but aligned initiatives. These are described fully later in the chapter and illustrated with case studies as appropriate in diagrammatic representation of this suite of initiatives and their relationship to one another and our over-arching philosophy is given below in Figure 1.

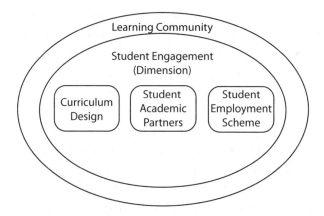

Figure 1: Relationship between initiatives and overarching philosophy.

Our activity, led from one of the university's central departments – the Centre for Enhancement of Learning and Teaching is best understood when presented under three headings – curriculum design, Student Academic Partners (SAP) and students employed by the university.

Introduction to the Initiatives

Our curriculum design initiative includes two projects: RoLEx (Redesign of the Learning Experience) – an overarching curriculum design – initiative and the T-SPARC project (Technology-Supported Processes for Agile and Responsive Curricula), a new technical system and institutional process for designing and approving academic programmes.

The Student Academic Partners (SAP) initiative is an employment scheme for students to work in partnership with academics on learning and teaching projects.

The Student Employment Scheme initiative offers general employment opportunities across the institution and also includes the Student Academic Mentoring Programme, a student employment activity whereby students are paid to mentor other students.

It is our view that for progress to be achieved in the area of quality enhancement through student engagement, ownership is needed at a number of levels including within programme teams of faculty and students.

In the early stages of our student engagement work a crucial step was to obtain the support of senior university managers and, as a sequel to that, the resource to underpin local initiatives. The first steps involved discussion at the University Senate and its sub-committees to ensure not only clarity of intention but also support from the full senior team for the direction of travel. When this had been achieved, the next step was to ensure a full range of opportunities for participation. These opportunities were made manifest through the parallel initiatives introduced above and expanded on below.

It is our view that three conditions are necessary for these project opportunities to deliver the aims of our coherent strategy. Firstly, the principal (though not exclusive) locus of student engagement activity should be close to curriculum design and delivery or, as Thomas (2012) describes it, having 'proximity to the academic sphere'. This is important because this is the area into which students are most likely to be attracted as they see a real opportunity to enhance their own learning experience.

Secondly, some central coordination is necessary so that resource may be provided equitably and synergies between different parts of the institution optimised. Finally, it is crucial that this central coordination comes from a centre associated with enabling enhancement and change through effective evaluation rather than through a culture of compliance and risk aversion that sometimes accompanies a purely assurance-focused paradigm. This setting up and coordination of our suite of initiatives has formed the basis of the 'deliberate steps' called for in the QAA's definition of quality enhancement.

Parallel Initiative: Curriculum Design

RoLEx

We have reported previously (Bartholomew *et al.*, 2010), how our institution embarked on a pan-university quality enhancement project (through curriculum redesign) in 2008. This project, known as RoLEx (Redesign of the Learning Experience), was tasked with facilitating the migration of the entire undergraduate portfolio from a 12-credit module structure to a 15-credit module structure whilst enhancing, and making more efficient, the programmes we offered our students. We learnt a great deal during this project. We learnt that student aspirations in relation to being involved in the redesign, and thus quality enhancement, of their own learning were set at a very low level, that faculty tended to engage with students, and other stakeholders, in a tokenistic way. We also learnt that our curriculum design and programme approval mechanisms, although robust in scrutinising the end *product* of curriculum design (as represented by the definitive documentation), were poor at having any oversight of the design *process* itself.

The low student expectations of involvement in quality enhancement through curriculum redesign were problematical and we soon realised that we needed to manage the expectations and aspirations of those entering Higher Education and to expand the ways in which students could engage with the university in the common aim of enhancing the student learning experience. A number of initiatives emerged from this intent which focused upon a new relationship with students and the Students' Union.

Technology-Supported Processes for Agile and Responsive Curricula (T-SPARC):

This project has run from October 2008 through to July 2012 and is one of just twelve projects funded in the UK to develop more effective approaches to designing curricula and approving programmes. Although an account of the details and technical specifications of the new on-line system is outside the scope of this chapter, it has made two important contributions to bolstering student engagement in quality enhancement through curriculum design:

- for programmes being submitted for approval through this system, artefacts that represent evidence of student engagement in the design process (for example through forums, videos, links to Facebook and survey data) are a *requirement*;

- by investment made in a range of audio-visual techno-logies to capture and share student views on their learning experiences.

Students' contributions to curriculum design activity allow for a very important set of experiences and perspectives to be considered as part of the quality enhancement process.

As part of the overarching T-SPARC project, colleagues piloting new processes to designing courses were asked to bring forward evidence of student engagement in curriculum design. The primary purpose of this requirement was to ensure that programme teams made full use of new opportunities, partly through the provision of new technology and partly through new policy-based expectations, to in-gather student perceptions of various aspects of their learning experience and to work with students to address issues raised through this in-gathering activity. An example of such can be found in the recent development of a Graduate Diploma in Psychology; this programme team used video-based technology to facilitate the virtual interviewing of students to learn about their perceptions of assessment practice. In this case, sixteen questions asking about experiences of assessment were put to twenty-five students yielding a total of three hundred and sixty-six clips. These clips formed a set of resources for the programme team to refer and to inform their design. This case offers an example of how, under the new approaches to curriculum design, such data can contribute to the auditable evidence of the student voice being incorporated into curriculum design decisions.

Curriculum Design: Summary of Quality Enhancement

We would contend that a better design process leads to better programmes and that the systematic inclusion of, and response to, the student voice at the point of designing (or redesigning) curricula will have the consequence of curriculum design outcomes that are fitter for purpose. Changing the institutional processes for curriculum design and approval so as to provide student-focused opportunities for the enhancement of curriculum quality can thus be seen as an 'institutional deliberate step' as referred to in the definition of quality enhancement we offered earlier in the chapter.

To give the reader an impression of the amount of online interaction our new system elicits, figures from a recent design cycle are included below as Table 1:

Provision	Online discussion posts	Number of artefacts uploaded
Suite of six overlapping programmes	494	166

Table 1: Online activity related to an online curriculum design and approval cycle.

Parallel Initiative: Student Academic Partners

The SAP scheme has been running since 2009 and has focused on providing funding and support for student and staff teams to enhance the quality of localised learning experiences. In the three years since its inception, over five hundred students and over two hundred faculty members have jointly shaped over one hundred and thirty innovations that impact upon the learning experiences of our students. For the university, not only does this refresh the curriculum, but it also provides a body of change agents who can impact on the wider student learning experience.

"I've not felt that we've been the students and they've been the staff, we haven't been told what to do, it has been refreshing and quite nice to have

this equal standing. I think it has worked well so far because we have a good mix of approaches, how we work and how we have learnt off each other... you feel like you are learning and growing rather than just being told, which is quite nice...we just feel like a team, there is no hierarchy or anything so it's great." (Student 1)

The university has embraced student engagement through partnership within the corporate plan and is delighted with the impact of these projects and the engagement of students and staff. We are nonetheless aware that the employment of 200 students per year on SAP activities is only a small proportion of the total student population at our university. However we do think that the introduction of this number of change agents into the student community every year does have a positive effect on the overall culture of the institution.

In the vast majority of cases the detailed proposals for participation in these initiatives arose in programme teams within individual schools or departments. Through such mechanisms it was possible for faculty/staff to pursue long-standing issues and for students to participate proactively in enhancement rather than merely being reactive contributors to institutional processes. In such ways, partnerships could be forged. An interesting by-product of this approach has been the emergence of not only shared agendas but also, pleasingly, the development of new perspectives. It has, for example, been a regular finding that faculty/staff report that they have gained new insights through working in partnership with their students. Mäensivu *et al.* (this volume) offer an interesting case study of the interpersonal dynamics of such ways of working.

The central SAP coordination team have adopted a contagion model for change and they charge all SAP participants, faculty and students, to 'infect' others in their locality with their enthusiasm and ideas. No project is ever funded for a second year as each project team is also charged with persuading those who have the local resources that their innovation is of such value that it needs to be embedded into normal operations the following year.

"...this SAPs thing has already started to infect ideas that are going on in the faculty about how we do define our relations with students .... Because we are stuck with this absolutely horrendous thing of customers which I think is so wrong. I think it could have a significance way beyond

the SAPs project itself in that we are entering uncharted waters about how students view themselves and how staff operate in academia and it is really up for grabs." (Faculty member 1)

The equality of the relationship between students and staff is key to the SAP development and reflects the philosophical underpinnings of trying to create a sense of belonging. Perhaps significantly, our students are paid for the work they do with us; the vast majority of students who study at our university require paid work to support their study. We believe that we would discriminate against those students who need to work if we did not pay because only those who could afford to engage (that is those not needing paid employment) would do so. To highlight the partnership, the induction process for all SAP partners emphasises the equality of development opportunity for both faculty and students.

Of course, ideas may originate with students or faculty but through the wider buy-in that comes with a partnership model we believe that more significant change will be delivered. To give the reader an impression of the sorts of projects that are delivered through SAP, we offer a sample (of titles) drawn from the 2011/12 academic year below:

- better Retention through Improved Orientation (BRIO);

- student Targeting Active Resources for Students (STARS);

- shaping the Administrative Services within a Faculty: supporting the 'student journey';

- using feed-forward feedback to enhance the Personal Tutor experience for students;

- teaching Mentoring and Curriculum Development Scheme;

- constructive Learning Activities for Analysis and Design with Lego MindStorm;

- developing a Real-Time Research Workshop for Undergraduate Research Methods Training.

The approach to innovation and change through SAP has been recognised through (UK) national awards (Times Higher Award for Outstanding Support for Students, 2010) and through adoption by the Higher Education Academy (HEA) in its 'Students as Partners' Change Programme

(2012) offered in conjunction with our university. This opportunity has seen ten universities join this HEA Students as Partners change programme, enabling them to explore how they might adopt and indeed reinterpret our student-as-partner approach to enhance the quality of their own education provision. As one of the sector leaders in the area of student engagement some may feel our university has developed a definitive recipe for effective furtherance of academic quality through influential student engagement. We believe however that we have only just started along this journey of change and are now seeking to learn from our experiences so that the broadening of student participation in such activity, through increased student numbers, can be achieved.

Analysis of the first three years of SAP cohorts shows that the SAP population broadly mirrors that of the university. Table 2 shows the average student attainment on their study programmes. This data is reassuring in that it demonstrates that student take-up of the SAP opportunity was not limited to the student educational elite; this may represent evidence that our decision to pay students for their work does result in a pattern of take-up representative of the wider university.

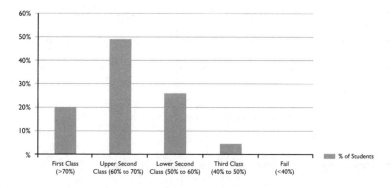

Figure 1: Three years' analysis of the average module performance of all SAP students.

Our contention that the SAP scheme fosters a sense of community is borne out in the comments students and staff made as part of their evaluation of the scheme:

> "Felt good to be part of the university – not just a student…very rewarding to be able to discuss issues with lecturers and staff as an equal – both trying to improve things." (Student 2)

"We are at the start of something that is really exciting in the University. We are beginning to see students starting to act as the flag bearers for student engagement and there is increasing good will and understanding. The Student Academic Partnership Scheme has helped to do that too. I think we are gathering a critical mass of people that see the value." (Faculty member 2)

As observed above, we consider our continuing work now is to build upon the success of the SAP initiative, to capitalise on the principles we have declared, and to cascade our philosophy and approaches more widely so as to deliver broader engagement of the student body.

Student Academic Partners: Summary of Quality Enhancement

These examples of active partnership between staff and students illustrate some of the ways we have sought to empower students to influence the design of curricula that they and their peers will go on to study. These types of student engagement activity are essential in generating a learning community where faculty-staff interactions are bolstered and process variables of quality enhancement can be addressed. It is critical that the deliberate steps we make to improve the learning experience include student agency since students bring a perspective to bear on issues of crucial importance that we, as academics, cannot bring – namely, the 'lived experience' of study. Through this they participate in the academic learning community and as one student partner highlighted:

"Yes, my attitude towards Birmingham City University has changed. As a student you take things at face value and don't fully appreciate nor understand the hard work staff members invest into the University to make students' experience and learning enjoyable. (Student 3)

This breaking down of the barriers between students and staff within the learning community enhances understanding and increases satisfaction of both students and staff. For the university, an overarching appreciation of the value of the student perspective and a respect of, and confidence in, students' collective ability to assist in enhancing the quality of their learning experience, goes beyond periodic activity relating to specific curriculum design work and underpins one of the major strands of our coherent strategy.

Parallel Initiative: Student Employment Scheme

In 2011 the University embarked on a strategic development to engage students further within the fabric of the university. Supported by the HEA and the Leadership Foundation, the university participated in a Change Academy initiative whereby it sought to devise a philosophy and plan that would see over one thousand students working in all aspects of the university's provision by 2015.

The desire to employ our own students was based upon the principle that we value our students so highly that we should wish to employ them ourselves. The simple, self-imposed question of 'if the university that educates the students is not willing to employ them, then how can it expect other employers to do so?' offers much food for thought. In addition to this overarching philosophical position, the university would also benefit from the affordances of a flexible workforce that could meet demand quickly, whilst providing our students with opportunities to develop the employability skills and experience that come from real employment. In that sense, an aim of curriculum design – to enhance the employability profile of our students – can be delivered through extra-curricular student engagement. These outcomes, related as they are to student abilities on exiting their programme, could be seen as 'product' variable deliverables in relation to our quality enhancement agenda. Huet et al. (this volume) also write about the value of extracurricular activities (in their case research grants) as opportunities to develop students' transferable skills.

A partnership with Northwest Missouri State University in the United States of America has shown us the wider benefits of student employment. These include greater student affiliation to the university, greater retention and improved student employee performance in their academic studies. Birmingham City University hopes to reap similar benefits as it seeks further to develop the creation of a vibrant and effective learning community. The university's senior management and Human Resources team have been persuaded of the benefits of the concept and have embedded student employment within operational plans so that, in forthcoming years, student employment will become the normal mode through which temporary employment opportunities are filled.

As we pilot our approaches to student employment, so we have been able to collect narrative accounts of some of the people involved. Some of these narrative accounts are shared below:

> "Working at BCU has enabled me to have greater respect towards the University. I feel proud to be a student and employee because it is a welcoming institution that is student focused. With this in mind, I look forward to the next day at work because I feel like a valued member of the team. I now appreciate students are not passive customers of their learning experience but are able to personally enhance their learning and social development." (Student 4)

We anticipate that student academic performance is also likely to improve, as students will be on campus for more sustained periods:

> "I enjoy my time at university now and spend more time inside the campus instead of just coming in to the library to do my assignment and leaving. I feel I am giving something back to the University community at BCU." (Student 5)

Students also report a sense of allegiance to their new employer, which drives improved performance. A Business School student reported that her job as an administrator in the Art and Design faculty has made her work more diligently on her academic subjects, as she "did not wish to embarrass her new employer with poor grades."

Within the Student Employment Scheme the university has also initiated a Student Academic Mentoring Programme that seeks to employ over sixty students in academic mentoring activities across the university. Once again, this scheme seeks to partner students and staff in activities that offer mentoring opportunities across our institution. As one student mentor stated:

"It gives students a sense of worth. It certainly gave me a sense of belonging and made me feel that I could have an idea for some interesting or cool project and if it was accepted I could go with it. It is motivating to be able to do that with the support of the University and for students to get involved." (Student 6)

Student Employment Scheme: Summary of Quality Enhancement

What better way could there be to improve the learning experience of students than to employ them to work within the offices that have imposed the systems and processes that the student has just experienced? The opportunity for direct and impactful feedback that leads to meaningful change is substantial. Through trust in our students, their abilities and their professionalism, we contend that the momentum to encourage further student engagement will grow and the value of employing students in various areas of the university's operation will become clearer. We believe that through this engagement, the sense of student belonging to an institution that values their views will develop and will facilitate the creation of a culture that encourages students to involve themselves in a shared quality enhancement agenda.

By complementing the activity relating to input into curriculum design and delivery with a more broad-based approach to student engagement in the institutional life of our university, we hope further to enhance the process and thus product variables of academic quality. We are convinced that such opportunities contribute to a bolstered sense of belonging that leads to greater engagement in a shared quality enhancement agenda.

Conclusion

Hardy and Bryson (2010) offered the view that student engagement increased student abilities and general thinking resulting in improved achievement and retention. This was extended to suggest engagement was a combination of intellectual application, diligence, and participation in the learning community supported by a sense of purpose. This viewpoint provides real resonance with notions of student engagement delivering enhancements in quality – in this case, product variables relating to student capability. Mainly the various initiatives put in place as part of a wider initiative seek to influence positively the lived experience of studying at our university and thus relate to the process variables of a quality enhancement agenda.

We conclude this chapter by offering some National Student Survey statistics (Figure 3) gathered over the past four years in response to the following survey inquiries:

1. I feel part of an academic community in my college or university

2. Within my course I feel my suggestions and ideas are valued

	2009	2010	2011	2012
Q1	65%	67%	72%	76%
Q2	65%	67%	75%	78%

Table 2: Responses to the questions above for last four years.

These figures are encouraging and support a conclusion that the initiatives we have described in this chapter have contributed to the realisation of a learning community and thus quality enhancement at an institutional level.

About the Authors

Paul Bartholomew is Director of Learning Innovation and Professional Practice at Aston University. He can be contacted at this email: p.bartholomew@aston.ac.uk

Stuart Brand is Director of Learning Experience at Birmingham City University, UK. He can be contacted at this email: stuart.brand@bcu.ac.uk

Luke Millard is Head of Learning Partnerships at Birmingham City University, UK. He can be contacted at this email luke.millard@bcu.ac.uk

A Comparison of Two Learning and Teaching Centres in the E.U. Area: Strategies for Quality Enhancement of Teaching and Learning

Lorenzo Vigentini and Laurent Ledouc

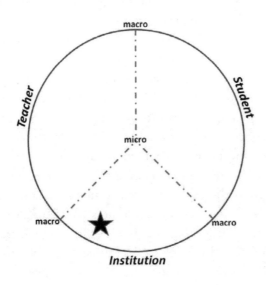

Introduction

The concept of quality in higher education has grown in importance in the past two decades driven by what Harvey and Askling (2003:69) called a *"package of simultaneous changes affecting higher education"* which include a large increase in students' numbers, devolution of authority, uncomfortable management shifts toward efficiency, a marked increase in external control directed by QA (Quality Assurance) agencies, and systematic evaluations of research, often affecting directly the allocation of funding (Williams, 2004, Kuenssberg, 2011). In the European context, the Bologna process has had a significant role in providing a unifying framework to direct quality. However, the concept of what quality entails is complex and multi-faceted. In practice, the issue of quality has shifted from an implicit aspect of learning and teaching – an expected responsibility of academics – to a formalised and complex set of strategies, processes and evaluations which is often imposed from the outside. These can fit under the umbrella terms of quality, Quality Assurance (QA) and Quality Enhancement (QE).

However, the issue of quality goes beyond simple definition. Krause (2012:285) called it the *"wicked problem"* of higher education and argued that: *"(...) quality in higher education constitutes a wicked, ill-defined problem that is under-theorised yet associated with high stakes policy-making and funding, particularly at the macro national level."*

Harvey (2006) suggested that quality in Higher Education (HE) embraces five conceptions; namely, excellence, consistency, fitness of purpose, value for money, and transformation. These conceptions are related to, but distinct from notions of standards (such as academic, competence, service and organisational standards). In fact, particularly in the past few years, the concept of quality has been portrayed as fundamentally separate from the processes used to monitor, assure, evaluate and enhance quality. One important question is whether QA should be measuring the transformation of quality in HE. However, the transformative value of both QA and QE for student learning has yet to be fully demonstrated, particularly in a rapidly changing environment. For these reasons we would argue that a myopic focus on narrow metrics of QE, rather than a broader overview, is actually detrimental.

To demonstrate such a position, this chapter depicts the reality of two

European universities which have organisational structures (i.e. Centres) dedicated to learning and teaching and compares how their operations drive the enhancement of learning and teaching in the respective institutions. Figure 1 provides an overview of how the Centres place themselves in the middle of a loop of influences which contributes to institutional development and leads to quality enhancement of the teaching and learning. Their work is instrumental in delivering training and development opportunities for lecturers, and improving students' experience and employability, ultimately supporting the delivery of a QE agenda. Nonetheless, we will argue that the metrics to evaluate QE have to be contextually different and specific to each institution.

The two centres, one at the University of Glasgow (GU) in Scotland and the other at the University of Liege (ULg) in the French-speaking area of Belgium, provide an opportunity to explore differences and similarities in the ways in which the institutions support academic development, promote innovation and align to EU policies.

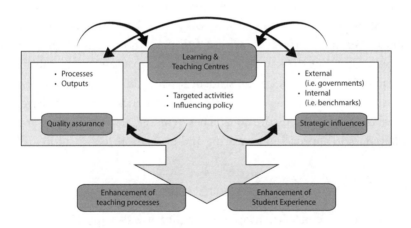

Figure 1. An overview of the loop of influence supported by a central Learning and Teaching Centre (LTC).
[Note: the positioning of the LTC is pivotal in the loop of influences to inform the activities leading to the enhancement, directly or indirectly, of students' learning experience]

The two centres can be considered at different stages of maturity, bound to their history and development and to the 'way in which things are done', and are embedded in the different cultures of the respective institutions. However, drawing a direct comparison of the strategic orientation, priorities, approaches and the activities, we are able to portray an interesting overview of the pivotal importance of such organisational entities to drive governance and strategic growth of the universities and in engaging with both students and academic staff.

In the course of this chapter we will first look at how the current literature on quality has shaped the authors' shared interpretation of quality and its enhancement. This does not necessarily represent the respective institutional perception of what QA and QE are, but will provide an essential interpretational lens for the remainder of the chapter. Then we describe the nature and activities of the two centres; once again, this is not intended to be a comprehensive review. Finally, we will argue that, despite the different national, institutional, cultural and linguistic factors, and the rather different organisational structures and dependencies, the range of activities offered to enable QE at the institutional level are essential to promote QE at programme or course level. This convergence of approaches and methods to achieve QE is an interesting observation in its own right, but the key outcomes of the comparison are: 1) the identification of a common focus on student learning and 2) the recognition of the strategic positioning and responsibility of such centres to drive real enhancement in the institutions. These emerge *despite* the fundamental differences in approach, monitoring and evaluation.

An Overview of QA and QE

In the authors' conceptualisation of quality, it was helpful to refer to the definition of quality (excellence, consistency, fitness of purpose, value for money, and transformation) proposed by Harvey and Knight (1996). Nevertheless, one of the overarching themes in the higher education literature on quality is how to define and measure it. As observed by Radford (1997) the reasons across countries why quality had become an issue in the late 80s and 90s are derived from ideologies founded on *accountability* or *improvement*. Many claim that accountability and improvement are incompatible (for an overview of the issue see Harvey

& Williams, 2010) because the openness, essential for improvement, tends to be absent if accountability is the aim. However, improvement and accountability can also be represented as inseparable, equal sides of a coin; accountability can always be looked at as one perspective driving improvements. An alternative view would be to consider accountability and improvement as opposite poles of a continuum in which the observer's perspective on transformational change is adjusted to focus more on the object (who/what is evaluated) or the subject (who is evaluating) as the actor of evaluation. What emerges is only like a snapshot; in reality the appraisal of quality is subject to change, shaped by both internal and external forces over time as much as the perspective or point of view taken.

An important aspect to consider is who are the stakeholders interested in quality and for what purpose. And this provokes even more questions. The following example is used to illustrate the problem. Assuming that departments from different universities were producing graduates with equivalent standards of achievement, the quote below demonstrates the complexity of quality as characterised/perceived by the stakeholders (i.e. government officials, employers, parents and students):

> *"Department A attracts students on entry with the highest possible grades, whereas Department B attracts students on entry with much lower grades. The public perception is that A is of higher quality than B. But because the achievements of the graduates are the same, it could be argued that B is of higher quality because the value added to its students is much greater. Department C has better qualified staff and better physical facilities than Department D. The public perception is that C is of higher quality than D. But C is more costly and, because the achievements of the graduates are the same, D is more efficient. Department E proclaims goals of high standards whereas Department F is more modest in its statements of what it intends. The public perception of E is that it is of higher quality than F, whereas F is more effective than E."* (Frazer 1994:104)

In these examples which compare pairs of universities it is striking that the key differences are concerned with the metrics and interpretations of quality. However, it is also evident that there is no such thing as an *objective characterisation* of quality; in each case a number of contextual variables affect the judgement and the evaluation and the same metrics are not relevant in all cases. The conditions affecting evaluation of quality will be referred to again later in this chapter with a focus on the importance of the reference criteria for the evaluation and the assessment of the impact of QE.

In their conceptualisation, the authors were also influenced by Biggs (2003:266) who, referring to the 'reflective institution', distinguished between two kinds of quality assurance: *"(...) retrospective QA which assures quality by requiring conformity to externally imposed standards; and prospective QA, which assures quality by continually striving to improve teaching and learning in the institution."*

Biggs also specified that retrospective quality assurance takes the role of a summative evaluation of what the institution does. This should lead to an evaluation with commitments to upgrade and improve teaching in the future by requiring that procedures are in place to lead quality enhancement. On the other hand, what is referred above as prospective QA could be named QE.

In this sense, QA encompasses all processes aimed at the monitoring and evaluation of quality. On the other hand, QE is intended as a strategic approach to quality presupposes the definition of priorities which strategically drive the concept of quality (for example the *Enhancement Themes* in Scottish Universities) focused on defining standards and setting them apart (with reference to the idea of excellence) from their international counterparts.

In our observations, most of the literature on quality assurance focuses on *processes*, but it seems to fall short of advocating action on the outcomes/findings of these QA processes. As an example, key performance indicators (KPIs), often used as valid representations of quality, tend to be viewed as somewhat abstract metrics. In a similar way that a grade assigned to a student is only a proxy indicating the achievement of a course learning outcomes, the use of KPIs as summary metrics are only one perspective towards quantifying the quality of learning and teaching whereas it should only be the starting point of the enhancement process.

Taking another example, in the EVALUE project (Dubois, 1998) – a 30-month European Community project including 11 institutions in eight countries – the author concluded that the evaluation process itself can cause improvement in university performance under certain conditions:

- cognitive, learning, cultural, identity and legitimating effects during the evaluation;

- the nature and presentation of the evaluation results, and the presence or otherwise of sanctions relating to these results;

- the institution and its members take ownership of the evaluation results;

- permanent mechanisms for internal evaluation are established.

Ideally these are also matching the principles behind the emergence of national and cross-national quality assurance agencies and external reviews. However, as indicated above, such entities and initiatives shift the attention on accountability and this often creates a defensive and emotional reaction in those who are the objects of the review or audit processes.

An interesting recent trend has been the growing need to counter external assessment exercises with the creation and establishment of strong internal processes to promote QE. This marks a shift from QA to QE. For example, the international mobility agreement (like the European Credit Transfer Scheme - ECTS) or national quality frameworks, provide a generic scaffold for a shared understanding of quality. Universities, at different organisational levels, become the subjects of QE, acting proactively in order to monitor, assure, assess and evaluate practice. Although formal processes are implemented differently in individual universities, they tend to align with external criteria to simplify the evaluation process.

Evaluation systems and entities (at institutional, national and international level) contributed to both convergence and divergence in the management and the formulation of HE policy (Sporn, 2003). However, as we will observe in this chapter, key differences in policies do not necessarily imply operational differences in what universities do.

Institutional Background

There are two main perspectives characterising the backgrounds of the cases presented in this chapter. The first is the Bologna Agreement and the second is the growing importance of academic development in the HE sector – in the UK in particular.

Much momentum for quality enhancement has been provided by a range of European policies and funding following the Bologna Agreement signed in June 1999 by 29 European countries. Its main objective was the harmonisation of programmes of study and the recognition of study titles in higher education (HE). However, Castells observed that "(...) *universities are social systems and historically produced institutions, all their functions take place simultaneously within the same structure, although with different emphases*" (Castells, 2001:211). Although the main focus has always been on mobility, there is an underlying agenda which pushes institutions in the EU area to harmonise the ways in which QA is performed and to provide tools allowing transparent and direct comparison and recognition of courses and degree programmes (i.e. the ECTS guide).

Alongside this, a common trend in the Higher Education sector has been the growing importance of *academic development*. This term is used intentionally in its most generic way; similar to Clegg (2009) the authors refer to both educational development and staff/professional development which are often interpretations based on the presence of individual roles in the institutions. We believe that both aspects contributed strongly to the creation and establishment of the two Centres and their activities.

In order to systematically consider the development of these entities it is useful to draw from the work of Palmer *et al.* (2011). In a study evaluating the roles of learning and teaching centres across Australia, they identified four factors critical to ensure the success of these organisational entities:

1) development of purpose (in liaison with the senior management or executive);

2) shared understanding of the purpose (emergent from senior academic leadership, head of divisions/faculties/schools and academic teaching staff);

3) capacity and capability to achieve purpose;

4) ability to demonstrate purpose achieved.

It should be noted that in the definition of factors Palmer and colleagues also provide explicit reference to the stakeholders, whose interests had been shown earlier to vary.

Palmer *et al.* (2011) also suggest that these key aspects can represent a 'maturity framework' which the leaders of the centres should use to reposition their centres in a rapidly changing environment. They see the role of such centres as pivotal in reaching maturation and moving from an embryonic stage (when the centres are created or restructured) to maturity (when the centres are seen as integral part of university activities and are valued in fostering teaching and learning practices across the institution).

To assist in the systematic description of the areas of practice and domains of influence in which the centres we are involved with, we will borrow from the benchmarking framework developed in Australia (see Table 1, CADAD 2010). This allows adoption of a broader international stance, but it also offers an opportunity to make this model more relevant to the EU context, in which some specific challenges are present.

The two centres described in the next section have some remarkable similarities in the range of activities they are involved with. However, there are some key differences with regards to institutional priorities, organisational structures and how the national contexts affect the work done 'on the ground' by staff belonging to the two centres.

In order to define how the activities or methods used to foster teaching and learning fit into institutional strategy and culture we have decided to focus specifically on two aspects; *staff/teacher development* – with the underlying assumption that better teachers can deliver better learning for the students – and *curriculum development*. The latter is also dependent on the fact that better teachers are more likely to be more aware of and better suited to the design of learning experiences which are effective. In the UK this is clearly referred to in the UK Professional Standards Framework (UK PSF) and a practical example can be also found in Lawrence and Corkill (this volume) who describe the central role of a specific programme for new lecturers. Klopper and Drew (this volume), focus on the individual development of teachers and demonstrate the impact of a peer review process to help the improvement in teaching practice in an Australian university.

1. Strategy, Policy and Governance	5. Credit-bearing Programs in Higher Education
Strategic Advice. Strategic Planning. Governance. Policy Development and Implementation. Strategic Initiatives.	Program and Course Design. Management. Delivery.
2. Quality of Learning and Teaching Standards	6. Curriculum Development
Evaluation and Improvement. Student Feedback. Peer Review. Curriculum Review.	Curriculum Planning and Design. Education Resource Development.
3. Scholarship of Teaching and Learning	7. Engagement
Grants and Awards. Significant Projects and Research into Learning and Teaching. Research into Academic Development.	Internal Engagement. External Engagement.
4. Professional Development	8. ADU Effectiveness
Planning. Management. Delivery.	ADU Mission and Strategy Alignment. ADU Leadership and Management. ADU Impact. ADU Quality Assurance and Improvement.

Table 1. Domains of practice for ADU (Academic Development Units) – table adapted from the CADAD report 2010.

The Scottish University

At the University of Glasgow (GU), there is evidence of a commitment to the enhancement of the quality of learning and teaching (L&T). There are formal L&T committees at School, College and University-wide level, but there is also an explicit management structure which includes a vice-principal for L&T, four college Deans of L&T and a student elected representative organisation that includes a vice-principal with a learning and teaching remit. According to McKenzie and Mann (2009) these are the products of an overarching quinquennial Learning and Teaching Strategy document which has been driving the quality agenda at this university since 2006. Using the wording from the document:

> "The Learning and Teaching Strategy is central to the maintenance and enhancement of an intellectually stimulating learning environment that delivers a truly excellent student experience.
>
> Our **vision** for Learning & Teaching remains, as originally set out in 2006, of a motivated, vibrant, diverse community of learners and teachers working in partnership to develop confident, skilled and highly valued graduates equipped for knowledge based society, enabled by a learning culture that values teaching and is shaped by our research rich environment." (GU L&T strategy 2011-16)

There are two unique aspects emerging from this quote. Firstly, *student experience* is a fundamental focus for all activities related to learning and teaching. The second aspect is the particular attention to the culture and an environment which are considered *enabling* for teachers and students to create a working partnership with the ultimate aim of developing graduate who will be ready for the 'real world'.

If we consider the framework suggested by Palmer *et al.* the strategic view and shared understanding of the purpose are clearly present.

The Learning and Teaching Centre (LTC) at GU was formally created in 2005 with the intention of bringing three existing and established services (the Teaching and Learning Service, the Learning Technology and the Media Services) under the same roof to promote the interrelations between these services, guided by the L&T strategy. Earlier we mentioned two areas of interest in terms of staff and curriculum development. Within these there are a number of activities in which the Centre plays a pivotal role: staff development, curriculum development via promotion/funding of innovation in teaching and college-specific support, the dissemination of good practice via CPDs and the L&T conference, and the reward of excellence in teaching.

Before the Centre was formed, the Teaching and Learning Service had already been responsible for staff development via both CPD and a New Lecturer Teaching Programme accredited by the Higher Education Academy (at Fellow level) and also offering students learning support. Since the late 90s, training has been compulsory for new lecturers, but this provision became a credit-bearing, Master level course in 2001. At approximately the same time, it was agreed that graduate teaching assistants (GTAs – also referred to as tutors, lab demonstrators or adjunct staff in some schools) should receive a minimum of a full day training to be split between the Learning and Teaching Centre and the Schools. The New Lecturer Teaching Programme (now the Postgraduate Certificate in Academic Practice, PgCAP) is a Masters level course running over two years and has an intake of about 80 new lecturers per annum phased over two entry points in September and January. Teaching is delivered via both face to face and online classes and it is assessed via an integrative portfolio comprising a number of elements which include reflective pieces, evaluation of their teaching and peer observations of teaching.

The GTA provision has changed over time but, in its current form, consists of a single half-day session; GTAs also expect to receive a further half day of support provided in the School in which they teach. The GTA statutory sessions cater for an average of 350 new GTAs every year. Aside from the compulsory training, further opportunities are provided through a GTA development series consisting of a range of fortnightly classes and workshops covering a range of topics in teaching and learning and focusing on the practical aspects of teaching appropriate to the GTA level. GTAs are encouraged to seek accreditation as Associate Fellows of the HEA and the development series is designed to support them in the process.

Another element, which is not included in the teaching approach described above, is a Continuous Professional Development (CPD) series of workshops which is offered to all staff and covers aspects of teaching and learning, learning technology and scholarship. These programmes are central to the QE agenda in order to develop teachers.

A second area of interest is the management of a Learning and Teaching Development Fund (LTDF) which was created to facilitate the support of initiatives to enhance teaching and/or promote scholarship of teaching in the different subjects. In the past few years, between 8-15 projects have been awarded an average of £10,000 via formal applications and review. The approximate figure for the number of projects is dependent on the amount requested and awarded to each project and this has varied over the years. Each application is scrutinised by a panel and feedback is provided to all applicants. In the case of a successful application a project is assigned a support officer who will be a member of the academic staff in the LTC, usually with a specific or cognate expertise in the area. Each funded project is expected to produce usable outcomes, produce a final report and be disseminated at least at the annual Learning & Teaching Conference. In terms of QE, the funding is specifically intended to promote initiatives to develop teaching and therefore affect directly the students' learning experience.

The third area of interest focuses on the dissemination of scholarship and good practice. This is mainly achieved with an annual Learning and Teaching conference and by rewarding good teachers at different levels of their careers with a Teaching Award scheme. Both are regulated by a robust peer-reviewing process which is designed to ensure that good practice is really recognised and valued appropriately to its merit. The conference has grown considerably from a local event to one which attracts submissions from other national and international scholars.

The dissemination of good practice is seen as another essential building block of QE as cases of excellent practice can gain visibility and move from specific courses to programmes in other disciplines.

All the activities listed above are the key aspects for building capacity as identified in Palmer's framework, however, even though we have pointed out some indicators of success, it is more difficult to demonstrate the impact of the LTC in a holist way. However, we can see that QE is emerging as a by-product of the activities rather than a specific target with a causal connection to a process/mechanism which affects the enhancement.

The Belgian University

At the University of Liege (ULg), the Service of Management and Support of Quality (SMAQ) has been led by the Vice-Rector for Quality Management since 2009. Its overall mission is to promote, coordinate and disseminate a culture of quality based on the values of the institution. The Institute for Research and Training in Higher Education (IFRES) was created in 2005 by the Management Board of the Institution. The key aim was to foster and support pedagogical initiatives and provide teacher training to meet the requirements of the Bologna Decree. This is a law passed by the Government of the French-speaking community in Belgium in 2004 and its aim is to encourage integration in the EU, to promote pedagogical initiatives, and advance teachers' development. In particular, the decree specified the objectives and missions of higher education (article 2) and defined that teaching staff in HE should be equipped with adequate "pedagogical skills and professionalism" (article 3).

The IFRES is also born out of the institutional will to strengthen and integrate the pre-existing initiatives aimed to promote innovation and teacher support; some were independently developed by academic staff since the early 2000s. Adequate resources have been deployed to amalgamate and sustain these initiatives and services and to benefit the academic and scientific community of the ULg. Some of these include:

- the *Methodological System of Help in Tests Realization* or SMART. This is responsible for supporting teachers in conceiving, implementing, analysing and evaluating student assessment methods and outputs (i.e. written exams and MCQs) and developing tools for the evaluation of teaching and students' feedback;

- the *Laboratory in Support of Telematic Learning* or LabSET is specialised in distance learning. Its main remit is to assists the university community (teachers and learners) to acquire the skills and technologies pertaining to high quality distance learning and to contribute to privately funded projects;

- the Complementary Master in Higher Education Pedagogy *Formasup* is a 60 credits (ECTS) programme. This is delivered both online or through a blended learning, including face-to-face sessions in French or English versions; its aims are to enhance the quality of higher education by 'professionalizing teaching';

- finally, considerable resources were channelled from various sources (some at institutional level and some from the IFRES) in order to mobilise a large number of teachers in order to support the implementation of Problem-Based Learning in the faculty of Medicine and other faculties and departments.

One of the most prominent missions of the IFRES is to coordinate the training provision in higher education pedagogy at the institution. It includes three strategic objectives: the first two are direct applications of the Bologna Decree. The academic mission to *"organise the Complementary Master in Higher Education Pedagogy"* (annex IV, article 18) was already implemented in 2001 as the DES (Diplôme d'Etudes Spécialisées) Formasup. Secondly, the decree prescribes the establishment of a *Centre de Didactique Supérieure* or CDS with the mandate to support, counsel and train staffs in charge of first-year students (article 83). Created as an integral part of the IFRES since inception, the CDS has taken charge of the organization of over 40 face-to face sessions, dealing with various pedagogical themes related to the enhancement of the First Year Experience, and has designed following 'application seminars' in a number of cases (offering online resources and individualised support for those who want to design a concrete activity/device related to these topics in a given course).

The third and most recent component of the IFRES training offer finds its origin in a decision taken by the University Management Board in 2007 to establish a compulsory training programme focusing on teaching in higher education for new academics during their probationary period and for teaching assistants in their first term. This obligation implies the participation in 10 half a day long training sessions with possible derogation for holders of specific credentials in education, and the submission of a short final reflective report. The fulfilment of the 10 units of training can be spread over two years (with no minimum requirement per year). Every new academic or assistant selects the thematic sessions of his/her own interest from a varied range of possibilities, which evolved from a total of 23 items in 2007-2008 (among which 5 were mandatory) to 59 in 2011-2012 (entirely free-to-chose entry). This catalogue is regulated yearly according to the feedback given by participants to in-session satisfaction questionnaires, and according to the new priorities identified within the university.

From this description it is evident that the QE remit of the IFRES is mainly focused on the development of teachers who have the responsibility of shaping students' learning experience.

However, in order to carry out its missions (supporting teachers and departments in their education of students; promoting research in higher education, implementing a quality approach in the evaluation of teaching and learning) the IFRES has also been developing other key activities:

- organising since 2007 a yearly one-day conference dedicated to sharing scholarship of teaching at the university (every year key themes are chosen and discussed by invited internal speakers/practitioners from faculties and international experts running workshops, round tables and plenary sessions);

- setting up since 2008 the "Faculties Anchoring" programme to enhance synergies between the IFRES and teaching actors from faculties, allowing them to submit (trough a standardised application form) an innovating pedagogical project directly related to their students' training, and for which they can receive funding and personalised support;

- funding and supporting (notably through the opening of an International Chair in higher education), from 2007-2008 to 2011-2012, projects carried out by groups of teachers belonging to the same training scheme and willing to implement educational practices aimed at the development of competences.

The emphasis of this overview is that the involvement of the IFRES has arisen from different levels of the organisation and was driven by different actors. Some were initiated by the authorities/management of the University, some came directly from within the IFRES and some originated from specific departments or academic with a particular expertise in higher education.

A Comparative Perspective

Considering an international perspective on the HE sector, which is not only becoming more competitive but is also affected by a decrease in public funding, the analysis of the work done in two very different universities provides a set of valuable lessons.

Firstly, from the descriptions of the two centres, it is apparent that the priorities and strategic approaches justifying their existence are different.

Despite the fact that efficiency and knowledge transfer might be the managerial justifications for pulling together rather different pre-existing organisational entities and initiatives, at the top level, their common aim is to enhance learning and teaching. In the case of GU, the Learning and Teaching Strategy drives activities and acts as a catalyst for shared understanding and purpose. At ULg, the Centre itself provides a physical reference to pivot the actions despite the fact that diverse forces act towards their own aims; in this case the shared understanding is implicit or pushed from the top. In both cases the Centres are in the middle of a loop of influence which affects the processes for monitoring quality and uses the outputs of QA to direct their activities. This loop also interacts and responds to strategic influences (both internal and external) to shape institutional policies and shape the university strategy. In this sense, the work with done with staff at different levels is the core focus leading to enhancement of teaching practices.

Secondly, by adopting the model presented in the CADAD report (Table 1), which offers a systematic scaffold to classify the activities presented, it is possible to show that both centres are actively involved in the specific QA processes and benchmarking of all the areas listed, and this indicates broad overlaps between their activities. Both centres are led in a transparent way and regularly report on their activities to various academic bodies. In both cases, using Palmer's framework, both centres present many elements which characterise their maturity. Of course, the logistic structures of the centres determines who is delivering the services, but the pivotal role in the enhancement of teaching and learning is a common denominator. The overlap of activities of the EU and Australian universities seems to suggest a theoretical alignment of what Academic Development Units and Learning and Teaching Centres should be doing, but the slight differences in implementations shown between GU and ULg should be the subject of further reflection.

Referring to the practical aspects considered in the previous section, for example, both centres are responsible for the delivery of programmes targeting new lecturers. At this point in time, a minimum training requirement is present in both universities to address aspects of strategy, professional development and the systematic management and design of credit-bearing programmes. In the Scottish university this is an accredited credit-bearing programme (PGCAP) and is a probationary requirement for all new lecturers. In the Belgian institution, although the content is very similar and it is a probationary requirement, unlike the PGCAP in which participants have a set curriculum, ULg staff are able to build their own curriculum by choosing the *courses* they want to attend. This model is more akin to the CPD series for the GTA development that is offered at GU.

Another aspect to keep in mind is that new lecturers and GTAs are considered differently at GU, but, at ULg, staff with different seniority (lecturers and 'assistants') attend the same sessions. Furthermore, whilst at GU there is a formal (summative) assessment associated with programme (but not for the CPD or the GTA development courses) this is not a requirement of the programme at ULg.

Considering the nature of the quality of these programmes, one could ask what is the real *impact* of the differences between the programmes? By taking a snapshot view of the past five years, if the number of individuals 'graduating' from these courses is used as metric – with the assumption that more qualified teachers will be better teachers – the institutional impact (or reach) of the sessions at ULg is higher than at GU where roughly the same number of people, including new appointments, took part every year. In comparison, the number of participants attending the 3-hours thematic sessions offered by the CDS has grown steadily from 108 to 148 between the first and second year. However if impact is measured as consistent engagement with teaching and learning (or transformative effect), the sessions at the CDS seem to be less effective; the increase in the number of attendees was not followed by any gain in the number of enrolments in the possible subsequent 'application seminars' (in some instances less with than four participants per seminar). At GU the course is spanning over two years with a number of sessions and the prolonged exposure is believed to provide a transformational experience.

Another key difference is the lack of a formal summative assessment at ULg. It is difficult to state whether, from attendance alone, the provision is leading to better teaching (in the transformative sense). This is also true for new lecturers attending the PGCAP at GU, but the opportunity offered to critically reflect on their practice for an extended period of time facilitates a deeper transformative process in new staff conceptions of teaching and learning and encourages them to take conscious steps in evaluating their practice. The evidence of this transformation comes from peer observation and peer review meetings, which provide a space for openly discuss how new lecturers develop (see also Klopper & Drew, this volume). Critically, this should produce more self-aware and reflective teachers, who will be more likely to engage proactively with their practice, students' feedback and quality enhancement. However, some only engage with the course because they have to.

Furthermore, considering the case studies/evaluations used in the summative assessment of the PGCAP (similar to those described by Lawrence & Corkhill, this volume), these small research projects concerned with teaching should facilitate continuous engagement with the scholarship of learning and teaching in the discipline. At the ULg the reflective reports submitted at the end of the programme provide some evidence of engagement with enhancement. In both cases evidence of a sustained engagement with learning and teaching is lacking and the authors are considering a follow-up review of how the programmes influence practice two or three years after 'graduation' from the courses to assess the long term value of the provision.

From a completely different perspective, one could argue that students' metrics (i.e. the strategic targets set for the teachers trained in engaging with students) would be more appropriate for evaluating the impact of these programmes. Retention and progression are typically used to assess the effects of 'quality teaching'. However, the number of recent graduates finding employment two years of economic recession is unlikely to make such comparisons straightforward. In this case, the assumption that better graduates are more likely to find a better job may be quite inaccurate. One could widen the scope and look at the comparison between graduates exiting different universities to ascertain whether those graduating from *this* university are considered better than the ones exiting courses elsewhere, but should the focus be regional, national or international? It is no surprise that benchmarking and reputation management are becoming more and more relevant in academic management jargon.

Another practical example of the effectiveness of staff engagement with scholarship of learning and teaching is the annual conference which both centres are organising. In both cases there has been a healthy increase in participation over the years. The main difference between them is in the process. For example, at ULg staff are invited to showcase examples of good practice which have been 'championed' within the academic community. At GU, staffs submit abstracts which are peer reviewed before acceptance; over time the number of submissions has grown making it more competitive to obtain presentation slots. Although these underlie a different philosophy, both methods reflect the institutional culture and have been effective in engaging staff in the scholarship of teaching and learning.

The most important difference emerging from the comparison, which brings the discussion back to the dyad of accountability and improvement, seems to be at the level of the evaluation of effectiveness of their activities and in the way in which they engage in the process of evaluation. Although both centres have undergone external reviews with self-evaluation reports summarising strengths and weaknesses of their activities, the data/reports are used quite differently. At the IFRES a recent external evaluation in 2009-10 encouraged the various units to produce relevant supporting evidence of their achievements. A list of recommendations was produced detailing at length what were the points requiring attention or action. At GU it seems that similar sources of data are used proactively as benchmarks not only to evaluate, but also to monitor interim progress towards the objectives set out in the Learning and Teaching Strategy document. We can observe this difference, but it is not possible to get a clear sense that the approaches lead to clear differences in terms of quality assurance or quality enhancements.

Very much like in the quote from Frazer earlier, the use of different metrics by different stakeholders leads to different views of quality. However, the focus on activities rather than outcomes might be more important to demonstrate the emergent value of enhancement, and strong similarities between activities have been observed. The fact that these seems to be driven by internal, strategic, but measurable objectives is in our view much more important than benchmarking comparisons between universities and certainly more effective in informing the Quality Assurance processes and impact in terms of Quality Enhancement.

The comparison of the Centres is useful to demonstrate a theoretical alignment of activities. However, the most important aspect of the arguments in this chapter is the fact that the positioning of the respective Learning and Teaching Centres is pivotal to produce the enhancement of student experience. This is achieved by shaping and mediating institutional strategies with QA mechanisms and actively engaging the learning community by developing better prepared teachers who are ultimately responsible to cater for students' diversity.

About the Authors

Lorenzo Vigentini is is Lecturer/Academic Developer at University of New South Wales. He can be contacted at this email: l.vigentini@unsw.edu.au

Laurent Leduc is the coordinator of the CDS (Centre de Didactique Supérieure de l'Académie Universitaire Wallonie) of the IFRES (Institute for Research and Training in Higher Education), Belgium. He can be contacted at this email: Laurent.Leduc@ulg.ac.be

Collected Bibliography

Adjieva, M. & M. Wilson (2002). Exploring the development of quality in higher education. *Managing Service Quality*, Vol. 12, No. 6, pp. 372-383.

Ahrens, T. & C. S. Chapman (2006). New Measures in Performance Management. In A. Bhimani (Ed.) *Contemporary Issues in Management Accounting*: 1-16: Oxford University Press.

Ahrens, T. & C. S. Chapman (2007). Management Accounting as Practice. *Accounting, Organizations and Society*, Vol. 32 No 1, pp 1-27.

Alderman, G. (2010). Reflections: Change, Quality and Standards in British Higher Education. *Journal of Change Management*. Vol. 10, No.3, pp. 243-252.

Allen, R. & G. Layer (1995). *Credit Based Systems as Vehicles for Change in Universities and Colleges*. London: Routledge.

Altricher, H. & P. Gsettner (1993). Action research: a closed chapter in the history of German social science? *Educational Action Research*, Vol.1, No. 3, pp. 329-360.

Andersson, P. H.; P. M. Hussmann & H. E. Jensen (2009). Doing the right things right – Quality enhancement in Higher Education. A paper presented at the *2009 SEFI conference*. Online resource: http://www.sefi. be/wp-content/abstracts2009/Andersson.pdf [Accessed 27 January 2013].

Andresen, L.; D. Boud & R. Cohen (2000). Experience-Based Learning. In G. Foley (Eds.) *Understanding Adult Education and Training*. Sydney: Allen & Unwin, pp. 225-239.

Ashby, A. (2004). Monitoring student retention in the Open University. *Journal of Open and Distance Learning*, Vol. 19, No. 1, pp. 65-77.

Askew, S. (2004). Learning about teaching through reflective, collaborative enquiry and observation. *Learning Matters*. Vol. 15, pp. 2-4.

Atherton, C. (2006). A-Level English Literature and the Problem of Transition. *Arts and Humanities in Higher Education*, Vol. 5, pp. 65 -76.

Atherton, C. (2012). Teaching English Literature Post-16. In A. Green (Ed.) *A Practical Guide to Teaching English in the Secondary School*. Abingdon: Routledge, pp. 85-93.

Atlay, M.; A. Gaitán & A. Kumar (2008). Stimulating Learning – Creating CRe8. In C. Nygaard & C. Holtham (Eds.) *Understanding Learning-Centred Higher Education*. Frederiksberg: Copenhagen Business School Press, pp. 231- 250.

Australian Government (2012). *MyUniversity*. Online resource: http://myuniversity.gov.au [Accessed 31 January 2013].

Baird, J. R. (1988). Quality: what should make higher education 'higher'? *Higher Education Research and Development*, Vol. 7, No. 2, pp. 141-152.

Ballinger, G. J. (2003). Bridging the Gap between A Level and Degree: Some Observations on Managing the Transitional Stage in the Study of English Literature. *Arts and Humanities in Higher Education*, Vol. 2, No. 1, pp. 99-109.

Bamber, V. & S. Anderson (2012). Evaluating learning and teaching: institutional needs and individual practices. *International Journal for Academic Development*. Vol. 17, No. 1, pp. 5-18.

Bandura, A. (1975). *Social Learning & Personality Development*. New York, NY: Holt, Rinehart & Winston Inc

Banks, F.; J. Leach & B. Moon (1999). New Understandings of Teachers' Pedagogic Knowledge. In J. Leach and B. Moon (Eds.) *Learners and Pedagogy*. London: Paul Chapman, pp. 89-110.

Barnard, A.; W. Croft; R. Irons; N. Cuffe; W. Bandara & P. Rowntree (2011). Peer partnership to enhance scholarship of teaching: a case study. *Higher Education Research & Development*. Vol. 30, No. 4, pp. 435-448.

Barrie, S. & P. Ginns (2007). The Linking of National Teaching Performance Indicators to Improvements in Teaching and Learning in Classrooms. *Quality In Higher Education*, Vol. 13, No. 3, pp. 275-286.

Bartholomew P. and N. Bartholomew (2011). Learning through Innovation. In C. Nygaard; C. Holtham & N. Courtney (Eds.) *Learning and Teaching in Higher Education: Beyond Transmission – Innovations in Learning and Teaching*. Oxfordshire: Libri Publishing Ltd.

Bartholomew, P.; S. Brand & D. Cassidy (2010). Distributed Approaches to Postgraduate Curriculum Design. In. C. Nygaard; N. Courtney & L. Frick (Eds.) *Postgraduate Education – Form and Function*. Oxfordshire: Libri Publishing Ltd.

Bartlett, L. (2005). Dialogue, knowledge, and teacher-student relations: Freirean pedagogy in theory and practice. *Comparative Education Review*, Vol. 49, No. 3, pp.344-364.

Baumeister, R. F. & M. R. Leary (1995). The Need to Belong: Desire for Interpersonal Attachments as a Fundamental Human Motivation. *Psychological Bulletin*, No. 117, pp. 497-529.

Becket, N. & M. Brookes (2006). Evaluating quality management in university departments. *Quality Assurance in Education*. Vol. 14, No. 2, pp.123-142.

Becket, N. & M. Brookes (2008). Quality Management Practice in Higher Education – What Quality Are We Actually Enhancing? *Journal of Hospitality, Leisure, Sport and Tourism Education*, Vol. 7, No. 1, pp. 40-54.

Bell, A. & R. Mladenovic (2008). The benefits of peer observation of teaching for tutor development. *Higher Education*. Vol. 55, No. 6, pp. 735-752.

Bell, M. (2001). Supported Reflective Practice: a program of peer observation and feedback for academic teaching development. *International Journal for Academic Development*. Vol. 6, No. 1, pp. 29-39.

Bennett, S. & J. Santy (2009). A window on our teaching practice: Enhancing individual online teaching quality though online peer observation and support. A UK case study. *Nurse Education in Practice*. Vol. 9, No. 6, pp. 403-406.

Biggs, J. B. & C. Tang (2007). *Teaching for Quality Learning at University*. Maidenhead: Open University Press/McGraw Hill. 3rd edition.

Biggs, J. B. & C. Tang (2011). *Teaching for Quality Learning at University*. Maidenhead: Open University Press/McGraw Hill. 4th edition.

Biggs, J. B. (1993). From theory to Practice: a cognitive systems approach. *Higher Education Research and Development*, Vol. 12, No. 1, pp. 73-85.

Biggs, J. B. (1996). Enhancing Teaching through Constructive Alignment. *Higher Education*. Vol. 32, no. 3, pp. 347-364.

Biggs, J. B. (1999). *Teaching for Quality Learning at University*. Buckingham: The Society for Research into Higher Education and Open University Press.

Biggs, J. B. (2001). The Reflective Institution: Assuring and Enhancing the Quality of Teaching and Learning, *Higher Education*, Vol. 41, No. 3, pp. 221-238

Biggs, J. B. (2003). *Teaching for quality learning at university*. London: Open University Press. 2nd edition.

Billing, D. (2004). International Comparisons and Trends in External Quality Assurance of Higher Education: Commonality or Diversity? *Higher Education*, Vol. 47, No. 1, pp. 113-137.

Birch, E. & P. Miller (2006). Student outcomes at university in Australia: a quantile regression approach. *Australian Economic Papers*, Vol. 45, No. 1, pp.1-17.

Bisbe, J.; J.-M. Batista-Foguet & R. Chenhall (2007). Defining Management Accounting Constructs: A methodological note on the risks of conceptual misspecification. *Accounting Organizations and Society*, Vol. 32 No 7/8, pp 789-820.

Blackwell, R. & P. Blackmore (Eds.) (2003). *Rethinking Strategic Staff Development*. Buckingham: Society for Research into Higher Education and Open University Press.

Bloom, B. S. (1956). *Taxonomy of Educational Objectives, Handbook I: The Cognitive Domain*. New York: David McKay Co Inc.

Bluett, J.; S. Cockcroft; A. Harris; J. Hodgson & G. Snapper (2004). *text : message: The Future of A Level English*. Sheffield: National Association for the Teaching of English.

Booth, A. (1997). Listening to Students: Experiences and Expectations in the Transition to a History Degree. *Studies in Higher Education*, Vol. 22, No. 2, pp. 205-220.

Boud, D. & G. Feletti (Eds.) (1997). *The Challenge of Problem-Based Learning*. Kogan Page, London.

Boud, D. (1999). Avoiding the traps: seeking good practice in the use of self assessment and reflection in professional courses. *Social Work Education*. Vol. 18, No. 2, pp. 121-132.

Bourdieu, P. & J-C. Passeron (1977). *Reproduction in Education, Society and Culture*. London: Sage.

Bourdieu, P. (1990). *Reproduction in Education, Society and Culture*. London: Sage.

Bowman, D. & P. Hughes (2005). Emotional Responses of Tutors and Students in Problem-Based Learning: Lessons for Staff Development. *Medical Education*, Vol. 39, No. 2, pp. 145-153.

Boyatzis, R. E. (1982). *The Competent Manager: A model for effective performance*. New York: John Wiley & Sons.

Boyer, E. L. (1990). *Scholarship Reconsidered: Priorities of the Professoriate*. Menlo Park, California: Carnegie Foundation for the Advancement of Teaching.

Bramming, P. (2007). An Argument for Strong Learning in Higher Education, *Quality in Higher Education*, Vol. 13, No. 1, pp. 45-56.

Brew, A. & E. Jewell (2012). Enhancing quality learning through experiences of research-based learning: implications for academic development. *International Journal for Academic Development*, Vol. 17, No. 1, pp. 47-58.

Brew, A. (2006). *Research and Teaching – Beyond the Divide*. Basingstoke: Palgrave MacMillan.

Brew, A. (2010). Imperatives and challenges in integrating teaching and research. *Higher Education Research & Development*, Vol. 29, No. 2, pp. 139-150.

Bridges, D. (1993). Transferable Skills: A Philosophical Perspective, *Studies in Higher Education*, Vol. 18 No. 1, pp. 43-51.

Britzman, D. P. (2009). The Poetics of Supervision: A Psychoanalytical Experiment for Teacher Education. *Changing English*, Vol. 16, No. 4, pp. 385-396.

Brown, R. B. & S. McCartney (1998). The link between research and teaching: Its purpose and implications. *Innovations in Education and Teaching International*, Vol. 35, No. 2, pp. 117-129.

Brown, S. (1999). How can threshold standards assure and enhance quality? In H. Smith, M, Armstrong & S. Brown (Eds.) *Benchmarking and Threshold. Standards in Higher Education*. London, Kogan Page, pp.35-52.

Brownlee, J. (2004). An investigation of teacher education students' epistemological beliefs: Developing a relational model of teaching. *Research in Education*, Vol. 72, pp. 1-17.

Bruce, M. A. & J. Stellern (2005). Building a caring community in teacher education. *The Teacher Educator*, Vol. 41, No. 1, pp. 34-53.

Bruner, J. S. (1986). *Actual Minds, Possible Worlds*. Cambridge, MA: Harvard University Press.

CADAD. (2010). Benchmarking Performance of Academic Development Units in Australian Universities. CADAD. Online resource: http://www.cadad.edu.au/pluginfile.php/119/mod_page/content/1/Resources_and_publications/Benchmarking_report/Benchmarking_Report.pdf [Accessed 17 January 2013].

Cambone, J. (1990). Teachers and teaching: Tipping the balance. *Harvard Educational Review*, Vol. 60, No. 2, pp. 217-236.

Carini, R.; G. D. Kuh & S. Klein (2006). Student Engagement and Student Learning: Testing the Linkages. *Research in Higher Education*. Vol. 47, No. 1, pp. 1-32.

Carr, W. & S. Kemmis (1986). *Becoming Critical: Education Knowledge and Action Research*. London: Routledge.

Chamberlain, J. M.; M. D'Artrey & D-A., Rowe (2011). Peer observation of teaching: A decoupled process. *Active Learning in Higher Education*. Vol. 12, No. 3, pp. 189-201.

Chapman, C. M. & R. S. King (2005). *Differentiated Assessment Strategies: One Tool Doesn't Fit All.* Thousand Oaks, CA: Corwin Press.

Chickering, A. W. & Z. F. Gamson (1987). Seven principles for good practice in undergraduate education. *AAHE Bulletin.* Vol. 39, p. 6.

Clayson, D. E., & D. A. Haley (2011). Are students telling us the truth? A critical look at the student evaluation of teaching. *Marketing Education Review.* Vol. 21, No. 2, pp. 101-112.

Clegg, S. (2009). Forms of knowing and academic development practice. *Studies in Higher Education*, Vol. 34, No. 4, pp. 403–416.

Clerehan, R. (2003). Transition to Tertiary Education in the Arts and Humanities: Some Academic Initiatives from Australia. *Arts and Humanities in Higher Education*, Vol. 2, No. 1, pp. 72–89.

Coates, H. (2005). The Value of Student Engagement for Higher Education Quality Assurance, *Quality in Higher Education*, Vol. 11, No. 1, pp. 25-36.

COBE (2005). *Action Research: A Guide for Associate Lecturers.* Milton Keynes: The Open University, Centre for Outcomes-Based Education.

Cohen, L.; L. Manion & K. Morrison (2005). *Research Methods in Education.* London: Routledge.

Cook, A. & J. Leckey (1999). Do Expectations Meet Reality? A Survey of Changes in First Year Student Opinion. *Journal of Further and Higher Education*, Vol. 23, No. 2, pp. 157–171.

Coppieters, P. (2005). Turning Schools into Learning Organizations, *European Journal of Teacher Education.* Vol. 28, No 2, pp 129-139.

Creswell, J. W. (2012). *Educational Research: Planning, conducting, and evaluating quantitative and qualitative research* (4th ed.). Boston: Pearson Education Inc.

Critical Integrative Teacher Education (2012). Available at https://www.jyu.fi/edu/laitokset/okl/integraatio/en [Accessed 6 August 2012].

Cuthbert, D.; D. Arunnachalam & D. Licina (2011). 'It feels more important than other classes I have done': an 'authentic' undergraduate research experience in sociology. *Studies in Higher Education*, Vol. 37, No. 2, pp. 129-142.

Dall'Alba, G. (2005). Improving teaching: Enhancing ways of being university teachers. *Higher Education Research & Development*, Vol. 24, No. 4, pp. 361-372.

D'Andrea, V. & D. Gosling (2005). *Improving Teaching and Learning in Higher Education: A Whole Institution Approach.* Berkshire: McGraw-Hill Education.

Dean, C. D.; D. Dunaway; S. Ruble & C. Gerhardt (2002). *Implementing problem-based learning in education*. Birmingham, AL: Samford University Press.

Deming, W. E. (2000). *Out of the crisis*. Massachusetts, MA: MIT Press.

Devlin, M. & G. Samarawickrema (2010). The criteria of effective teaching in a changing higher education context. *Higher Education Research & Development*, Vol. 29, No. 2, pp. 111-124.

Dewey, J. (1986). Experience and Education. *The Educational Forum*, Vol. 50 No 3, pp 241-252.

Dexter, B. & R. Seden (2012). "It's really making a difference": How small-scale research projects can enhance teaching and learning. *Innovations in Education and Teaching International*, Vol. 49, No. 1, pp. 83-93.

Dobozy, E. (2011). Resisting Student Consumers and Assisting Student Producers. In C. Nygaard; N. Courtney & C. Holtham (Eds.) (2011) *Beyond Transmission – Innovations in University Teaching*. Oxfordshire: Libri Publishing Ltd., pp. 11-25.

Donnelly, R. (2007). Perceived impact of peer observation of teaching in higher education. *International Journal of Teaching & Learning in Higher Education*. Vol. 19, No. 2, pp. 117-129.

Dubois, P. (1998). EVALUE, Évaluation et auto-évaluation des universités en Europe. *Rapport final. Projet financé par la communauté européenne*.

Dunbar-Hall, P. (2009). Ethnopedagogy: culturally contextualised learning and teaching as an agent of change. *Action, Criticism and Theory for Music Education*, Vol. 8, No. 2, pp. 60-78.

Dunbar-Hall, P. (2010). Learning and Teaching Balinese Gamelan: An experiential investigation of cultural diversity in music education. *Proceedings of the Tenth International Conference on Cultural Diversity in Music Education*, University of Sydney, January, pp. 39-44.

Dunbar-Hall, P.; J. Rowley; M. Webb & M. Bell (2010). ePortfolios for music educators: parameters, problems and possibilities. *Proceedings of the 29th World Conference of the International Society for Music Education*, Beijing, pp. 61-64.

Durkin, K. & A. Main (2002). Discipline-Based Study Skills Support for First-Year Undergraduate Students. *Active Learning in Higher Education*, Vol. 3, No. 1, pp. 24–39.

Elliott, J. (1991). *Action research for educational change*. Buckingham: Open University Press.

Ellis, D. (2008). *In at the Deep End*. London: Higher Education Academy English Subject Centre, Royal Holloway University of London.

Emirates24/7 (2012). Expats make up over 88% of UAE population. Online resource: http://www.emirates247.com/news/expats-make-up-over-88-of-uae-population-2011-04-17-1.381853 (Accessed 11 January 2013).

Entwistle, N. (1988). *Styles of Learning and Teaching*. London: David Fulton Publishers.

Erskine, J. A., M. R. Leenders & L. A. Mauffette-Leenders (1998). *Teaching with Cases*. Ontario, Canada: Ivey Publishing, Richard Ivey School of Business.

European Commission. (2010). *Europe 2020: A Strategy for Smart, Sustainable and Inclusive Growth*: Communication from the Commission. Publications Office.

Falchikov, N. (2001). *Learning Together-Peer Tutoring in HE*. London: Routledge.

Fallows, S. & C. Steven (Eds.) (2000). *Integrating Key Skills in Higher Education*. London: Kogan Page.

Felder, R. M. & L. K. Silverman (1988). Learning and Teaching Styles in Engineering Education. *Engineering Education*, Vol. 78. No. 7, pp. 674-681.

Filippakou, O. & T. Tapper (2008). Quality assurance and quality enhancement in higher education: contested territories? *Higher Education Quarterly*, Vol. 62, No. 1-2, pp. 84-100.

Fincher, R-M. E. & J. A. Work (2006). Perspectives on the scholarship of teaching. *Medical Education*, Vol. 40, pp. 293-295.

Fogarty, R. (Ed.) (1998). *Problem-based learning*. Arlington Heights, IL: IRI/ Skylight Training and Publishing, Inc

Frazer, M. (1994). Quality in higher education: an international perspective. In D. Green (Ed.) *What is Quality in Higher Education?* Buckingham: Open University press and Society for Research into Higher Education, pp. 101–111.

Freire, P. (1978). *Pedagogy in Process*. New York: Seabury.

Freire, P. (1990). *Pedagogy of the Oppressed*. New York: Continuum.

Geraldo, J. L. G.; C. Trevitt; S. Carter & J. Fazey (2010). Rethinking the Research-Teaching Nexus in Undergraduate Education: Spanish laws pre- and post-Bologna. *European Education Research Journal*, Vol. 9, No. 1, pp. 82-91.

Gerlander, M. & P. Isotalus (2010). Professionaalisten viestintäsuhteiden ääriviivoja [Outlines of Professional Communication Relationships] *Puhe ja kieli [Speech and Language]* , Vol. 30, No. 1, pp. 13–19.

Gibbs, G. (2010). *Dimensions of Quality*. York. Higher Education Academy.

Ginns, P., J. Kitay & M. Prosser (2010). Transfer of academic staff learning in a research-intensive university. *Teaching in Higher Education*. Vol. 15, No. 3, pp. 235-246.

Goffman, E. (1986). *Frame Analysis. An Essay on the Organization of Experience*. Boston: Northeastern University Press.

Goleman, D. (1995). *Emotional Intelligence*. New York: Bantam Books.

Good Universities Guide (2012). *The Good Universities Guide*. Online resource: http://www.gooduniguide.com.au/?gclid=CI_mpXZ768CFVGApAodv3TJXg [Accessed 8 January 2013].

Goodenow, C. (1993). Classroom belonging among early adolescent students: relationships to motivation and achievement. *Journal of Early Adolescence*, Vol. 13, No. 1, pp. 21-43.

Gordon, S. & K. Fittler (2004). Learning by teaching: A cultural historical perspective on a teacher's development. *Outlines*, Vol. 6, No. 2, pp. 35-46.

Graneheim, U.H. & B. Lundman (2004). Qualitative content analysis in nursing research: concepts, procedures and measures to achieve trustworthiness. *Nurse Education Today*, Vol. 24, pp. 105-112.

Granovetter, M. (1992). *Economic Action and Social Structure: The Problem of Embeddedness*. In M. Granovetter & R. Swedberg (Eds.) The Sociology of Economic Life (1992). Boulder CO: Westview Press.

Grebennikov, L. & I. Skaines (2008). University of Western Sydney students at risk: profile and opportunities for change. *Journal of Institutional Research*, Vol. 14, No. 1, pp. 58-70.

Grebennikov, L. & M. Shah (2012). Investigating attrition trends in order to improve student retention. *Quality Assurance in Education*, Vol. 20. No. 3, pp. 223-236.

Green, A. (2005a). English Literature: From Sixth Form to University. *International Journal of Adolescence and Youth*, Vol. 12, No. 4, pp. 253–280.

Green, A. (2005b). *Four Perspectives on Transition: English Literature from Sixth Form to University*. London: Higher Education Academy English Subject Centre, Royal Holloway University of London.

Green, A. (2006). University Challenge: Dynamic Subject Knowledge, Teaching and Transition. *Arts and Humanities in Higher Education*, Vol. 5, No. 3, pp. 275–290.

Green, A. (2009). *Starting an English Literature Degree*. Basingstoke: Palgrave Macmillan.

Green, A. (2010). *Transition and Acculturation*. London: Lambert Academic Publishing.

Green, A. (2011). English in Transition. *English Drama Media*, Vol. 20, pp. 57-62.

Green, L. (Ed.) (2011). *Learning, teaching, and musical identity: voices across cultures*. Bloomington: Indiana University Press.

Greenwood, J. D. (1994). A Sense of Identity: Prologomena to a Social Theory of Personal Identity. *Journal for the Theory of Social Behavior*, Vol 24, No 1, pp 25-46.

Griffith University (2012). Teaching quality enhancement. Online resource: http://www.griffith.edu.au/gihe/teaching-quality-enhancement [Accessed 17 January 2013].

Grossman, P. L.; S. M. Wilson & L. S. Shulman (1989). Teachers of Substance: Subject Matter Knowledge for Teaching. In M. C. Reynolds (Ed.) *Knowledge Base for the Beginning Teacher*. Oxford: Pergamon, pp. 23-36.

Guterman, L. (2007). What good is undergraduate research, anyway? *The Chronicle of Higher Education*, Vol. 53, No. 50, pp. 1-6.

Gvaramadze, I. (2008). From Quality Assurance Quality Enhancement in the European Higher Education Area, *European Journal of Education*, Vol. 43, No. 4, pp. 443-455.

Gvaramadze, I. (2008). From Quality Assurance to Quality Enhancement in the European Higher Education Area. *European Journal of Education*, Vol. 43, No. 4, pp. 443-455.

Habermas, J. (1984). *The theory of communicative action. Vol. 1: reason and the rationalisation of society*. Boston: Beacon Press.

Habermas, J. (1991). *The Structural Transformation of the Public Sphere: An Inquiry into a Category of Bourgeois Society*. Cambridge, MA: MIT Press.

Habermas, J. (2001). *Moral Consciousness and Communicative Action*. Harvard: MIT Press.

Hall, G. & K. Hooper (2008). Australia's Exports of Education Services, 2012. Online resource: http://www.rba.gov.au/publications/bulletin/2008/jun/2.html [Accessed 8 January 2013].

Halldorsdottir, S. (1990). The Essential Structure of a Caring and an Uncaring Encounter with a Teacher: The Perspective of the Nursing Student. In M. Leininger & J. Watson (Eds.) *The Caring Imperative in Education*. New York: National League for Nursing, pp. 95-108.

Hamachek, D. (1999). Effective Teachers: What they do, how they do it, and the Importance of Self-knowledge. In R. P. Lipka & T.M. Brinthaupt (Eds.) *The Role of Self in Teacher Development*. Albany, NY: State University of New York Press, pp. 189-224.

Hämäläinen, K.; J. Kangasniemi & K. Hämäläinen (2011). Finnish State-funded Continuing Professional Development System for Education Personnel. Annual conference of the Association for Teacher Education in Europe. Online resource: www.ppf.lu.lv/pn/files/articles/ATEE%20 2011%20Hamalainen.doc [Accessed 21 January 2013].

Hamilton, D. (1989). *Toward a Theory of Schooling*. London: Falmer.

Hammar Chiriac, E. (2008). A Scheme for Understanding Group Processes in Problem-Based Learning. *Higher Education*, Vol. 55, No. 5, pp. 505-518.

Hardy, C. & C. Bryson (2010). The Social Life of Students: support mechanisms at university. Presented at the *Society of Research into Higher Education Conference*. Celtic Manor, Wales, December 14-16.

Harvey L. & P. T. Knight (1996). *Transforming Higher Education*. Buckingham: Open University Press.

Harvey, L. & B. Askling (2003). Quality in Higher Education. In R. Begg (Ed.) *The Dialogue between Higher Education Research and Practice*. Springer Netherlands, pp. 69–83.

Harvey, L. & J. Newton (2004). Transforming Quality Evaluation, *Quality in Higher Education*, Vol. 10, No. 2, pp. 149-165.

Harvey, L. & J. Williams (2010). Fifteen years of quality in higher education. *Quality in Higher Education*, Vol. 16, No. 1, pp. 3-36.

Harvey, L. & P. T. Knight (1996). *Transforming Higher Education*. Bristol: Open University Press/Taylor & Francis.

Harvey, L. (2002). The End of Quality? *Quality in Higher Education*, Vol. 8, No. 1, pp. 5-22.

Harvey, L. (2004). Analytic quality glossary. *Quality Research International*. Online resource: http://www.qualityresearchinternational.com/glossary/ [Accessed 27 January 2013].

Harvey, L. (2006). Understanding Quality. *EUA Bologna Handbook: Making Bologna work*. Online resource: http://www.qualityresearchinternational. com/Harvey%20papers/Harvey%202006%20Understanding%20quality. pdf [Accessed 17 January 2013].

HEA (2008). *Quality enhancement and assurance – a changing picture?* York: Higher Education Academy.

Healey, M. & A. Jenkins (2009). *Developing undergraduate research and inquiry*. UK: Higher Education Academy.

Healey, M. (2000). Developing the Scholarship of Teaching in Higher Education: A discipline-based approach. *Higher Education Research & Development*. Vol. 19, No. 2, pp. 169-189.

Heidegger, M. (1968). *What is called thinking?* [Trans. F.D. Wieck & J.G. Gray]. New York: Harper & Row.

Heikkenen, H. & L. Huttunen (2004). Teaching and the dialectic of recognition. *Pedagogy, Culture and Society*, Vol. 12, No. 2, pp. 163-173.

Helle, L.; P. Tynjälä & E. Olkinuora (2006). Project-Based Learning in Post-Secondary Education – Theory, Practice and Rubber Sling Shots. *Higher Education*, Vol. 51, No. 2, pp. 287-314.

Higher Education Academy (2008). *Quality enhancement and assurance – a changing picture?* York: Higher Education Academy.

Hil, R. (2012). Whackademia: An Insider's Account of the Troubled University, New South, Sydney.

Hmelo-Silver, C.E. (2004). Problem-Based Learning: What and How Do Students Learn? *Educational Psychology Review*, Vol. 16, No. 3, pp. 235-266.

Hodgkinson, M. & G. Brown (2003). Enhancing the Quality of Education: A case study and some emerging principles, *Higher Education*, Vol. 45, No. 3, pp. 337-352.

Hodgson, A. & K. Spours (2003). *Beyond A Levels: Curriculum 2000 and the Reform of 14-19 Qualifications.* London: Kogan Page.

Hodgson, J. (2010). *The Experience of Studying English in UK Higher Education.* London: Higher Education Academy English Subject Centre, Royal Holloway University of London.

Hodson, P. & T. Harold (2003). Quality Assurance in Higher Education: Fit for the New Millennium or Simply Year 2000 Compliant? *Higher Education*, Vol. 45, No. 3, pp. 375-387.

Hofman, J. E. & L. Kremer (1980). Attitudes Toward Higher-Education and Course-Evaluation. *Journal of Educational Psychology*, Vol. 72, No. 5, pp. 610-617.

Honey, P. & A. Mumford (1986). *A Manual of Learning Styles.* Maidenhead: Peter Honey.

Horsburgh, M. (2010). Quality Monitoring in Higher Education: the impact on student learning. *Quality in Higher Education*, Vol. 10, No. 1, pp. 37-41.

Hsieh, H.-F. & S. Shannon (2005). Three Approaches to Qualitative Content Analysis. *Qualitative Health Research*, Vol. 15, No. 9, pp. 1277-1288.

Huet, I.; A. V. Baptista; N. Costa; A. Jenkins & M. Abelha (2009). Evaluation of Undergraduate Students' Involvement in Research Projects. *International Journal of Learning*, Vol. 16, No. 9, pp. 575-588.

Huet, I.; C. Figueiredo; O. Abreu; J. M. Oliveira; N. Costa; J. A. Rafael & C. Ferreira (2011). Linking a Research Dimension to an Internal Quality Assurance System to Enhance Teaching and Learning in Higher

Education. In Z. Bekirogullari (Eds.) *Procedia - Social and Behavioral Journal*, Vol. 29, pp. 947-956.

Huet, I.; J. A. Rafael; N. Costa & J. M. Oliveira (2010). Quality Assurance System to monitor the teaching and learning process at the University of Aveiro (Portugal), 5th *European Quality Assurance Forum*. Conference organized by the EUA, ENAQ, EURASHE and ESU. França, Lyon, 18-20 November. Online resource: http://www.eua.be/Libraries/ EQAF_2010/WGSII_5_Papers_Huet_et_al.sflb.ashx [Accessed 27 January 2013].

Huisman, J. & D. F. Westerheijden (2010). Bologna and Quality Assurance: Progress Made or Pulling the Wrong Cart? *Quality in Higher Education*, Vol. 16, No. 1, pp. 63–66.

Huisman, J.; P. Maassen & G. Neave (Eds.) (2001). *Higher Education and the Nation State: The International Dimension of Higher Education*. Enschede: CHEPS.

Hunter, A-B.; S. L. Laursen & E. Seymour (2007). Becoming a scientist: The role of undergraduate research in students' cognitive, personal, and professional development. *Science Education*, Vol. 91, No. 1, pp. 36-74.

Hunter, A-B.; T. J. Weston; S. T. Laursen & H. Thiry (2009). URSSA: Evaluating student gains from undergraduate research in the sciences. *Council on Undergraduate Research Quarterly*, Vol. 29, No. 3, pp. 15-19.

Jackson, D. & R. Tasker (2003). *Professional Learning Communities*. Nottingham: National College for School Leadership.

Jackson, N. & R. Ward (2004). A fresh perspective on progress files – a way of representing complex learning and achievement in higher education. *Assessment & Evaluation in higher Education*, Vol. 29, No. 4, pp. 423-449.

Jackson, N. (2006). Creativity in higher education: 'Creating tipping points for cultural change'. *SCEPTrE Scholarly Paper* 3 (March), pp. 1-26.

Jahangiri, L.; T. Mucciolo; M. Choi & A. Spielman (2008). Assessment of Teaching Effectiveness in U.S. Dental Schools and the Value of Triangulation. *Journal of Dental Education*. Vol. 72, No. 6, pp. 707-718.

James Cook University (JCU) (2012). Quality Enhancement Framework. Available at http://www.jcu.edu.au/quality/ [Accessed 17 January 2013].

Jeliazkova, M. & D. F. Westerheijden (2002). Systemic Adaptation to a Changing Environment: Towards a Next Generation of Quality Assurance Models. *Higher Education*, Vol. 44, No. 3/4, pp 433–448

Jenkins, A. & M. Healey (2010). Undergraduate Research and International Initiatives to Link Teaching and Research. *Council on Undergraduate Research Quarterly*, Vol. 30, No. 3, pp. 36-42.

Jiang, K. (2009). A Critical Analysis of Accountability in Higher Education: Its Relevance to Evaluation of Higher Education. *Chinese Education & Society*, Vol. 42 No 2, pp 39-51.

JISC (2009). *Managing Curriculum Change*. Online resource: http://www.jisc.ac.uk/media/documents/publications/managingcurriculumchange.pdf [Accessed 28 January 2013].

Johnston, L. (2006). Software and Method: Reflections on Teaching and using QSR Nvivo in Doctoral Research. *International Journal of Social Research Methodology*, Vol. 9, No. 5, pp. 379-39.

Jones, G. A. & A. Oleksiyenko (2011). The internationalization of Canadian university research: a global higher education matrix analysis of multi-level governance. *Higher Education*. Vol. 61, No. 1, pp. 41-57.

Jönsson, S. (1996). *Accounting for Improvement*. Oxford: Pergamon Press.

Kahn, P.; R. Young; S. Grace; R. Pilkington; L. Rush; B. Tomkinson & I. Willis (2008). Theory and legitimacy in professional education: a practitioner review of reflective processes within programmes for new academic staff. *International Journal for Academic Development*, Vol. 13, No. 3, pp. 161-173.

Kandlbinder, P. & T. Peseta (2009). Key concepts in postgraduate certificates in higher education teaching and learning in Australasia and the United Kingdom. *International Journal for Academic Development*, Vol. 14, No. 1, pp.19-31.

Kaplan, R. S., & D. P. Norton (1996). Using the Balanced Scorecard as a Strategic Management System. *Harvard Business Review*, Vol. 74 No 1, January-February, pp 75-85.

Karlsen, S. (2011). Using Musical Agency as a Lens: researching music education from the angle of experience. *Research Studies in Music Education*, No. 33, pp. 107-122.

Keller, F.S. (1968). 'Good-bye, teacher...' *Journal of Applied Behavior Analysis*, Vol. 1, No. 1, pp. 79-89.

Kember, D. (2000). *Action Learning and Action Research – Improving the Quality of Teaching and Learning*. London: Kogan Page.

Kember, D. (2009). Promoting student-centered forms of learning across an entire university. *Higher Education*, Vol. 58, No. 1, pp. 1-13.

Kemmis, S. & R. McTaggart (Eds.) (1992). *The Action Research Planner*. Geelong, Victoria, Australia: Deakin University Press, 3rd edition.

Kidd, S. A. & M. J. Kral (2005). Practicing Participatory Action Research. *Journal of Counselling Psychology*, Vol. 52, No. 2, pp. 187-195.

Kindall-Smith, M.; C. McKay & S. Mills (2011). Challenging exclusionary paradigms in the traditional musical canon: implications for music education practice. *International Journal of Music Education*, Vol. 29, No. 4, pp. 374-386.

Knight, P. (2006). Quality enhancement and educational professional development. *Quality in Higher Education*, Vol. 12, No. 1, pp. 29-40.

Knowles, M. (1984). *Andragogy in Action.* San Francisco: Jossey-Bass.

Knowles, M. (1990). *The adult learner: A neglected species.* Houston, TX: Gulf Publishing.

Kolb, D. A. (1984). *Experiential Leaning.* Englewood Cliffs: Prentice Hall.

Korthagen, F. A. J. (2004). In search of the essence of a good teacher: Towards a more holistic approach in teacher education. *Teaching and Teacher Education*, Vol. 20, No. 1, pp. 77-97.

Koshy, S. (2011). Poster Presentation: An effective assessment for large communication classes? In C. Nygaard; N. Courtney & C. Holtham (Eds.) (2011). *Beyond Transmission: Innovations in University Teaching.* Oxfordshire: Libri Publishing.

Koshy, V. (2010). *Action Research for Improving Educational Practice.* (2nd edition.). London: Sage.

Krathwohl, D. R.; B. S. Bloom & B. M. Bertram (1973). *Taxonomy of Educational Objectives, the Classification of Educational Goals. Handbook II: Affective Domain.* New York: David McKay Co. Inc.

Krause, K.-L. (2012). Addressing the Wicked Problem of Quality in Higher Education: Theoretical Approaches and Implications. *Higher Education Research & Development*, Vol. 31, No. 3, pp. 285–297.

Kristjánsson, K. (2006). 'Emotional intelligence' in the classroom?: An Aristotelian critique. *Eductional Theory*, Vol. 56, No. 1, pp. 39-56.

Kuenssberg, S. (2011). The discourse of self-presentation in Scottish university mission statements. *Quality in Higher Education*, Vol. 17, No. 3, pp. 279–298.

Kuh, G. D. (2003). What We're Learning About Student Engagement from NSSE: Benchmarks for Effective Educational Practices. *Change.* Vol. 35, No. 2, pp. 24-32.

Kuh, G. D. (2009). What Student Affairs Professionals need to know about student engagement. *Journal of College Student Development*, Vol. 50, No. 6, pp. 683-706.

Langbein, L. (2008). Management by results: Student evaluation of faculty teaching and the mis-measurement of performance. *Economics of Education Review.* Vol. 27, pp. 417–428.

Lather, P. (1998). Reaction to "disrupting hegemonic writing practices in school science". *Journal of Research in Science Teaching*, Vol. 35, No. 4, pp. 363-364.

Laursen, S. L.; A-B. Hunter; E. Seymour; H. Thiry & G. Melton (2010). *Undergraduate Research in the Sciences: Engaging students in Real Science.* San Francisco, CA: Jossey-Bass.

Laursen, S. L.; E. Seymour & A-B. Hunter (2012). Learning, Teaching and Scholarship: Fundamental Tensions of Undergraduate Research. *Change: The Magazine of Higher Learning*, Vol. 44, No. 2, pp. 30-37.

Lave, J. & E. Wenger (1991). *Situated Learning: Legitimate peripheral participation.* Cambridge: Cambridge University Press.

Lawrence, L. (2010). "Making It So: A case study in CRe8ing". In M. Atlay (Ed.) *Creating Bridges: A Collection of Articles Relating to Implementing the Curriculum Review 2008 (CRe8) from practitioners across the University of Bedfordshire*, pp. 211-224. Luton: University of Bedfordshire.

Lawson, T. (1997). Situated rationality. *Journal of Economic Methodology*, Vol. 4, No. 1, pp. 101-125.

Leadbeater, C. (2004). Personalisation through Participation: A new script for public services. London: Department for Education and Skills in association with National College for School Leadership.

Lewin, K. (1946). Action Research and Minority Problems. *Journal of Sociological Issues.* Vol. 2, No. 4, pp. 34-46.

Likert, R. (1932). A technique for the measurement of attitudes. *Archives of Psychology.* Vol. 22, No. 140, pp. 1-55.

Little, B. & R. Williams (2010). Students' Roles in Maintaining Quality and Enhancing Learning – Is There a Tension? *Quality in Higher Education*, Vol. 16, No. 2, pp. 115-127.

Livingston, T. S. (1971). Myth of the Well-Educated Manager. *Harvard Business Review.* January-February pp. 79-89.

Lomas, L. & G. Nicholls (2005). Enhancing Teaching Quality Through Peer Review of Teaching. *Quality in higher education.* Vol. 11, No. 2, pp. 137-149.

Lomas, L. & I. Kinchin (2006). Developing a Peer Observation Program with University Teachers, *International Journal of Teaching and Learning in Higher Education*, Vol. 18, No. 3, pp. 204-214.

Lomas, L. (2004). Embedding quality: the challenges for higher education. *Quality Assurance in Education.* Vol. 12, No. 4, pp. 157-165.

Lopatto, D. (2003). The essential features of undergraduate research. *Council on Undergraduate Research Quarterly*, Vol. 24, No. 2, pp. 139-142.

Lopatto, D. (2007). Undergraduate research experiences support science career decisions and active learning. *Cell Biology Education*, Vol. 6, No. 4, pp. 297-306.

Lopatto, D. (2009). *Science in Solution: The impact of Undergraduate Research on Student Learning*. Tucson: Research Corporation for Science Advancement.

Lowe, H. & A. Cook (2003). Mind the Gap: Are Students Prepared for Higher Education? *Journal of Further and Higher Education*, Vol. 27, No. 1, pp. 53–76.

Lundberg, C. A. & A. A. Schreiner (2004). Quality and frequency of faculty-student interaction as predictors of learning: An analysis by student race/ethnicity. *Journal of College Student Development*, Vol. 45, No. 5, pp. 549-565.

MacDougall, M. (2012). Research-Teaching Linkages: Beyond the Divide in Undergraduate Medicine. *International Journal for the Scholarship of Teaching and Learning*, Vol. 6, No. 2, pp. 1-21.

McGregor, D. (1960). The Human Side Of Enterprise, McGraw Hill.

McKenzie, J. & S. Mann (2009). Changing Academic Practice at a UK Research-Intensive University through Supporting the Scholarship of Teaching and Learning (SoTL). *Transformative Dialogues*. Online resource: http://kwantlen.ca/TD.html [Accessed 21 January 2013].

Mäensivu, M. (2012). Auktoriteettisuhteen vankina? Tapaustutkimus luokanopettajaksi opiskelevista [Prisoner of an Authority Relationship? A Case Study of Class Teacher Students] *Aikuiskasvatus* [*Adult Education*], Vol. 32, No. 2, pp. 107-115.

Mantei, J. & L. Kervin (2011). Turning into teachers before our eyes: the development of professional identity through professional dialogue. *Australian Journal of Teacher Education* Vol. 36, No. 1, pp. 1-17.

Marcus, L. R.; A. O. Leone & E. D. Goldberg (1983). The Path to Excellence: Higher Education Quality Assurance in ASHE-ERTC. Higher Education Research Report. Washington, D.C.: Association for the Study of Higher Education

Marginson, S. (2007). Global Position and Position Taking: The Case of Australia. *Journal of Studies in International Education*. Vol. 11, No. 1, pp. 5-32.

Marginson, S. (2011). Global Position and Position-taking in Higher Education: The Case of Australia. In S. Marginson, S. Kaur & E. Sawir (eds.), *Higher Education in the Asia-Pacific: Strategic Responses to Globalization*, pp. 375-392. Springer: Netherlands.

Marland, M. (2003). The Transition from School to University: Who Prepares Whom, When and How? *Arts and Humanities in Higher Education*, Vol. 2, No. 2, pp. 201–11.

Marsh, K. (2000). Making connections: a case study of pre-service music education students' attitudinal change to indigenous music. *Research Studies in Music Education*, Vol. 15, No. 1, pp. 58-67.

Martin, G. A. & J. M. Double (1998). Developing Higher Education Teaching Skills Through Peer Observation and Collaborative Reflection. *Innovations in Education & Training International*. Vol. 35, No. 2, pp. 161-170.

Marton, F. & R. Säljö (1976). On Qualitative Differences in Learning - Outcome and process. *British Journal of Educational Psychology*, Vol. 46, No. 1, pp 4-11.

Marton, F. & R. Säljö (1984). Approaches to Learning. In F. Marton, D. Hounsell & N. Entwistle (Eds.) *The Experience of Learning*. Edinburgh: Scottish Academic Press, pp. 36-55.

Marton, F. (1994). Phenomenography. In T. Husén & N. Postlethwaite (Eds.) *The International Encyclopedia of Education*, Vol. 8, pp. 4424–4429. Oxford: Pergamon.

Maslow, A. (1968). Some Educational Implications of the Humanistic Psychologies. *Harvard Educational Review*. Volume 38, No. 4, pp. 685-696.

Mayer, J. D.; P. Salovey & D. R. Caruso (2000). Competing Models of Emotional Intelligence. In R. J. Steinberg (Ed.) *Handbook of Human Intelligence*. New York: Cambridge University Press, 2nd edition, pp. 396-420.

Mayeroff, M. (1971). *On Caring*. New York: Harper & Row.

McCulloch, A. (2009). The Student as Co-producer: learning from public administration about the student university relationship, *Studies in Higher Education*, Vol. 34, No. 2, pp. 171-83.

McGill, I. & L. Beaty (1995). *Action Learning: A guide for professional, management, and educational development*. London: Kogan Page.

McKimm, J. (2009). Teaching quality, standards and enhancement. In H. Fry; S. Ketteridge & S. Marshall (eds.). *A Handbook for Teaching And Learning in Higher Education. Enhancing Academic Practice*. (3rd edn.). pp. 186-197. Abingdon: Routledge.

McLoone, S. (2007). On the Use of Multiple Class Test Assessments to Promote and Encourage Student Learning. *Case Studies of Good Practices in Assessment of Student Learning in Higher Education. Dublin: AISHE, pp. 64-67.*

McTaggart, R. (1997). Guiding principles for participatory action research. In R. McTaggart (Ed.), *Participatory action research: International contexts and consequences*. New York: State University of New York, pp. 25–44.

Meyer, J. W. & B. Rowan (1977). Institutionalized Organizations: Formal Structure as Myth and Ceremony. *American Journal of Sociology*, Vol. 83 No 2, pp 340-363.

Meyers, D. (2012). Australian Universities: A Portrait of Decline. Online resource: http://www.australianuniversities.id.au/Australian_ Universities-_Portrait_of_Decline.pdf [Accessed October 7, 2013].

Middlehurst, R. (1995). Quality Enhancement in Higher Education. *Engineering Science and Education Journal*, Vol. 4, No. 6, pp. 244-248.

Middlehurst, R. (1997). Enhancing quality. In F. Coffield & B. Williamson (Eds.) *Repositioning Higher Education*. Buckingham: SRHE/Open University Press.

Miliband, D. (2004). Personalised Learning: Building a New Relationship with Schools. Online resource: https://www.education.gov.uk/ publications/eOrderingDownload/personalised-learning.pdf [Accessed 13 January 2013].

Mintzberg, H. (1973). *The Nature of Managerial Work*. New York: Harper Row.

Mintzberg, H. (2004). *Managers Not MBAs: A Hard Look at the Soft Practice of Managing and Management Development*. San Francisco, Calif: Berrett-Koehler Publishers, Inc.

Mishra, S. K. (2008). Possibilities of Quality Enhancement in Higher Education by Intensive Use of Information Technology, *Proceedings of the National Conference on Impact of Assessment and Accreditation of Educational Institutions of Higher Education in India*, Shillong College Academic Society, Shillong (India), 2008, pp. 92-111.

Moore, G. (1973). Towards a Theory of Independent Learning and Teaching. *The Journal of Higher Education*, Vol. 44, No. 9, pp. 661-679.

Morley, L. (2012). Gender and Access in Commonwealth Higher Education. In W. Allen (Ed.), *Achieving Diversity in tertiary and Higher Education: Cross-National Lessons, Challenges and Prospects*. London: Emerald Group Publishing, pp. 41-69.

Moss, P. A. (2005). Understanding the other/understanding ourselves: Toward a constructive dialogue about 'principles' in educational research. *Educational Theory*, Vol. 55, No. 3, pp.263-283.

Murtonen, M.; E. Olkinuora; P. Tynjälä & E. Lehtinen (2008). "Do I need research skills in working life?": University students' motivation and difficulties in quantitative methods courses. *Higher Education*, Vol. 56, No. 5, pp. 599-612.

Nagda, B. A.; S. R. Gregerman; J. Jonides ;W. V. Hippel & J. S. Lerner (1998). Undergraduate student faculty research partnerships affect student retention. *The Review of Higher Education*, Vol. 22, No. 1, pp. 55-72.

National Committee of Inquiry into Higher Education [NCIHE] (1997). *Higher Education in the Learning society. Main report.* London, NCIHE. http://www.leeds.ac.uk/educol/ncihe/ [Accessed 23 June 2012].

National Science Foundation (2003). *Exploring the concept of undergraduate research centers: A report on the NSF workshop.* Arlington, VA: Division of Chemistry, Office of Special Projects, Office of Multidisciplinary Activities, MPS Directorate.

National Survey of Student Engagement (2007). *Experiences That Matter: Enhancing Student Learning and Success.* Bloomington, Indiana University, Center for Postsecondary Research. Available online at: http://nsse. iub.edu/NSSE_2007_Annual_Report/docs/withhold/NSSE_2007_Annual_Report.pdf [Accessed 1 February 2013].

New South Wales Institute of Teachers (NSWIT) (2012). National Professional Standards for Teachers. Online resource: http://www.nswteachers.nsw.edu.au/Initial-Teacher-Education [Accessed 17 January 2013].

Nikkola, T. (2011). *Oppimisen esteet ja mahdollisuudet ryhmässä. Syyllisyyden kehittyminen syntipukki-ilmiöksi opiskeluryhmässä ohjaajan tulkitsemana [Learning in a Group: Obstacles and Opportunities. A Supervisor's Interpretation of How Guilt Becomes Scapegoating in a Study Group].* Jyväskylä Studies in Education, Psychology and Social Research 422.

Nikkola, T.; P. Räihä; P. Moilanen; M. Rautiainen & S. Saukkonen (2008). Towards a Deeper Understanding of Learning in Teacher Education. In Nygaard C. & C. Holtham (Eds.) (2008). *Understanding Learning-Centred Higher Education.* Frederiksberg: Copenhagen Business School Press, pp. 251-263.

Noddings, N. (1984). *Caring: A Feminine Approach to Ethics and Moral Education.* Berkeley: University of California Press.

Noddings, N. (1986). Fidelity in teaching, teacher education, and research for teaching. *Harvard Educational Review*, Vol. 56, No. 4, pp. 496-510.

Noddings, N. (1988). An ethic of caring and its implications for instructional arrangements. *American Journal of Education*, Vol. 96, No. 2, pp. 215-230.

Norton, L. (2009). *Action Research in Teaching and Learning.* London: Routledge.

Nulty, D. (2001). Evaluation of educational programs: Issues for an effective policy framework. Paper presented at the *Teaching Evaluation Forum - Student Feedback on Teaching: Reflections and Projections*, August 2000, Perth, Australia.

Nye, B.; S. Konstantopoulos & L. V. Hedges (2004). How large are teacher effects? *Educational Evaluation and Policy Analysis*, Vol. 26, No. 3, pp.237-257.

Nygaard, C. & D. Z. Belluigi (2011). A proposed methodology for contextualised evaluation in Higher Education. *Assessment and Evaluation in Higher Education*. Vol. 36, No. 6, pp. 657-671.

Nygaard, C. & I. Andersen (2005). Contextual Learning in Higher Education. In Milter; V. S. Perotti & M. S. R. Segers (Eds.) *Educational Innovation in Economics and Business IX*. Breaking Boundaries for Global Learning. pp 277-294. Springer.

Nygaard, C. & M. B. Serrano (2010). Students' Identity Construction and Learning. Reasons for Developing a Learning-Centred Curriculum in Higher Education. In L. E. Kattington (Ed.) *Handbook of Curriculum Development*. New York: Nova Science Publishers Inc., pp. 233-254.

Nygaard, C.; T. Højlt & M. Hermansen (2008). Learning-based Curriculum Development. *Higher Education*, Vol. 55, No. 1, pp. 30-55.

Nygaard, C.; T. Højlt & M. Hermansen (2008). Learning-based curriculum development. Higher Education, Vol. 55, No. 1, pp. 33-50.

Oliver, M. (2007). Quality Assurance and Quality Enhancement in e-learning. Higher Education Academy EvidenceNet. Online resource: http://evidencenet.pbworks.com/w/page/19383515/Quality%20 assurance%20and%20quality%20enhancement%20in%20e-learning [Accessed 22 December 2012].

Otley, D. (2005). Trends in budgetary control and responsibility accounting. In A. Bhimani (Ed.) *Contemporary Issues in Management Accounting*. Oxford: Oxford University Press, pp. 291-307.

Palmer, S.; D. Holt & D. Challis (2011). Strategic Leadership of Teaching and Learning Centres: from Reality to Ideal. *Higher Education Research & Development*, Vol. 30, No. 6, pp. 807–821.

Papinczak, T.; T. Tunny & L. Young (2009). Conducting the Symphony: a Qualitative Study of Facilitation in Problem-Based Learning Tutorials. *Medical Education*, Vol. 43, No. 4, pp. 377-383.

Patall, E. A.; H. Cooper & S. R. Wynn (2010). The Effectiveness and Relative Importance of Choice in the Classroom. *Journal of Educational Psychology*, Vol. 102, No. 4, pp. 896-915.

Perkins, D. (1999). The many faces of constructivism. *Educational Leadership*, Vol. 57, No. 3, pp. 6-11.

Peters, O. (2000). The transformation of the university into an institution of independent learning. In T. Evans & D. Nation (Eds.) *Changing University Teaching – Reflections on Creating Educational Technologies*. London: Kogan Page, pp. 10-23.

Power, A. & P. Dunbar-Hall (2001). My views on teaching strengthened: Perceptions of the problems and benefits of international practicum by pre-service music educators. *Pacific-Asian Education*, Vol. 13, No.2, pp. 55-67.

Prosser, M. & K. Trigwell (1999). *Understanding Learning and Teaching: The experience in higher education*. Buckingham: Open University Press.

PRO-Teaching Project (2012). *Guidelines for Peer Review and Observation of Teaching to Improve Learning and Teaching*. Online resource: http://www.ict.griffith.edu.au/~sdrew/PRO-Teaching/PRO-Teaching-Standard [Accessed 23 January 2013].

QAA (2006). Handbook for institutional audit: England and Northern Ireland, paragraph 46. Online resource: http://www.qaa.ac.uk/reviews/institutionalaudit/handbook2006/handbookcomments.asp [Accessed 15 January 2013].

QAA (2012). UK Quality Code for Higher Education. Chapter B5: Student Engagement. Online resource: http://www.qaa.ac.uk/Publications/InformationAndGuidance/Documents/Quality-Code-Chapter-B5.pdf [Accessed 15 January 2013].

QAA (2012). *UK Quality Code for Higher Education*. Gloucester: Quality Assurance Agency for Higher Education. Online resource: www.qaa.ac.uk/assuringstandardsandquality/quality-code [Accessed 29 November 2012].

Quellmalz, E. S. (1985). Developing Reasoning Skills. In J. R. Baron & R. J. Sternberg (Eds.) *Teaching Thinking Skills: theory and practice*. New York: Freeman, pp. 86-105.

Race, P. (2003). Why Assess Innovatively?. In S. Brown & A. Glasner (Eds.) *Assessment Matters in Higher Education*. Buckingham: Open University Press.

Radford, J. (1997). *Quantity and Quality in Higher Education*. London: Jessica Kingsley Publishers.

Raiker, A. (2010). Creativity and reflection: some theoretical perspectives arising from practice. In C. Nygaard; C. Holtham & N. Courtney (Eds.) *Teaching Creativity - Creativity in Teaching*. Oxfordshire: Libri Publishing Ltd.

Ramsden, P. (1992). *Learning to Teach in Higher Education.* London: Routledge.

Ramsden, P. (2008). *The Future of Higher Education Teaching and the Student Experience.* London: Department of Business, Innovation and Skills. Online resource: http://www.bis.gov.uk/assets/BISCore/corporate/docs/H/he-debate-ramsden.pdf [Accessed 27 January 2013].

Rasmus, D. W. (2011). *Management by Design: Applying Design Principles to the Work Experience.* Hoboken, New Jersey: John Wiley & Sons, Inc.

Renwick, J. & M. Webb (2008). Going global: a pilot project in diversifying the musical experiences of Conservatoire students in non-performance-based programs. *Proceedings of the 17ᵗʰ International Seminar of the Commission for the Education of the Professional Musician (CEPROM), International Society for Music Education,* pp. 91–95.

Revans, R. W. (1982). *The Origin and Growth of Action Learning.* Brickley: Chartwell-Bratt.

Richards, L. (2002). Rigorous, Rapid, Reliable and Qualitative? Computing in Qualitative Method. *American Journal of Health Behavior,* Vol. 26, No. 6, pp. 425-430.

Rizvi, F. & B. Lingard (2011). Social equity and the assemblage of values in Australian higher education. *Cambridge Journal of Education.* Vol. 41, No. 1, pp. 5-22.

Rock, M. L.; M. Gregg; E. Ellis & R. A. Gable (2008). Framework for Differentiating Classroom Instruction, *Preventing School Failure,* Vol. 52, No. 2, pp. 31-47.

Rodgers, C. R. & M. B. Raider-Roth (2006). Presence in teaching. *Teachers and Teaching,* Vol. 12, No. 3, pp. 265-287.

Rogers, C. (1969). *Freedom to Learn.* Columbus, Ohio: Charles Merrill.

Roper, E. (1992). Quality in course design: Empowering students through course processes and structures in a professional development scheme. Paper presented at the *AETT conference on 'Quality in Education',* University of York.

Rosslyn, F. (2005). Literature for the Masses: The English Literature Degree in 2004. *The Cambridge Quarterly,* Vol. 34, No. 3, pp. 313-322.

Røvik, K. A. (1998). *Moderne organisasjoner: Trender i organisasjonstenkningen ved tusenårsskiftet.* Bergen-Sandviken: Fagbokforlaget.

Rowley, J. & P. Dunbar-Hall (2012). A case study of shifting musical identity: the lens of cultural diversity in music learning and teaching. *Proceedings of the Hawaii International Conference on Arts and Humanities 2012,*

Hawaii, pp. 1316-1317. Online resource: http://www.hichumanities.org/proceedings_hum.php [Accessed 17 January 2013].

Rowley, J. (2010). Beginning music teachers' expectations of teaching. *Proceedings of the 29th World Conference of the International Society for Music Education*, Beijing, pp. 78-79.

Rowley, J. (2011). Technology, innovation and student learning: ePortfolios for music education. In C. Nygaard; N. Courtney & C. Holtham (Eds.) *Beyond Transmission - Innovations in University Teaching*. Oxfordshire: Libri Publishing Ltd., pp. 45-62.

Ruohoniemi, M. & S. Lindblom-Ylänne (2009). Students' experiences concerning course workload and factors enhancing and impeding their learning – a useful resource for quality enhancement in teaching and curriculum planning. *International Journal for Academic Development*, Vol. 14, No. 1, pp. 69-81.

Russell, S. H. (2006). Evaluation of NSF Support for Undergraduate Research Opportunities. Follow-up Survey of Undergraduate NSF Program Participants. National Science Foundation.

Russell, S. H.; M. Hancock & J. McCullough (2007). The pipeline: Benefits of undergraduate research. *Science*, 316, pp. 548-549.

Ryan, R. M. & E. L. Deci (2000). Self-determination theory and the facilitation of intrinsic motivation, social development, and well-being. *American Psychologist*, Vol. 55, No.1, pp. 68-78.

Sachs, J.; N. Mansfield & B. Kosman (2011). Implementing a Teaching Standards Framework. *Workshop presented at The Australian Quality Forum*, 29 June – 1 July 2011, Melbourne, Australia.

Sarrico, C.; M. Rosa, P. Teixeira & M. Cardoso (2010). Assessing Quality and Evaluating Performance in Higher Education: Worlds Apart or Complementary Views? *Minerva: A Review of Science, Learning & Policy*, Vol. 48, No. 1, pp 35-54.

Sayles, L. (1970). Whatever Happened to Management? *Business Horizon*, April pp 25-34.

Schuck, S.; S. Gordon & J. Buchanan (2008). What are we missing here? Problematising wisdoms on teaching quality and professionalism in higher education. *Teaching in Higher Education*, Vol. 13, No. 5, pp. 537-547.

Scott, G. (1999). *Change Matters. Making a difference in education and training*. St Leonards, NSW: Allen & Unwin.

Senge, P. (2006). *The Fifth Discipline. The Art & Practice of the Learning Organisation*. London: Random House.

Seymour, E.; A. B. Hunter; S. L. Laursen & T. DeAntoni (2004). Establishing the benefits of research experiences for undergraduates: First findings from a three-year study. *Science Education*, Vol. 88, No. 4, pp. 493-534.

Shah, M. & C. S. Nair (2011). Renewing quality assurance at a time of turbulence. *Perspectives: Policy and Practice in Higher Education.* Vol. 15, No. 3, pp. 92-96.

Shah, M. & C. S. Nair (2012). The changing nature of teaching and unit evaluations in Australian Universities. *Quality Assurance in Education.* Vol. 20, No. 3, pp. 1-13.

Shor, I. (1996). *When students have power. Negotiating authority in a critical pedagogy.* Chicago: The University of Chicago Press.

Shortland, S. (2004). Peer observation: a tool for staff development or compliance? *Journal of Further and Higher Education.* Vol. 28, No. 2, pp. 219-228.

Shulman, L. S. (1986). Those Who Understand: Knowledge Growth in Teaching. *Educational Researcher.* Vol. 15, No. 2, pp. 4-14.

Shulman, L. S. (1987). Knowledge and Teaching: Foundations of the New Reform. *Harvard Educational Review.* Vol. 57, No. 1, pp. 1-23.

Simons, R. (1990). The Role of Management Control Systems in Creating Competitive Advantage: New Perspectives. *Accounting, Organizations and Society,* Vol. 15 No 1/2, pp. 127-143.

Simons, R. (1995). *Levers of Control - How Managers Use Innovative Control Systems to Drive Strategic Renewal.* Boston, Massachusets: Harvard Business School Press.

Sin, C. (2012). Academic Understandings of and Responses to Bologna: A Three-Country Perspective. *European Journal of Education,* Vol. 47, No. 3, pp. 392-404.

Sizer, T. R. & N. F. Sizer (1999). *The Students are Watching: Schools and the Moral Contract.* Boston: Beacon Press.

Smeyers, P. (2005). Idle research, futile theory, and the risk for education: Reminders of irony and commitment. *Educational Theory,* Vol. 55, No. 2, pp.165-183.

Smith, C. (2008). Building effectiveness in teaching through targeted evaluation and response: connecting evaluation to teaching improvement in higher education. *Assessment & Evaluation in Higher Education.* Vol. 33, No. 5, pp. 517-533.

Smith, K. (2003). School to University: Sunlit Steps, or Stumbling in the Dark? *Arts and Humanities in Higher Education,* Vol. 2, No. 1, pp. 90–98.

Smith, K. (2004). School to University: An Investigation into the Experience of First-Year Students of English at British Universities. *Arts and Humanities in Higher Education*, Vol. 3, No. 1, pp. 81–93.

Snapper, G. (2009). Beyond English Literature A level: The silence of the seminar? *English in Education*, Vol. 43, No. 3, pp. 192-210.

Snapper, G. (2011). Teaching post-16 English. In A. Green (Ed.) *Becoming a Reflective English Teacher*. Maidenhead: Open University Press, pp. 185-203.

Sporn, B. (2003). Convergence or Divergence in International Higher Education Policy: Lessons from Europe. Online resource: http://www. educause. edu/ir/library/pdf/F FPFP0305.Pdf [Accessed 17 January 2013].

Srikanathan, G. & F. Dalrymple (2002). Developing a Holistic Model for Quality in higher Education. *Quality in Higher Education*, Vol. 8, No. 3, pp. 215-224.

Stenhouse, L. (1975). *An Introduction to Curriculum Research and Development*. London: Heinemann.

Stenhouse, L. (1975). *An introduction to curriculum research and development*. London: Heinemann.

Stewart, J. & C. McCormack (1997). Experiencing and Supporting Change: From Lecture to Interactive Groupwork. *Teaching in Higher Education*, Vol. 2, No. 2, pp. 99-109.

Stiggins, R. (2002). Assessment Crisis: The Absence of Assessment. *Learning, Kappan Professional Journal*. Online resource: http://www.pdkintl.org/kappan/k0206sti.htm [Accessed 11 January 2013].

Stiggins, R. (2007). Assessment through the Student's Eyes, *Educational Leadership*, Vol. 64, No. 8, pp. 22-26.

Swann, J. & K. Ecclestone (1999). Improving lecturers' assessment practice in higher education: a problem-based approach. *Educational Action Research*, Vol. 7, No. 1, pp. 63-87.

Swinglehurst, D.; J. Russell & T. Greenhalgh (2008). Peer observation of teaching in the online environment: an action research approach. *Journal of Computer Assisted Learning*, Vol. 24, No.5, pp. 383-393.

Tarc, A. M. (2006). In a dimension of height: Ethics in the education of others. *Educational Theory*, Vol. 56, No. 3, pp. 287-304.

Teaching Agency (2012). *Continuing your professional development*: Online resource: http://webarchive.nationalarchives.gov.uk/20111218081624/http://tda.gov.uk/teacher/developing-career/professional-development.aspx [Accessed 21 January 2013].

Teaching Quality Enhancement Committee [TQEC] (2003). *Final Report of the TQEC on the Future Needs and Support for Quality Enhancement of Learning and Teaching in Higher Education.* HEFCE/UUK/SCOP (The Cooke Report). Online resource: http://tinyurl.com/czt7q7e [Accessed 20 July 2012].

Tennant, M., C. McMullen & Kaczynski, D. (2010). *Teaching, Learning, and Research in Higher Education – Enhancing Practice through Critique.* London: Routledge.

TEQSA (2012). *Higher Education Standards Framework.* Online resource: *http://www.teqsa.gov.au/higher-education-standards-framework* [Accessed 25 January 2013].

The Higher Education Academy (2008). *Quality enhancement and assurance – a changing picture.* York: The Higher Education Academy.

Theodoropoulou, S. (2010). Skills and education for growth and well-being in Europe 2020: are we on the right path? *European Policy Centre.*

Thomas, L. (2012). *Building Student Engagement and Belonging in Higher Education at a Time of Change: final report from the What Works? Student Retention and Success programme.* York. Higher Education Academy.

Thomas, L. (2012). *Building student engagement and belonging in Higher Education at a time of change: final report from the What Works? Student Retention & Success programme.* Higher Education Academy. Online resource: http://www.heacademy.ac.uk/resources/detail/what-works-student-retention/What_Works_Summary_Report [Accessed 18 January 2013].

Tieso, C. (2001). Curriculum: Broad brushstrokes or paint-by-the numbers? *Teacher Educator,* Vol. 36, No. 3, pp. 199–213.

Tinto, V. (1993). *Leaving college: Rethinking the causes and cures of student attrition.* Chicago: University of Chicago Press.

Tomlinson, C. A. & M. L. Kalbfleisch (1998). Teach me, Teach my Brain: A call for differentiated classrooms. *Educational Leadership,* Vol. 56, No. 3, pp. 52-55.

Tomlinson, C. A. (2000). Differentiated Instruction: Can it work? *Educational Digest,* Vol. 65, No. 5, pp. 25–31.

Townley, B.; D. J. Cooper & L. Oakes (2003). Performance Measures and the Rationalization of Organizations. *Organization Studies,* Vol. 24, No. 7, pp. 1045-1071.

Trigwell, K & M. Prosser. (1991). Relating Learning Approaches: perceptions of context and learning outcomes. *Higher Education,* Vol. 22, pp 251-266.

Trowler, P. & V. Bamber (2005). Compulsory Higher Education Training: Joined-up Policies, Institutional Architectures and Enhancement Cultures. *International Journal for Academic Development*, Vol. 10, No. 2, pp. 79-93.

Tuning Project (2002). Tuning general brochure. Online resource: http://www.unideusto.org/tuningeu/images/stories/publications/English_brochure_for_website.pdf [Accessed 1 February 2013].

UK PSF (2011). *The UK Professional Standards Framework for teaching and supporting learning in higher education 2011.* http://www.heacademy.ac.uk/assets/documents/ukpsf/ukpsf.pdf [Accessed 2 May, 2012].

University of Bedfordshire (2008). *Education Strategy 2008-13.* Internal document: unpublished.

University of Bedfordshire (2009a). *External examiner report 2008-9.* Internal document: unpublished.

University of Bedfordshire (2009b). *Module specification Postgraduate Certificate in Academic Practice.* Internal document: unpublished.

University of Bedfordshire (2010). *External examiner report, 2009-10.* Internal document: unpublished.

University of Bedfordshire (2011a). *External examiner report, 2010-11.* Internal document: unpublished.

University of Bedfordshire (2011b). *Assessment Brief Postgraduate Certificate in Academic Practice.* Internal document: unpublished.

University of Bedfordshire (2011c). *CRe8 - Stimulating Learning,* (2nd edition). Luton: University of Bedfordshire. Online resource: http://www.beds.ac.uk/__data/assets/pdf_file/0016/26530/cre8_and_soar_summary.pdf [Accessed 29 November 2012].

University of Waterloo (2012). Promoting and Assessing Critical Thinking. Online resource: http://cte.uwaterloo.ca/teaching_resources/tips/promoting_and_assessing_critical_thinking.html [Accessed 27 December 2012].

Valsan, C. & R. Sproule (2008). The Invisible Hands Behind the Student Evaluation of Teaching: The Rise of the New Managerial Elite in the Governance of Higher Education. *Journal of Economic Issues (Association for Evolutionary Economics),* Vol. 42, No. 4, pp. 939-958.

van Vught, F.A. (1994). Intrinsic and Extrinsic Aspect of Quality Assessment in Higher Education. In D. F. Westerheijden; J. Brennan & P. A. M. Maassen (Eds.) *Changing Context of Quality Assessment.* Utrecht: LEMMA, pp. 31–50.

Vlasceanu, L.; L. Grünberg, & D. Parlea (2004). *Quality assurance and accreditation: A glossary of basic terms and definitions.* Bucharest: UNESCO-CEPES. Papers on Higher Education. Online resource: http://

unesdoc.unesco.org/images/0013/001346/134621e.pdf   [Accessed 27 January 2013].

Vygotsky, L. S. (1978). *Mind and Society: The Development of Higher Mental Processes*. Cambridge, MA: Harvard University Press.

Vygotsky, L. S. (1987). *The Collected Works of L. S. Vygotsky. Volume 1: Problems of General Psychology*. London: Plenum Press.

Walker, L. O. & K. C. Avant (2004). *Strategies for Theory Construction in Nursing*. Englewood Cliffs, NJ: Prentice Hall, 4th edition.

Webb, M. (2010). Reviewing listening: 'clip culture' and cross-modal listening in the music classroom. *International Journal of Music Education*, Vol. 28, No. 4, pp. 313-340.

Weiskopf, R. & S. Laske (1996). Emancipatory action research: a critical alternative to personal development or a new way of patronising people? In O. Zuber-Skerritt (Ed.) *New directions in action research* London: Falmer.

Wenger, E. (1998). *Communities of Practice. Learning, Meaning and Identity*. Cambridge: Cambridge University Press.

Wenger, E.; N. White & J. D. Smith (2009). *Digital Habitats: stewarding technology for communities*. Portland, OR: CPsquare.

Whitehead, J. (1985). An analysis of an individual's educational development: the basis for personally orientated action research. In M. Shipman (Ed.) *Educational research: principles, policies and practices*. Lewes: Falmer.

Williams, G. (2004). The higher education market in the United Kingdom. In P. Texeira; B. Jongbloed; D. Dill & A. Amaral (Eds.) *Markets in Higher Education: Rhetoric or Reality?* Dordrecht: Klüwer Academic Publishers.

Wilson, A.; S. Howitt; K. Wilson & P. Roberts (2012). Academics' perceptions of the purpose of undergraduate research experiences in a research-intensive degree. *Studies in Higher Education*, Vol. 37, No. 5, pp. 513-526.

Wingate, U. (2007). A Framework for Transition: Supporting 'Learning to Learn' in Higher Education. *Higher Education Quarterly*, Vol. 61, No. 3, pp. 391-405.

Witmer, M. M. (2005). The fourth R in education – Relationships. *The Clearing House*, Vol. 78, No. 5, pp. 224-228.

Wong, V. Y-Y. (2012). An alternative view of quality assurance and enhancement. *Management in Education*. Vol. 26, No. 1, pp38-42.

Wormeli, R. (2006). Principal Leadership: Busting Myths about Differentiated Instruction. Online resource: http://teachingss.pbworks.com/f/BustingMythsaboutDI.pdf [Accessed 13 January 2013].

Yin, R. (1994). *Case study research: Design and methods.* Thousand Oaks: Sage Publishing.

Yorke, M. & B. Longden (2008). *The First Year Experience of higher education in the UK.* York: Higher Education Academy.

Yorke, M. (1994). Enhancement-led Higher Education. *Quality Assurance in Education,* Vol. 2, No. 3, pp. 6-12.

Young, S. & D. G. Shaw (1999). Profiles of Effective College and University Teachers. *The Journal of Higher Education.* Vol. 70, No. 6, pp. 670.

Zhao, C. & G. Kuh, (2004). Adding Value: Learning Communities and Student Engagement. *Research in Higher Education,* Vol. 45, No. 2, pp. 115–138.

Zuber-Skerritt, O. (1996). Introduction. In O. Zuber-Skerritt (Ed.) *New directions in action research.* London: Falmer.

About the Editors

Claus Nygaard is Professor in Management Education at Copenhagen Business School, Denmark. Originally trained in business economics and administration, where he holds a PhD, he first became Associate Professor in Economic Sociology at Department of Organization at Copenhagen Business School. In 2000 he changed position to CBS Learning Lab, and began to work with Quality Enhancement of Higher Education. He was a driving force behind the formulation and implementation of the "Learning Strategy" for Copenhagen Business School in 2005. Claus is currently Professor at Department of Management, Politics and Philosophy at Copenhagen Business School focusing his educational research on the link between identity and learning. He has received distinguished research awards from Allied Academies, outstanding paper awards from Students in Free Enterprise, and he was voted "best teacher" at Copenhagen Business School in 2001. His research has resulted in several books and anthologies, and he has published in leading journals such as Higher Education, International Studies of Management & Organization, International Journal of Public Sector Management, and Assessment & Evaluation in Higher Education. He can be contacted at this email: lihe-support@gmail.com

Nigel Courtney is Honorary Senior Visiting Fellow at Cass Business School, City University London, UK, where he gained the MBA and was awarded his PhD. He is a Visiting Fellow at the University of Technology, Sydney. Nigel is a chartered engineer, a certified management consultant and a certified IT professional with extensive experience in project and general management. Clients of his firm, Courtney Consulting, include the European Commission, Deloitte & Touche, Metropolitan Police, Transport for London, The Post Office and the UK National Endowment for Science Technology and the Arts. Nigel co-authored PD7502 on Knowledge Management for the British Standards Institute and is co-originator of the Skills Framework for the Information Age (SFIA.org.uk). Nigel's teaching practice includes MBA programmes and MSc courses in Economics and on Information Leadership. His research interests include innovation in education, business innovation, the extraction of business value from ICT, and the use of communications technologies for social change. He can be contacted at this email: nigel@courtneynet. com

Paul Bartholomew is Professor of Learning and Teaching and Head of Curriculum Design & Academic Staff Development at Birmingham City University (BCU), UK. He is currently academic lead for BCU's MEd Learning and Teaching in Higher Education. He is a member of the JISC's Learning and Teaching Experts Group and has designed and managed a major project relating to institutional approaches to curriculum design. He has also worked as Consultant for e-Learning for the Health Sciences and Practice Subject Centre of the Higher Education Academy. He was awarded a National Teaching Fellowship in 2004 as well as having been awarded Learning and Teaching Fellowships at University and School level. He has delivered workshops on 'Woven Learning' at the University of Pittsburgh, at Copenhagen Business School and at a number of UK universities. His doctoral research is in the field of co-located computer supported collaborative learning and he has a particular interest in using video methods to study collaborative learning behaviour. He has published on the topics of institutional change, curriculum design, innovation in Higher Education and quality and capacity of clinical placement education. He can be contacted at this email: Paul.Bartholomew@bcu.ac.uk.

For more information on the International Academic Association for the Enhancement of Learning in Higher Education (LiHE) visit: www.lihe. info